Our Maryland Heritage

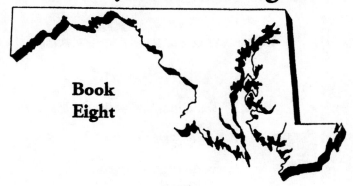

**Book
Eight**

The
Brandenburg
Families

William N. Hurley, Jr.

**HERITAGE BOOKS
2006**

HERITAGE BOOKS
AN IMPRINT OF HERITAGE BOOKS, INC.

Books, CDs, and more—Worldwide

For our listing of thousands of titles see our website
at
www.HeritageBooks.com

Published 2006 by
HERITAGE BOOKS, INC.
Publishing Division
65 East Main Street
Westminster, Maryland 21157-5026

International Standard Book Number: 978-0-7884-0842-9

OUR MARYLAND HERITAGE

Book Eight

BRANDENBURG FAMILIES

Primarily of
Montgomery & Frederick Counties

But Including Members of the Family
Found in Other Counties of Maryland
and in Other States.

HERITAGE BOOKS, INC.

ALSO BY W. N. HURLEY, JR.

Available from the publisher: Heritage Books, Inc.

Neikirk-Newkirk-Nikirk, Volume 1

Neikirk-Newkirk-Nikirk, Volume 2

Hurley Families in America, Volume 1

Hurley Families in America, Volume 2

John William Hines 1600, And His Descendants

Maddox, A Southern Maryland Family

Pratt Families of Virginia and Associated Families

Lowder Families in America

Our Maryland Heritage Series:

    Book One: The Fry Families

    Book Two: The Walker Families

    Book Three: The Fulks Families

    Book Four: The Watkins Families

    Book Five: The King Families

    Book Six: The Burdette Families

    Book Seven: The Soper Families

INTRODUCTION

This is the eighth in our series of families having their origins in Maryland, with descendants now found in all sections of the United States. This study of the Brandenburg families has been limited somewhat to those members of the family having their origins primarily in Frederick and Montgomery Counties, Maryland, although others will be mentioned as they are found in other locations.

As colonists continued to arrive in the early years, seven original counties were formed in Maryland under the Colonial Governor: being Anne Arundel; Charles; Kent; Somerset; St. Mary's; Calvert; and Talbot. As settlers moved steadily westward, and took up new lands, it was necessary to form new centers of government to serve them and, over time, sixteen new counties were formed from the original seven, as well as the City of Baltimore. The researcher must be familiar with this formation, in order to know the sources of information for any given time-frame. The following tabulation demonstrates the formation of each of the counties of Maryland:

Formation of the Counties of Maryland

Name of County	Formed	Source County or Counties
Allegany	1789	Washington
Anne Arundel	1650	Original County
Baltimore	1660	Anne Arundel
Calvert	1654	Original County
Caroline	1773	Dorchester & Queen Anne's
Carroll	1837	Baltimore & Frederick
Cecil	1674	Baltimore & Kent
Charles	1658	Original County
Dorchester	1669	Somerset & Talbot

Name of County	Formed	Source County or Counties
Frederick	1748	Prince George's & Baltimore
Garrett	1872	Allegany
Harford	1773	Baltimore
Howard	1851	Anne Arundel
Kent	1642	Original County
Montgomery	1776	Frederick
Prince George's	1695	Calvert & Charles
Queen Anne's	1706	Dorchester, Kent & Talbot
Somerset	1666	Original County
St. Mary's	1637	Original County
Talbot	1662	Original County
Washington	1776	Frederick
Wicomico	1867	Somerset & Worcester
Worcester	1742	Somerset

ORDER OF PRESENTATION

Our studies deal primarily with descendants of one distinct ancestral individual, Solomon Brandenburg, born 1700 in Germany. His descendants are found in both Frederick and Montgomery Counties of Maryland; in Kentucky, Ohio, Indiana, Illinois, and elsewhere.

First, in Chapter 1, we will discuss some of the ancient background and immigration of members of the Brandenburg family, and the accepted children of Solomon, with records of their movements from Germany to Pennsylvania, Maryland and points west.

Chapters 2, 3 and 4 are each devoted to one of the sons of Wilhelm Heinrich Brandenburg, all of them being grandsons of Solomon. These individuals, and their descendants, were found primarily in Frederick County, Maryland, and in Ohio, Kentucky, Indiana, Illinois and other points further west, although many of them remained in Maryland.

Chapters 5 and 6 are devoted to two more of the sons of the original Solomon. These two and their descendants were also found primarily in Frederick County, Maryland.

Chapters 7 and 8 deal with later generations of the descendants of Solomon, through his son Alexander Henry Brandenburg, who died in 1793. Alexander's children were all born in Frederick County, and many of his descendants lived there, but he was also the progenitor of many of those who are later found in Montgomery County; in Howard, Carroll and other nearby counties.

Chapters 9 thru 13 contain members of the Brandenburg family found in Baltimore, Carroll, Frederick, Howard and Montgomery Counties, who have not been identified within the framework of the principal families discussed earlier, but we believe a connection does exist, and the information is presented for further review.

Finally, in Chapter 14 can be found extensive notations relative to family members who have yet to be placed in the framework of any of the Brandenburg families discussed in the first thirteen chapters, with a lengthy list of miscellaneous births, deaths and marriages of individuals bearing the Brandenburg name.

The work is followed by a Bibliography of sources searched, and an all-name, every page, index.

CONTENTS

Solomon Brandenburg
1700
Germany
*
*
*   *   *   *   *   *   *
*
*   *   Wilhelm Heinrich Brandenburg 1722
*
*   *   Mathias Brandenburg 1744
*
*   *   Alexander Henry Brandenburg
*
*   *   John Martin Brandenburg

CHAPTER 1

Early Brandenburg Origins

The Brandenburg families are of German descent, having their ancient origins in the province of Brandenburg. It has been reported that Prince Bismark was a member of the family, and came into possession of the family estates after they were confiscated by the crown. In later years, the estate was restored to the Brandenburg family, and efforts were made to regain possession, apparently with little success.

In *History of Frederick County, Maryland,* Volume II, 1910, by T. J. C. Williams, and continued from 1861 by Folger McKinsey, it is reported that one Jacob Brandenburg immigrated to America, with his two brothers; Mathias, who settled in Kentucky; and William, who settled in the Middletown valley of Frederick County, where his descendants yet live. This may be true, but on the surface, it looks suspiciously like the well-known, and often repeated, "Three Brothers story." Numerous family histories relate that three brothers came together to America; usually, one went south or west (or returned home) and was never heard from again. We have heard the story on so many occasions, but still do not know its origin, and how it became so widespread in genealogy.

However, it is recorded fact that several individuals who bore the name Brandenburg, in any of its several variations, did arrive in America quite early.

As discussed just above, one Jacob Brandenburg is said to have been born in Germany, and immigrated to America in company with two of his brothers: Mathias, who settled in Kentucky; and William, who settled in Middletown valley, Frederick County, Maryland. The family files of the Montgomery County Historical Society contain several papers relative to the Brandenburg family, and among them, there is a chart setting forth the ancestry and descent of Jacob and his wife, Elizabeth Rine. Its accuracy is unknown, but it will be set forth here for reference. There is a recorded marriage between Jacob Brandenburg and Elizabeth Rein, dated February 13, 1787 in Frederick County, Maryland.

According to the chart, we begin the family with Solomon Brandenburg, born c.1700, apparently in Germany. He is said to have had at least four sons: Mathias, Alexander Henry, John Martin, and William Henry. It is perhaps from this generation that the "three brothers" story should have its origins. Of the brothers, Alexander Henry is reported as having been married to Anna, and the father of: Barbara, John Conrad, and our Jacob Brandenburg. From the chart, one would guess that Jacob was born in America, and was the son of one of the original "three brothers," rather than being among them.

In *More Palatine Families*, by Henry Z. Jones, Jr., it is reported that Wilhelm Heinrich Brandenburger of Winkelbach in the parish of Hochstenbach went to America in 1752 aboard the ship, *Two Brothers*, arriving in Philadelphia. At the courthouse in Philadelphia, September 15, 1752, the immigrants arriving on the ship *Two Brothers*, Thomas Arnot, Master, from Rotterdam, but last from Cowes, in England, took the Qualifications to the Government in the usual form. Among them was Willem Henrich Brandenburger.

In *Pennsylvania German Pioneers*, by Ralph Beaver Strassburger, LL.D, we find other references to early arrivals in the colonies, through the port of Philadelphia. Qualified there on September 30, 1740, arriving on the ship *Samuel and Elizabeth*, List 77A included one Anthony Brandeburger, aged 29 years. List 77B, the same day, includes Johann Andonges Brondenburg, no age given; both arriving from Rotterdam. He may well be the same Johann Anton Brandenburger who is discussed in *More Palatine Families*, by Henry Z. Jones, Jr. It is there reported than Johann Anton was from

Niederhattert in the parish of Alstadt, and that he sold his estate to someone in Kirburg, and then moved to America in 1740. It should be noted that in the report first referenced here, only the male immigrants were listed. On the ship *Samuel and Elizabeth*, there were fifty-six males identified by name, and a notation that there were twenty-eight women aboard. We do not then know if Johann Anton was married at the time. At the courthouse in Philadelphia, on September 30, 1740, a number of immigrants arriving on the *Samuel and Elizabeth* subscribed their names to Oaths to the Government. Among them was Johan Andonges Brandenburg.

At the Mayor's house, in Philadelphia, on November 4, 1766, several individuals subscribed the "usual qualifications" having been imported on the ship *Sally*, John Davidson, Master, from Rotterdam, but last from Portsmouth. Among them was Jacob Brandenburger.

There is information of interest relative to the early background of the Brandenburg family found in *Eighteenth Century Emigrants from German-Speaking Lands to North America*, Volume 1, by Annette Kunselman Burgert. She reports relative to the influx of certain religious sects into the German states after the Thirty Year's War. Among them were immigrants from Switzerland in the canton of Zurich. In 1661, one Jagli Graf from Weertzweil went to the Pfaltz in Germany, with his wife, and seven children. His brother also went in 1651, with a wife and child, and two young men named Hans Graf and Heinrich Brandenburger, both single.

Ultimately, although their economic contribution was welcomed, the religion of these Palatines was not acceptable, and they were severely persecuted. By 1717, the burden of high rents, tributes and taxation resulted in the movement of many of these people into Holland, and later to Pennsylvania.

Having arrived there, it was relatively easy to move across the southern boundary of that colony along what was known by 1751 as the Great Philadelphia Wagon Road. It probably followed an old Indian trail, or a bison track, and ran from Philadelphia to the western areas of Maryland. Near Hagerstown, the traveler could continue on into the Ohio country, or turn south on the Wagon Road, down through the valley of Virginia, as far south as Charlotte. The first real accurate map of the Atlantic Coast and the existing roads, trails, villages, ordinaries, streams and other features was made by Peter Jefferson and Colonel Joshua Fry in 1751, and the Great Wagon Road is clearly defined in its entirety.

Our Brandenburg ancestors joined numerous others of the German groups in settling in the valleys of western Maryland, down into Virginia, and in western Pennsylvania. There they built their stone homes, cleared land for cultivation, and had their numerous children. They were typically farmers, hard-working, scrupulously honest, and devoted to their Church. It is these people and their descendants with whom we will be concerned, and we will repeat following what we now know or believe to be the facts relative to the earliest identified ancestor of the family.

Solomon Brandenburg
1700-

According to Ancestral Family files of the Mormon Church, Solomon Brandenburg was born in Germany, and most sources list his birth year as about 1712. From all available records, he appears to have had at least these children:
1. Wilhelm Heinrich Brandenburg, born August 24, 1722 at Berlin, Germany, and of whom more following.
2. Mathias Brandenburg, born c.1744 in Germany, and of whom more in Chapter 5.
3. Alexander Henry Brandenburg, perhaps born in Germany, and of whom more in Chapter 6.
4. John Martin Brandenburg, perhaps.

CHILD 1

Wilhelm Heinrich Brandenburg
1722-1796

Wilhelm Heinrich, a good German name, appears in the early records of Frederick County, Maryland. As discussed in Chapter 1, above, it appears that he was the son of Solomon Brandenburg (1700), and that he was born August 24, 1722 in Berlin. In *More Palatine Families*, by Henry Z. Jones, Jr., it is reported that Wilhelm Heinrich Brandenburger of Winkelbach in the parish of Hochstenbach went to America in 1752 aboard the ship, *Two Brothers*, arriving in Philadelphia in 1752. We may here be dealing with that same individual.

If the "three brothers" story is correct, it appears that we have now correctly identified them as being the first three listed sons of Solomon Brandenburg: Wilhelm Heinrich; Mathias; and Alexander Henry.

Ancestral records of the Mormon Church report that Wilhelm was born August 24, 1722 at Berlin, Germany, a son of Solomon Brandenburg, born there c.1696, although that appears to be more likely about 1700. Wilhelm was married to Ann, and by some records, reportedly had as many as nine children, the first four being born in Middlesex County, New Jersey, and the final five in Frederick County, Maryland. It appears from other records, however, that there were at least ten children, and that most of them were probably born at or near Middletown, Frederick County, Maryland, including:

1. Maria Brandenburg.
2. Samuel Brandenburg, born April 6, 1756 at Middletown, Maryland, of whom more in Chapter 2.
3. William Brandenburg, born October 8, 1758, of whom more following.
4. Henry Brandenburg.
5. John Brandenburg, born c.1760.

6. Aaron Brandenburg, born February 18, 1761, of whom more in Chapter 3.
7. Mathias Brandenburg, born 1763, of whom more in Chapter 4.
8. Eve Brandenburg, born c.1763.
9. Elizabeth Brandenburg, born c.1764.
10. Catherine Brandenburg, born c.1765

William Brandenburg
1758-

This son of Wilhelm Heinrich Brandenburg (1722) was born October 8, 1758. Married c.1781 to Catherine Beyer in Frederick County, Maryland. They had children, whose birth dates are as found in the IGI records of the Mormon Church, but in need of correction:

1. Enoch P. Brandenburg, born c.1782
2. Mary Ann Brandenburg, born c.1782
3. Henry T. Brandenburg, born March 29, 1782; married April 15, 1804 to Elizabeth Gephart, Frederick County.
4. Samuel Brandenburg, born April 11, 1783
5. William Brandenburg, born May 26, 1785
6. Katharine Brandenburg, born c.1789

Solomon Brandenburg
1700-
Germany
*
*
Wilhelm Heinrich Brandenburg
1722-
*
*
Samuel Brandenburg
1756-1833
*
*   *   *   *   *   *   *
*
* * Hannah Brandenburg 1789
*
* * Susannah Brandenburg 1790
*
* * Samuel Brandenburg, Jr. 1793
*
* * Henry Brandenburg 1795
*
* * Ann Maria Brandenburg 1797
*
* * John Brandenburg 1799
*
* * Mary Brandenburg
*
* * Catherine Brandenburg
*
* * Jacob Brandenburg

CHAPTER 2

Samuel Brandenburg
1756-1833

In at least one family group sheet found at the Mormon Church Family History Center, Samuel is said to have been a son of Wilhelm Heinrich Brandenburg. No mother is listed, and the dates relative to Samuel and his children are as we have found them elsewhere. Samuel was born April 6, 1756. Married in Frederick County, May 8, 1780 to Mary Magdalena Hargerhymer, born May 17, 1759, died January 2, 1817. There is a burial at the Christ Reformed Church in Middletown which is apparently this couple, considering the dates of birth. The Samuel buried there was born c.1756 and died October 30, 1833 at the age of 77 years, 6 months and 24 days, and was a Revolutionary soldier. His wife was Mary, born c.1760 and died January 2, 1817 at the age of 57 years, 7 months and 13 days.

As reported in *History of Frederick County*, Volume 1, by T. J. C. Williams, Samuel was father of at least one son, Henry. Williams reports, however, that the maiden name of the wife of Samuel was Bear, or something similar. He appears to be incorrect. Samuel Brandenburg, Jr. (1793) was married May 22, 1818 to Mary Baer, born May 1, 1800, as will be noted following, and Henry was probably his brother, rather than his son. Family group sheets of the Mormon Church report Henry as a son of Samuel and Mary Magdalena Hargerhymer, placing him in this family. There is a will of Samuel Brandenburg, dated May 19, 1832 and probated November 19, 1833, filed in liber GME1 at folio 507 in Frederick County. He had at least nine children:

1. Hannah Brandenburg, born December 18, 1789; married Frederick County, September 15, 1808 to George Wiles. At least one son:
   a. Peter Wiles, born January 19, 1795, died October 22, 1869. (Although date of birth of this child, and marriage date of parents does not fit, they are reported here as found.) Married Rebecca Byerly.
2. Susannah Brandenburg, born December 25, 1790. Married October 18, 1809 to John Cramer.
3. Samuel Brandenburg, Jr., born May 6, 1793, died January 19, 1866, who received under his father's will the plantation containing 128 and 3/4 acres, with the proviso that he pay certain funds into the estate over time, amounting to a value of $30 per acre. Those sums would then be distributed in one-sixth shares. The descendants of this Samuel will be discussed in detail, following.
4. Henry Brandenburg, born on his father's farm June 17, 1795, and died August 2, 1845, and of whom more.
5. Ann Maria Brandenburg, born July 12, 1797.
6. John Brandenburg, born March 19, 1799
7. Polly Brandenburg, actually Mary, married in Frederick County, April 23, 1801 to Jacob Michael.
8. Catherine Brandenburg, married December 3, 1804 to George Dehaven (or John Dehaven).
9. Jacob Brandenburg, who did not inherit under the will, having already received "more than a child's portion"

Samuel Brandenburg, Jr.
1793-1866

This son of Samuel Brandenburg (1756) and Mary Magdalena Hargerhymer (1759) was born May 6, 1793 in Frederick County, Maryland, and died there January 19, 1866. He was married May 22, 1818 to Mary Baer, born May 1, 1800, died September 18, 1855. Buried at Middletown Reformed Church. They had children, born in Frederick County:

1. Maria Ann Brandenburg, born January 11, 1820, died March 27, 1871. Married William Smith, born September 3, 1819, died January 11, 1856. After marriage, they removed to Warren County, Indiana. Children:

    a. Sarah Jane Catherine Smith, born January 9, 1840. Married McAlister; no children.

    b. Lawson H. Smith, born September 25, 1841, died September 18, 1913. Married Sarah Ann Lucinda Routzahn, born December 25, 1845, died January 16, 1928, daughter of Jacob Routzahn. They had nine children:

        (1) Will Smith.

        (2) Charles E. Smith, born October 17, 1867, died January 29, 1924.

        (3) John Smith.

        (4) Harvey K. Smith, married December 25, 1902 to Alice Stewart, and had children.

        (5) Mary Catherine Smith, born September 19, 1871, died May 6, 1962. Married August 30, 1899 to Charles Reuben Remsburg, born December 31, 1869, died June 18, 1954. They had five children.

        (6) Rose M. Smith, born October 16, 1876, died February 7, 1905, single.

        (7) David A. Smith, born April 5, 1879, and died July 15, 1955, single.

        (8) Carrie Belle Smith, born October 1, 1881, died September 10, 1962. Married May 14, 1912 to Frank Oswalt and had two children.

        (9) Bessie Smith, married Beach; three children.

    c. Mary Ellen Smith, born May 27, 1845.

    d. Amanda Elizabeth Smith, born January 10, 1848. Married William Poffenbarger and had four children.

e. Jane Rebecca Smith, born August 2, 1850

f. George Washington Smith, born December 26, 1852 and died March 9, 1926. Married March 19, 1874 to Catherine Margaret Fout, born September 9, 1848 and died August 15, 1911. He married second Agnes Webster of Tennessee, where he died. He had five children from his first marriage:

(1) Mary Ann Elizabeth Smith, born December 20, 1874, died June 3, 1952. Married to William Alpheus Perry, and secondly to Wilhite. She had two children from her first marriage.

(2) Amy Eugenia Smith, born April 11, 1876 and died January 9, 1962. Married December 20, 1892 to Michael Oliver Golden, born January 18, 1862, died 1941.

(3) Elmer Vernon Smith, born September 3, 1877 and died March 15, 1955. Married December 24, 1902 Clara Leone Crawford, born January 1, 1880.

(4) Clara Viola Smith, born February 20, 1879 and died January 22, 1949.

(5) Leslie Washington Smith, born October 25, 1881, died January 18, 1965. He was married November 2, 1902 to Grace Ann Lape, born January 3, 1884, and had three children.

g. Josiah W. Smith, born February 23, 1853. Returned to Maryland. Married with two daughters:

(1) Mollie Smith.

(2) Lola Smith.

2. Elizabeth Brandenburg, born May 13, 1821, and died September 12, 1855, single.

3. John Nathaniel Brandenburg, born October 10, 1822 and of whom more following.

4. Ann Rebecca Brandenburg, born November 20, 1823, died January 15, 1905 in West Lebanon, Indiana. Mar-

ried in Frederick County, Maryland, January 9, 1851 to Lewis Hamilton Remsberg, born July 6, 1828, died July 5, 1911, son of John Remsberg and Catherine Coblentz. They moved to West Lebanon, Indiana in 1859 where he became a successful farmer. Five children:

a. Mary Elizabeth Remsburg, born November 27, 1855 and died June 26, 1932. Married October 21, 1875 to Isaac Hoff, born June 9, 1852, died September 11, 1882. They had three children. She was married second February 16, 1887 to Samuel Warrenfels. Her children were:

    (1) Lewis Calvin Hoff, born November 24, 1876, died June 12, 1934. Married December 1, 1897 to Pearl Bowlus. Married second January 1, 1900 to Lula Bowlus, born September 11, 1880. Four children.

    (2) Lillie Montrose Hoff, born October 3, 1878, died May 30, 1956. Married February 1, 1899 to Clarence Melvin Bowlus, born May 30, 1876 and died October 4, 1951. Four children.

    (3) Blanche Viola Hoff, born June 30, 1880. She married Omer Hamblen and moved to Grant County, Ohio.

b. Malissa Catherine Remsburg, born June 24, 1857, died March 9, 1924. Married November 17, 1886 to George Daniel Pierce, born February 8, 1856, died December 21, 1930. One son:

    (1) Raleigh Pierce, born October 15, 1890. Married 1912 to May Palmer McClintock, who died November 4, 1935. He married second January 7, 1938 to Pearl B. Miller, born March 15, 1885, died May 27, 1965. Three children.

c. Jennie Rebecca Remsburg, born March 27, 1859, died July 6, 1938. Married June 12, 1879 to Jacob

Hugh Brenner, born April 23, 1859, died January 1, 1938. Four children:

(1) Monta Viola Brenner, born October 16, 1880, died August 19, 1964. Married July 17, 1907 to L. P. Coblentz at Quinton, Oklahoma.

(2) Kathryn Estella Brenner, born June 20, 1882, died June 7, 1934. Married G. W. Stephenson at Winter, Wisconsin.

(3) Allen Lewis Brenner, born April 2, 1884, died January 1, 1964. Married Opal K. Salts at Macon, Georgia.

(4) Bertha Ann Brenner, born April 24, 1888. Married June 12, 1912 to Ray Walter Fleming, born September 24, 1885, died August 16, 1950.

d. Annie Malinda Remsburg, born September 27, 1861, died December 16, 1888. Married April 14, 1881 to Chancellor Livingston Crone, born June 15, 1857 and died February 25, 1925. Four children:

(1) Frederick Lewis Crone, born June 6, 1882. Married December 24, 1906 to Nettie Niswonger, born September 30, 1878, and died August 16, 1907. He married second Carrie Biniger, born September 22, 1886, and died January 29, 1915. One child.

(2) Flora Rebecca Crone, born April 2, 1884. Married January 20, 1904 to George Moore.

(3) Alta Susan Crone, born April 12, 1886.

(4) Charles Thomas Crone, born June 9, 1888, died July 17, 1944. Married Phyllis M. Waddell and moved to Pennsylvania.

e. Charles Edward Remsburg, born May 20, 1863, died May 21, 1945. He was an attorney at law and lived for a time, at least, in Seattle, Washington. Married October 21, 1891 to Belle Farquhar, born

November 14, 1863, and died October 2, 1954. Two children:

(1) Mabel R. Remsburg, born December 25, 1892. Married April 29, 1917 to Alfred Finney Stone, born May 2, 1887, died November 28, 1933. Two children.

(2) Helen R. Remsburg, born May 13, 1895.

5. Cornelius E. Brandenburg, perhaps, born c.1824, and of whom more.

6. George Martin Brandenburg, born July 31, 1825 and died February 9, 1907 near Frederick, Maryland. Buried at Middletown Reformed Church, with his wife. He was married May 21, 1861 in Frederick County to Minerva Warrenfels, born July 19, 1842 and died March 19, 1923. The couple appear in the 1880 census for Middletown, in Frederick County, Maryland, with seven children, and in the 1900 census of the county, with five. In the 1920 census for Frederick, Minerva appears at age seventy-eight, apparently a widow. With her is her daughter, Josephine; her son, Leslie, born c.1887; and a grandson, George H. Stone, born c.1906. Their children included:

a. Annie E. Brandenburg, born December 21, 1861, died November 9, 1945. Buried at the Christ Reformed Church, Middletown.

b. Emma C. Brandenburg (or Emma K.) born October 13, 1864, died February 13, 1952. Buried at Middletown Reformed Church.

c. Mary E. Brandenburg, born c.1867

d. Josephine L. Brandenburg, born December 25, 1869 and died May 4, 1954. Buried at Middletown Reformed Church.

e. George W. Brandenburg, born December 28, 1873 and died November 18, 1899. Buried at Jefferson Union.

f. Effie May Brandenburg, born c.1877

g. Carrie E. Brandenburg, born c.1880
h. Clarence Brandenburg, born February 5, 1883. Married Bessie V., born Setember 25, 1880, died November 12, 1956. She is buried at Mt. Olivet cemetery in Frederick. They appear in the 1920 census for Frederick County, with three children:
   (1) William L. Brandenburg, born c.1906
   (2) Helen V. Brandenburg, born c.1907
   (3) Frank E. Brandenburg, born c.1910
i. Leslie F. Brandenburg, born c.1886
j. Virgie H. Brandenburg, born c.1892
7. James Adam Brandenburg, born February 28, 1830 and died February 10, 1906 in West Lebanon, Indiana. (Some reports list his name as John Adam Brandenburg.) Married March 21, 1859 to Mary Ann Rebecca Warrenfels, born c.1836, died 1908. Eight children:
   a. Laura V. Brandenburg, born April 21, 1860, died September 18, 1862. Buried at Middletown Reformed Church.
   b. Jacob Samuel Brandenburg, born April 27, 1863, died May 3, 1948. Married June 27, 1888 to Cora Frances Perry, born April 6, 1870, died November 5, 1954. One son:
      (1) Roy Vern Brandenburg, born February 13, 1890. Married January 31, 1913 to Naomi Bell Talbot, born May 7, 1891, died April 19, 1926. Two children. He married second April 28, 1929 to Catherine Finney, and was divorced after having three children. Married third April 8, 1950 to Lou Ellen Hershberger, born February 9, 1899, died January 16, 1953. Roy married third November 25, 1959 to Daisy Laurine Wilhite, born October 17, 1896.
      (2) Archie Brandenburg, born May 18, 1893, died August 21, 1893.

(3) Jacob Earl Brandenburg, born April 18, 1896. Married March 9, 1917 to Mabel Christine Whorley, born January 5, 1901, and had two children:
  (a) Lois Marie Brandenburg, born March 7, 1926. Married October 26, 1945 to Robert G. Stevenson, born October 22, 1918. Children.
  (b) Forrest Dean Brandenburg, born June 12, 1933. Married September 16, 1951 Mary Lou English, born December 9, 1934.
(4) Archie Lowell Brandenburg, born August 22, 1901 and died May 22, 1919.
c. Rufus Mahlon Brandenburg, died July 4, 1917. Married December 24, 1890 to Margaret M. Young, born November 7, 1864, died December 29, 1948. Three children:
(1) Ruth Gwenn Brandenburg, born December 26, 1894. Married April 28, 1923 to Rodger B. Paul.
(2) Clyde Sanderson Brandenburg, born November 13, 1897. Married September 28, 1935 to Muriel Gough and had a child.
(3) Marjorie Eva Brandenburg, born June 26, 1901, died January 2, 1929.
(4) Clifford Earl Brandenburg, born August 26, 1906, died September 9, 1906.
d. Harley Brandenburg.
e. Frances Cecelia Brandenburg, born December 13, 1865, died December 27, 1931. Married January 25, 1888 to Simon David Haupt, born October 14, 1852, died January 28, 1889. One son:
(1) Simon Jacob Haupt, born February 15, 1888. Married Della May Clark, born May 19, 1890, died April 19, 1960. Seven children.

f.   Carleton William Brandenburg, born May 3, 1872, died February 10, 1942. Married February 22, 1911 to Ruth K. Lucas, born September 25, 1883, died March 10, 1932. Members of this family apparently lived on or near the border between Indiana and Illinois. Four children:

(1)   Laura Mary Brandenburg, born February 23, 1913. Married August 31, 1935 to Frank Frederick Bahrns, born March 1, 1937, and had three children.

(2)   Charles Emerson Brandenburg, born November 1, 1916. Married June 10, 1938 to Nila Roberts, and had three children.

(3)   Audrey Brandenburg, born May 23, 1920. Married December 21, 1940 to John Jordan, born October 10, 1918, died August 22, 1957. Five children. She married second October 21, 1961 to James Miller.

(4)   Musetta Berniece Brandenburg, born October 20, 1925. Married July 14, 1943 to Vernon Taylor, and had six children.

g.   Frank Brandenburg.

h.   John T. Brandenburg.

8.   Rosanna Catherine Magdalena Brandenburg, born December 10, 1838.

9.   Lucinda C. Brandenburg, born c.1843 and died near Dayton, Ohio. Married in Frederick County, November 2, 1858 to Enos Marker and had children:

a.   Samuel Marker.

b.   Edward Marker.

c.   Rella Marker.

10.   Cornelius Brandenburg, perhaps, who died in Ohio.

John Nathaniel Brandenburg
1822-1891

This son of Samuel Brandenburg, Jr. (1793) and Mary Baer (1800) was born October 10, 1822 in Frederick County, Maryland, and died September 19, 1891. He was married twice, first in Frederick County, March 26, 1846, to Mary Barbara Smith, born March 26, 1845 and died November 11, 1852, daughter of Jacob and Ellen Smith. Five children, and perhaps two infant deaths as listed following. He was married second May 9, 1856 to Mary Magdalene Aultman, born March 21, 1830 at Bennicheim, Wurtenburg, in Germany, and died of heart disease and dropsy, May 8, 1904 in Frederick County. According to her obituary, her parents immigrated to America when she was twelve years old, landed at Baltimore, and settled in Middletown Valley. John and his second wife are buried together at Middletown Reformed Church. There are also two children buried with them. There were eight children born to the union, for a total of thirteen. John Nathaniel and his second wife appear in the 1880 census for Frederick County, with five of their children. There appear to have been as many as sixteen children in total:

1. Manzella Ellen Brandenburg, born January 16, 1847. Married Joseph E. Castle. They had children, including:
    a. Rebecca Castle.
    b. George Castle.
    c. Mary Castle.
    d. Effie Castle.
2. John William Edward Brandenburg, born October 13, 1849; buried at Mt. Olivet cemetery in Frederick. His tombstone states that he was born October 13, 1849 and died August 27, 1920. His wife is buried there also; she was Ida V. Taylor, born March 27, 1849 and died January 31, 1917. There are two sons buried with them; three others are buried at Mt. Pleasant Reformed Church. The

family appears in the 1880 census for Frederick County, with the first five children, and in the 1900 census for Woodsboro in Frederick County, with two more. Their children included, at least:

a. George William Brandenburg, born c.1871. George is listed in his own household in the 1900 census for Frederick County. Cemetery records of Ladiesburg, Maryland, at Haughs cemetery, state that George William was born 1871 and died 1939. His wife, Mary Catherine, is buried with him, born 1875 and died 1909. There are also two sons. The couple are listed in the 1900 census of Frederick County, with three children. They appear to have had at least four. It appears possible that George may have been married a second time after the early death of his wife. In the 1920 census of Frederick County, there is a George W. Brandenburg of the proper age to be this one. He there has a wife, Annie B., born c.1872 and a daughter, listed following. Also in the household is one Claude L. Smith, born c.1905, listed as a stepson, perhaps from a first marriage of Annie. If all this is true, then there were five children from his first marriage:

(1) Maude G. Brandenburg, born c.1889
(2) Edgar Allen Brandenburg, born 1896, died 1912.
(3) Amy M. Brandenburg, born c.1898
(4) John William Brandenburg, born 1901, died 1912.
(5) Zelda I. Brandenburg, born c.1904.

b. John R. Brandenburg, born c.1873. This may be the same John who died c.1947, and is buried at Bush Creek Brethren Church in Frederick County, with his wife. She was Laura S., born c.1875 and died c.1958. Their eldest son is buried with them. The couple appear in the 1900 census for Frederick County, with three children. In the 1920 census of New Market, in Frederick County, there are two children in the household:

    (1)   Paul C. Brandenburg, born 1895, died 1910
    (2)   Helen C. Brandenburg, born c.1897
    (3)   Charles L. Brandenburg, born c.1899
    (4)   Rodger J. Brandenburg, born c.1901
    (5)   William H. Brandenburg, born c.1909

c.   Mary A. Brandenburg, born c.1874

d.   Grayson E. Brandenburg, born November 17, 1877 and died April 15, 1947

e.   Marcellus E. Brandenburg, born June 10, 1879 and died July 20, 1903

f.   Charles S. Brandenburg, a twin, born September 11, 1883 and died September 6, 1892.

g.   Clayton E. Brandenburg, a twin, stillbirth September 11, 1883

h.   Sarah Brandenburg, born c.1886

i.   Bradley F. Brandenburg, born c.1888

j.   Charles Brandenburg, born 1889, died 1892.

3.   Mary Magdalena Clementine America Brandenburg, born March 10, 1848, died October 3, 1848.

4.   Mary Barbara Brandenburg, who died September 11, 1852, perhaps also an infant death.

5.   Cornelius Edward Brandenburg, born July 7, 1852, and died September 19, 1852 at two months.

6.   Mary Elizabeth Brandenburg, born November 1, 1853, died August, 1856 at the age of two years. She is buried at Middletown Reformed Church.

7.   James Buchanan Brandenburg, born November 30, 1856, died March 14, 1858 at the age of 1 year, 3 months and 14 days. Buried at the Middletown Reformed Church.

8.   Charles Malocton Brandenburg, born November 14, 1858, of whom more.

9. Thomas Hamilton Brandenburg, born July 24, 1860
10. Sarah Ann Rebecca Brandenburg, born May 4, 1862 in Frederick County. Married to James L. Gaver.
11. Alice Catherine Brandenburg, born June 14, 1864, died January 3, 1927. Married to Charles L. Cline and had children:
    a. John Cline.
    b. Elmer Cline.
    c. Charles Cline.
    d. Harry Cline.
12. Julia E. Brandenburg, born c.1865
13. Samuel Clayton Brandenburg, born April 22, 1866, died May 21, 1938. Married Clara M. Alexander, born 1863, died 1942. Both are buried at Middletown Reformed Church, with two of their sons. The couple appears in the 1900 census for Frederick County, with seven children. According to the report of a family reunion, found in the Frederick County Historical Society, there were several children. In the 1920 census for the county, there are additional children identified. Those known from the various sources included:
    a. Sarah M. Brandenburg, born c.1890
    b. Harry Roscoe Brandenburg, born c.1896 and killed at El Vallee, Mexico, November 16, 1916, while serving in Troop L, US Cavalry.
    c. James A. Brandenburg, died January 21, 1906. Does not appear in the census records.
    d. John F. Brandenburg, born c.1891, of whom more.
    e. Gorman C. Brandenburg, born c.1893
    f. Leslie Clarence Brandenburg, born c.1894 and died 1947; buried with his wife at Middletown Lutheran cemetery. Leslie C. is found in the 1920 census for Frederick County, with a wife, Anna Jane, born c.1897. No children are listed in the census. They had children, however, including at least these two:

(1) Clarence C. Brandenburg, died September 14, 1923, perhaps young. Buried Middletown Lutheran Church.

(2) R. Lamar Brandenburg, born May 24, 1913 and lived for five days. Buried Middletown Reformed Church.

g. Mary E. Brandenburg, born c.1898

h. Alice C. Brandenburg, born c.1899

i. Charles A. Brandenburg, born c.1902

j. Russell R. Brandenburg, born c.1905

k. Leo Brandenburg, born c.1908

14. Glencora Elizabeth Brandenburger, born October 15, 1868, died 1940. Married to George Alexander, and had children:

a. Mary Alexander.

b. Guy Alexander.

15. Mary L. Brandenburg, born May 11, 1871, died 1953. Married William H. Summers, born 1866, died 1940, son of Isaac J. Summers (1838) and Lucinda C. Brandenburg (1840). Isaac and Lucinda were married in Frederick County, July 21, 1862, but she has not yet been placed within the framework of the families under study at this time. Children:

a. Katie Summers.

b. Charles Summers.

c. Chester Summers.

16. George Washington Brandenburg, born April 15, 1875, died October 4, 1942. Married to Frances (Fannie) M. Wise, born c.1883. The young couple appear in the 1900 census for Frederick County, without children. His mother, Mary Magdalene, is living with them at the age of seventy, and the record confirms that she was born in Germany. In the 1920 census of the county, the couple again appear, with eight children. The children included:

a. Raymond L. Brandenburg, born 1905, died 1926. He is buried at Middletown Reformed Church.
b. Robert F. Brandenburg, born c.1905, perhaps a twin of Raymond.
c. Charles A. Brandenburg, born c.1907
d. Eva Blanche Brandenburg, born February 12, 1909, and died August 1, 1912. Buried Christ Reformed Church, at Middletown, Maryland.
e. Mildred I. Brandenburg, born c.1911
f. Lillian G. Brandenburg, born c.1913
g. Ethel B. Brandenburg, born c.1915
h. Arline E. Brandenburg, born c.1918
i. Erma Brandenburg, born c.1920
j. George Washington Brandenburg, Jr., apparently born after 1920.

John F. Brandenburg
1891-1945

This son of Samuel Clayton Brandenburg (1866) was born c.1891 in Frederick County, Maryland, and died there 1945. He was married to Bertha E. Hartsock, born 1892. Both are buried at the Middletown Lutheran Church. He appears in the 1920 census of Frederick County, with his wife, Bertha E, born c.1893, and one child. There were other children born to the couple:

1. Hilda C. Brandenburg, died July 14, 1914; buried with her parents.
2. Marianna Jane Brandenburg, born August 28, 1916. She married Paul Austin Routzahn, born 1914, son of Calvin Wesley Routzahn (1873). He was a master carpenter and in retirement, caned chairs. Three children:
    a. Clark Austin Routzahn, born March 25, 1940, died February 28, 1983 at Frederick. Married Clara Belle

Moss of Burkittsville, born September 19, 1943. One child:

 (1) Kelly Lynn Routzahn, born March 14, 1962. Married Blaine Edward Clem, and divorced.

 b. Harold Francis Routzahn, born July 2, 1949. Married March 20, 1969 to Judy Floretta Morgan, born November 7, 1949, daughter of Paul Irving Morgan (1921) and Vera Naomi Kline (1924). Children:

  (1) Chad Paul Routzahn: February 2, 1972
  (2) Wesley Davis Routzahn: April 9, 1978
  (3) Shannon Morgan Routzahn: May 20, 1982

 c. Sarah Jane Routzahn, born April 28, 1955. Married September 20, 1975 to Kevin Dean Spade, born September 26, 1953, son of Floyd Curtis Spade and Leah Page Leatherman. Two children:

  (1) Melissa Gail Spade: July 4, 1980
  (2) Kristen Danielle Spade: November 20, 1984

3. Margarita J. Brandenburg, born c.1917
4. Grace Ellen Brandenburg, married Glenn Earl Routzahn, died January 28, 1975. He was a son of Oscar John Routzahn (1873) and Margaret Rebecca Feaga (1871). Glenn served under Patton in Germany, and worked as a lab techician at Ft. Detrick. They had two children:

 a. Ricky Routzahn.
 b. Randy Routzahn.

Charles Malocton Brandenburg
1858-1917

 This son of John Nathaniel Brandenburg (1822) and his second wife, Mary Magdalene Aultman (1830) was born November 14, 1858 in Frederick County, Maryland, died June 19, 1917. Buried at the Middletown Christ Reformed Church. Married December 25, 1883 to Mary Jane Burton, born June

12, 1862 in Stafford County, Virginia, and died September 13, 1951 in Arlington, Virginia. Children:

1. Clarence Marshall Brandenburg, born March 7, 1885 at Stafford, Virginia, died c.1917 and buried at Arlington National Cemetery. Married Estella Cordi, born August 23, 1886, and had children:
    a. Clarence Millard Brandenburg, born c.1906; married Jeannette Wells, and had two children.
    b. Columbia May Brandenburg, born June 6, 1912. Married William O. Pigott and had a daughter.

2. Charles Frederick Brandenburg, born c.1892. Married to Mary Alice Myers, born c.1891, and had children:
    a. Charles Emory Brandenburg, born November, 1912. Married Betty and had three children:
        (1) Gloria Edwina Brandenburg, a twin, married Russell Hickman and had three children.
        (2) Juanita May Brandenburg, a twin, married to James Drummond and had three children.
        (3) Freddie Brandenburg.
    b. Eleanor Brandenburg, married first to Paul Dwyer and had one infant death, and a living son. Married second Francis Russell. Her son was:
        (1) Ronald Paul Dwyer, married, three sons.
    c. Zelda Brandenburg, married George Nash, and had a son and daughter, both married with children.
    d. Mary Alice Brandenburg, born c.1918, married Joe Berger and had a son and daughter:
        (1) Joe Berger, Jr.
        (2) Rosalee Berger, married and had a daughter.
    e. Frances Ollie Brandenburg, married Fred Bell and had two daughters:
        (1) Alice Bell, married and had a daughter.
        (2) Diane Bell, married and had two children.
    f. Myrtle Oneida Brandenburg, married George Snyder and had five children.

g.   Clarence Frederick Brandenburg, born September, 1925. Married and had two sons.

3.   Kurtz Aloysious Brandenburg, born January 19, 1897, died January 20, 1957. Married c.1920 to Myrtle Boone of Greensboro, North Carolina. They had a daughter:

a.   Neta Brandenburg, born 1921. Married first Vincent Dabbadanza and had one child. Married second R. P. Mansfield, no children. Her daughter was:

(1)   Betty Dabbadanza, married with two children.

4.   Myrtle Oneida Brandenburg, born August 17, 1901. Married October 7, 1922 to Robert Louis Meadows, born September 12, 1894 in Atlanta, Georgia. They had a son:

a.   Marshall Robert Meadows, born December 15, 1924 at Washington, D. C. Married June 14, 1952 to Margaret Jane Bennett, born February 27, 1924 at Covington, Virginia. They had three children, born in Arlington, Virginia:

(1)   Angela Kay Meadows, born September, 1954 and lived one month.

(2)   Martin Robert Meadows: July 27, 1957

(3)   Marsha Lynne Meadows: December 10, 1960.

Cornelius E. Brandenburg
1824-1891

Cornelius was born between 1824 and 1828 in Frederick County, Maryland, son of Samuel Brandenburg. We have not positively identified which Samuel was his father, but it seems possible that the parents may have been Samuel Brandenburg, Jr., born 1793, and Mary Baer, born c.1800, which see above. The time frame fits comfortably, and some of their children are known to have moved to Ohio, as did Cornelius. He died December 18, 1891 near Fletcher, Ohio. Cornelius was married April 1, 1850 in Frederick County, Maryland to

Elizabeth Ann Yaste, a twin, born July 22, 1830 in Maryland, and died October 27, 1894 near Fletcher, Ohio. Her parents were Samuel Yaste, born c.1800 in Middletown Valley, Frederick County, Maryland, and Mary Youtsey, born c.1800. They had moved to Ohio about 1850, which is approximately the time that their daughter and Cornelius were married, and in all likelihood members of the Yaste and Brandenburg families made the trip together. Cornelius and Elizabeth Ann had two children in Miami County, Ohio:

1. Florence Brandenburg.
2. Laura Brandenburg.

Henry Brandenburg
1795-1845

Believed to have been a son of Samuel Brandenburg (1756) and Mary Magdalena Hargerhymer (1759), Henry was born on his father's farm June 17, 1795, and died August 2, 1845 on his farm located along Brandenburg Hollow Road at Wolfsville, Maryland. He remained on the family farm until his marriage, at which time he began farming for himself on a tract of timber land purchased for him by his father, located a mile and a half north of Wolfsville. Married March 17, 1823 to Mary Kemp, born in 1794, died October 21, 1863. Henry and Mary are buried in the family burying ground on the farm. The will of Henry was dated May 1, 1869 and probated May 31, 1869 in Frederick County, although it is obvious that the date of death in 1869 does not conform with the death date first reported above from other sources, which is apparently incorrect. We are surely here dealing with the proper individual, in that he names his wife, Mary (deceased in 1863), and his son Eli, and two of his daughters, Annie (probably Mary A. of 1826), and Harriet. He provides that his wife is to inherit his house and lot containing two acres, three roods and nineteen perches, and known as part of *Michael's*

Fancy, together with personal property and the sum of one thousand dollars, in lieu of dowry. He leaves his plantation to his son, Eli, valued at eighty dollars per acre, and provides that Eli is to pay that sum into the estate, over time, which is to be then divided between Eli and his two sisters, who apparently were the only living children. There were other children as well:

1. Malinda C. Brandenburg, born c.1822, married in Frederick County, October 18, 1860 to Daniel Toms and lived in Kansas.
2. Samuel Brandenburg, born May 21, 1824, and of whom more.
3. John Brandenburg.
4. Mary E. Brandenburg, born c.1826. Married February 15, 1849 to Henry Poffenberger.
5. Eli Brandenburg.

Samuel Brandenburg
1824-1888

This son of Henry Brandenburg (1795) and Mary Kemp was born May 21, 1824 on his father's farm near Wolfsville, in Frederick County, Maryland, and died July 6, 1888. He remained on the family farm until the death of his father, at which time he assumed management on behalf of his mother. Later, he purchased the two hundred acre farm and timber land, clearing additional acreage. He owned a sawmill and dealt in lumber, in addition to actively farming. Married in Frederick County December 24, 1849 to Julia Ann Catherine Grossnickle, born c.1829 and died June 10, 1916 at the age of 87 years. Both are buried at Ellerton Church of the Brethren. Samuel left a will, dated May 14, 1885 and probated August 6, 1888, filed in liber HL1 at folio 21 in Frederick. In the will, he calls his wife Julia Ann Catharine, leaving her all his property for her lifetime. At her death, the estate was to be divided between eight children, all named, apparently the only ones then surviving. The family is listed in the 1880 census of Frederick County, with seven of the children. In the 1900 census of the county, Julia Ann appears as head of the household, with one granddaughter living with her; Nellie M. Brandenburg, born c.1882. Ten children, nine of whom reached maturity:

1. Cornelius Upton Brandenburg, a carpenter and building contractor. Born December 9, 1850, died July 7, 1928. Married to Cordelia A., born August 31, 1859, and died September 4, 1913. In the 1880 census for Frederick County, the young couple appear with one child, a daughter. They appear in the 1900 census for the county, with the same daughter, her husband, and their three grandchildren living in the houshold. In the 1920 census, Cornelius Upton (listed simply as Upton) is a widower, living with his daughter and her husband. The daughter known to us through the census was:

   a. Elsie V. Brandenburg, born c.1878 and married to Rooklyn Pryor, born c.1874. Three children appeared in the census, but there were more:

      (1) Milton A. Pryor, born c.1897
      (2) James D. Pryor, born c.1898
      (3) Jasper V. Pryor, born c.1899
      (4) Donna Louise Pryor, born 1910, married 1928 to Herman Kline.

2. Henry Levi Brandenburg, born December 13, 1853, and of whom more.

3. Martin Rufus Brandenburg, a farmer, born December 25, 1856, of whom more.

4. Samuel Tracy Brandenburg, born May 29, 1858, a farmer, of whom more.

5. Cyrus P. Brandenburg, (or Cyrus C.), born c.1861, who moved to North Dakota.

6. Alvey Raymond Brandenburg, born July 21, 1863, and of whom more.
7. Elmer Caleb Brandenburg, a carpenter and contractor, born November 13, 1865, and of whom more.
8. Mary Ellen Brandenburg, born April 5, 1867, died March 9, 1948. Married November 29, 1894 to Jacob Ludwig Routzahn, born near Ellerton, November 10, 1864, died March 25, 1950. They had eight children, born in Frederick County, Maryland:
    a. Mary Catherine Routzahn, born 1895, died November 14, 1969. Married Frederick Edward Ahrens and had one son:
       (1) Kent Ahrens.
    b. Samuel Ludwig Routzahn, born February 12, 1897, died May 24, 1990 at Hagerstown. Married Geraldine Reba Hays, born April 27, 1901 at Wolfsville, daughter of Albert E. Hays and Jennie Stottlemyer. They had a daughter.
    c. Cyrus Raymond Routzahn, born April 16, 1900, died May 18, 1900.
    d. Martha Grace Routzahn, born December 9, 1901, died August 7, 1928 at Boonsboro.
    e. William Floyd Routzahn, born 1904, died 1985.
    f. Anna Elizabeth Routzahn, born 1907, died 1963. Married June 9, 1926 to John Petre Nicodemus and had three children.
    g. Ruth Julia Routzahn, born April 26, 1908, died February 4, 1979.
    h. Maynard Jacob Routzahn, born November 2, 1912, died September 17, 1954. Married Louise Wachtel, born July 9, 1916, died May, 1987, daughter of Clyde C. Wachtel and Elsie Wilhide. Two children:
       (1) Marilyn Routzahn.
       (2) Ann Ludwig Routzahn.

9.   Chester Robert Brandenburg, a farmer, born June 7, 1870, of whom more.

Henry Levi Brandenburg
1853-

This son of Samuel Brandenburg and Julia Ann Catharine Grossnickle was born December 13, 1853 on his father's farm in Catoctin District of Frederick County, Maryland, and died April 12, 1928. He is buried at the Ellerton Brethren Church, with his wife. He worked on the family farm prior to purchasing a ninety-three acre farm about a half mile north of Wolfsville. He operated a large sawmill on his property, providing lumber for many of the buildings in the valley. He was married to Louisa C. Grossnickle, born July 5, 1856, died May 16, 1914, daughter of George P. Grossnickle and Sarah Ann Grossnickle. Levi, listed only by that name, appears as head of household in the 1880 census for Frederick County, Maryland, born c.1855. His wife was Louisa, born c.1857, and they then had three children. There is a will of one L. H. Brandenburg, dated February 17, 1926 and probated April 25, 1928; filed in liber GES2 at folio 351 in Frederick; which we believe to be that of Henry Levi. In fact, although it has only initials in the will, it is indexed under the given name Levi. Henry Levi was married second to Lucretia Shuff, born 1862, died 1941, daughter of Benjamin Shuff, Jr. (1837) and Sarah Ann Stottlemyer (1842). She had been married twice previously, first to John William Hooper (1862) and second to David Barkman, Jr. (1830). In the will of Henry Levi the wife is named Lucretia, and Lloyd R. Brandenburg is named as Executor. In the 1900 census for Frederick County, we found the family again, although the Soundex film at the Archives was very faint and difficult to read. He appeared to have been listed there as Harry L. Brandenburg, with his first wife, Louisa C., and ten of his children. The couple appear in the 1920 census for Frederick County, with just one son, Harry, still living at home. Henry Levi and Louisa had as many as sixteen children, all but one reaching maturity:

1. Esta R. Brandenburg, born c.1878, and married Charles Harshman.
2. Calmeda Brandenburg, born c.1879, and married Harry Grossnickle. In the 1900 census for Hagerstown, in Washington County, Maryland, when she was 21 years of age, she appeared in the household of John H. Jones, listed as a servant.
3. Levi Brandenburg, born c.1880
4. Roy R. Brandenburg.
5. Keefer Brandenburg, born c.1881 to 1883. In the 1880 census with his parents, he is listed as Samuel K. In the 1900 census, in his own household, he is listed as Keefer S., with a wife, Nellie L., born c.1885. They have five children living with them, and John T. Gaver, born c.1842, listed as father in law. The children were:
   a. Beulah J. Brandenburg, born c.1909
   b. Merhl H. Brandenburg, born c.1910
   c. Herman E. Brandenburg, born c.1912
   d. Bruce W. Brandenburg, born c.1914
   e. Gale W. Brandenburg, born c.1919
6. Clara E. Brandenburg, born c.1884
7. Sarah E. Brandenburg, married William Gaver of Middletown District.
8. Jennie Brandenburg, married Charles Blickenstaff.
9. Cyrus P. Brandenburg, born c.1885
10. Ira Brandenburg, born c.1888 a merchant of Chewsville, Maryland
11. Estelle H. Brandenburg, born c.1889
12. Otha Charles Brandenburg, born c.1890. He is found in the 1920 census for Washington County, Maryland, with his wife, Annie E., born c.1892, and three children:
    a. Pauline F. Brandenburg, born c.1916

b. Pearl E. Brandenburg, born c.1918
c. Ernest L. Brandenburg, born c.1919
13. Emmet G. Brandenburg, born c.1892
14. Lloyd R. Brandenburg, born c.1895. He appears in the 1920 census of Frederick County with a wife, Elizabeth M., born c.1895, and one son. Also in the household is Charles F. Arsherman, born c.1866, listed as his father-in-law. The known son was:
a. C. Edward Brandenburg, born c.1917; died September 18, 1917 at the age of 4 months and 27 days.
15. Harry E. Brandenburg, born c.1898
16. Earl H. Brandenburg.

Martin Rufus Brandenburg
1856-1911

This son of Samuel Brandenburg and Julia Ann Catharine Grossnickle was born December 25, 1856, and died October 1, 1911. Buried at Monrovian Brethren Church with his wife. He was married in Frederick County, December 19, 1882 to Emma D. Bussard, born February 13, 1863 and died January 26, 1955, daughter of Gideon B. Bussard and Sophia Recher. The family is found in the 1900 census for Frederick County, with nine of their children. They had children, born in Maryland, including:
1. George Keifer Brandenburg, born August 4, 1883, died January 16, 1928. Married to Hattie Tabler. They had at least thirteen children, two of whom were:
a. George Brandenburg, twin, born December, 1918
b. Harriett Brandenburg, twin, born December, 1918
2. Annie Virginia Brandenburg, born September 17, 1884, and died March 30, 1958. Married December 22, 1910 to Henry Frank Main, born December 22, 1883, died April 29, 1957. At least three children.

3. Mary Catherine Brandenburg, born May 18, 1886. Married December 8, 1910 to Walter Hipkins, born February 11, 1890. At least five children, one of whom was:
   a. Rufus Burkett Hipkins, born July 18, 1911. Married Bessie Louise McElfresh, born October 26, 1909.
4. Martha Sophia Brandenburg, born May 31, 1888. Married James Wesley Geisler, born August 6, 1896. Seven children, six of whom were:
   a. William Wesley Geisler, born November 14, 1927. Married November 19, 1949 to Almeda Riggs, born August 23, 1931, the daughter of Lester Baker Riggs (1903) and Evelyn Crothers Brandenburg (1907). Four children:
      (1) Gary Lee Geisler, born November 3, 1952. Married June 7, 1980 Vicki Marie Boone, born June 7, 1953, a daughter of Charles and Jean Boone of Mt. Pleasant, Maryland. Gary and Vicki drive tractor-trailer trucks together. One child:
         (a) Amy Marie Geisler, born September 14, 1982, and lived two days.
      (2) Donna Kay Geisler, born October 1, 1956
      (3) Carole Jean Geisler, born November 27, 1961
      (4) Lori Ann Geisler, born May 7, 1963
   b. Edwin B. Geisler, married Barbara.
   c. Emma S. Geisler, married Biser.
   d. M. Frances Geisler, married John A. Shafer.
   e. Mary Lucille Geisler.
   f. Elizabeth Geisler, born January 31, 1914 near Urbana, and died March 22, 1996. Married Wilcom, and had several children:
      (1) Ruth Elizabeth Wilcom, married Weast of Gaithersburg, and had children:
         (a) Tracy Ann Weast.
         (b) Susan Elizabeth Weast.

(2) Donald Lee Wilcom, married Mary; a son:

    (a) Daniel Christopher Wilcom.

5. Lavada E. Brandenburg, born August 4, 1889, died December 29, 1963. Her given name appears in some records as Lovetta. Married March 16, 1913 George Jacob Henry Kanode, born March 16, 1878, died March 6, 1956, son of Charles E. Kanode and Hester A. M. Zimmerman (1851). Two children:

  a. Charles Edward Kanode, born March 25, 1914.

  b. George Martin Rufus Kanode, born March 20, 1916

6. Samuel Gideon Brandenburg, born August 18, 1891 and died March 3, 1974. Married to Lola M. Haines, born May 7, 1896, died January 23, 1973. They are found in the 1920 census for Frederick County, with their first child. Two children, born in Maryland:

  a. Rufus Edgar Brandenburg, born April 28, 1914 in Maryland, died October 14, 1972. Married Margaret Werking, born September 1, 1908. He had a son:

    (1) Lee Edward Brandenburg, born November 26, 1941. Married July 5, 1961 to Connie Rose, born October 27, 1942, and had children:

      (a) Kimberly Brandenburg, born September 9, 1963

      (b) Kelly Brandenburg: February 22, 1965

  b. Dorothy Brandenburg. Married Thomas Steel, and second to Leo Summers.

7. Rufus Edgar Brandenburg, born November 6, 1893 and died August, 1971. Married February 17, 1915 to Lola Virginia Keller, born February 17, 1897. Three children:

  a. Jefferson Brandenburg, born November 7, 1915 and died August 8, 1970. Married Ruth Eaves, born July 22, 1917 and had a son:

    (1) Patrick Brandenburg, born July 21, 1957

b. William Aubrey Brandenburg, born May 12, 1917. Married Elizabeth Stup, born July 30, 1917. They had children:
  (1) Bonnie Lee Brandenburg: May 13, 1942
  (2) Carol Ann Brandenburg: January 30, 1945
  (3) William Aubrey Brandenburg, Jr., born October 15, 1948.
  (4) Veronica M. Brandenburg: October 24, 1955
c. Irving T. Brandenburg, born March 5, 1922. Married and had children:
  (1) Norma Brandenburg.
  (2) Michael Brandenburg, born April 11, 1956.
  (3) Keith Brandenburg.
8. Julia Emma Brandenburg, born August 8, 1895 and died September 25, 1895. Buried Monrovia Brethren Church.
9. Atlee Francis Brandenburg, born October 12, 1896 and died February 18, 1963, single.
10. Laura Priscilla Brandenburg, born October 21, 1898 and died June 20, 1977, single.
11. Charles Tyson Brandenburg, born November 22, 1900. Died March 16, 1966. Married May 14, 1921 to Carrie Manzella Plunkard, born December 11, 1902, and had nine children:
  a. C. Upton Caldwell Brandenburg, born June 9, 1922. Married April 7, 1945 to Betty Jane Rice, born November 3, 1926. Children:
    (1) Charles Franklin Brandenburg, born September 8, 1946, died in Vietnam August 5, 1967. Married August 15, 1965 to Connie Simpson, born May 23, 1946.
    (2) Phyllis Elaine Brandenburg, born June 9, 1949 and married April 14, 1973 to Gary Welsh, born February 26, 1947.

(3)   Ernie Lee Brandenburg, born October 20, 1951. Married June 28, 1970 Gail Lee Poole, born August 3, 1948. A son:

    (a) Ernie Lee Brandenburg, Jr., born August 6, 1971

b.   Mary Emma Brandenburg, born October 2, 1923. Married April 27, 1946 to Jonathan Forrest Covell, born April 26, 1916. They had children:

(1)   Lorna Jean Covell, born December 28, 1946. Married August 27, 1966 to Edwin Rhinehart and had children:

    (a) Lauri Ann Rhinehart: April 1, 1967

    (b) Kelly Marie Rhinehart: July 3, 1968

(2)   Thomas Bernard Covell, born July 21, 1948. Married September 3, 1970 to Iedje Buchens, born October 22, 1948 in the Netherlands.

(3)   Jonathan Wayne Covell, born April 1, 1950. Married June 5, 1971 to Donna Jean Werking, born July 30, 1952. One daughter:

    (a) Carrie Lynn Covell: August 13, 1972

c.   Edythe Charlotte Brandenburg, born July 24, 1925 at Urbana, Frederick County. Married October 27, 1945 in Frederick to Harold David Harshman, born April 21, 1923 near New Market, son of Harry Herbert Harshman and Ella Lavinia Burrier. They had children, born in Frederick County:

(1)   Harold David Harshman, Jr., born August 9, 1946. Married November 24, 1967 Monrovia to Patricia Ann Fox, born December 26, 1950 in Frederick, daughter of John Lewis Fox and Mary Catherine Graser. Two children:

    (a) Jeffrey Allen Harshman: October 8, 1968

    (b) Leslie Ann Harshman: January 16, 1971

(2)   Ronald Lee Harshman, born November 25, 1947. Married October 8, 1964 at Monrovia

to Linda Jean Blank, born January 3, 1948, daughter of Ralph Leon Blank and Evelyn Annabelle Morgan. They had children, born in Montgomery County:

    (a) Christie Dawn Harshman: May 4, 1966

    (b) Kimberly Diane Harshman: June 21, 1967

    (c) Gaylen Patrick Harshman: June 19, 1968

(3) Gareth Wayne Harshman, born November 27, 1950. Married February 29, 1968 in Frederick to Anna Margaret Himes, born April 5, 1949, daughter of Richard Maxwell Himes and Juanita Virginia Smith. Children:

    (a) Elizabeth Ann Harshman, born September 14, 1968 in Frederick County

    (b) Katherine JoAnn Harshman, born June 27, 1970 at McPherson, Kansas

    (c) Monica Jean Harshman, born January 30, 1975

(4) Charles Daniel Harshman, born March 16, 1955. Married June 16, 1979 to Joann Marie Heffner, born March 11, 1956, daughter of Paul Luther Heffner and Verna Elizabeth Burrier. At least one child:

    (a) Amy Jo Harshman, born August 25, 1982

(5) Melissa Ann Harshman, born July 6, 1959

d. Marshall E. Brandenburg, born February 9, 1927. Married April 30, 1949 to Dorothy White; divorced. Married second May 30, 1971 to Kathleen Newton Heller, born May 5, 1922. Children:

(1) Faye Elizabeth Brandenburg, born August 8, 1950. Married October 27, 1968 to Larry Repass, born August 18,1950. A daughter:

    (a) Anita Repass, born January 30, 1970

(2)　Larry Eugene Brandenburg, born August 6, 1952. Married 1970 to Jean Brashear, born March 24, 1953.

(3)　Tyson Willard Brandenburg: August 19, 1956

(4)　Timothy Wayne Brandenburg, born January 28, 1959.

(5)　Lori Ann Brandenburg: September 15, 1960

(6)　Carrie Naomi Brandenburg: August 21, 1962

e.　Gloria Irene Brandenburg, born December 4, 1930. Married May 14, 1955 to Daniel Bruce McFadyen, born December 20, 1932. A daughter:

(1)　Linda Sue McFayden: December 31, 1959

f.　Ira Franklin Brandenburg, born March 13, 1933. Married December 22, 1953 to Peggy Lou Rippeon, born November 20, 1933. Two daughters:

(1)　Sharon Lee Brandenburg: January 24, 1956

(2)　Norma Jean Brandenburg: August 9, 1966

g.　Barbara Ann Brandenburg, born November 15, 1934. Married September 16, 1955 Thomas Henry Payne, Jr., born November 25, 1932. They had four children:

(1)　Rex Allen Payne: June 11, 1956

(2)　Daniel Thomas Payne: December 7, 1958

(3)　Janet Marie Payne: August 4, 1961

(4)　Sherri Lynn Payne: August 16, 1969

h.　Norman Edward Brandenburg, born November 16, 1939. Married June 19, 1960 to Mary Margaret Williams, born December 6, 1941. Children:

(1)　Michael Edward Brandenburg, born September 30, 1962

(2)　Laura Patricia Brandenburg: January 17, 1966

i.　Martha Adelaide Brandenburg, born August 6, 1943 and married September 14, 1963 to Otis Calvin Norwood, born February 12, 1942. Childlren:

(1)　Stephen Douglas Norwood: February 7, 1968

12. William Elmer Brandenburg, born June 8, 1904. Died September 2, 1908.

Samuel Tracy Brandenburg
1858-1926

This son of Samuel Brandenburg and Julia Ann Catharine Grossnickle was born May 29, 1858 on his father's farm in Catoctin District of Frederick County, Maryland, and died June 20, 1926. Buried at Wolfsville Lutheran Church. After marriage Samuel began farming for himself on part of his father's farm, and later purchased from the estate that part on which he was living, containing one hundred and twenty-six acres of farm and timber land, located two miles north of Wolfsville. He was married to Susan Elizabeth Gaver, born March 21, 1860 and died May 10, 1945, daughter of Henry Gaver and Malinda Kline. Ten of their eleven children reached maturity, according to *History of Frederick County*; it appears that there may have been as many as twelve, one who died as a young man, and an infant, both buried with them. The family also appears in the 1900 census for Frederick County, found in the Soundex files at the National Archives. The film was exceptionally poor, and very difficult to read, but included the parents, and seven children. They appear again in the 1920 census of the county, with four of their children. He is listed there as Tracy Brandenburg; she is called Elizabeth, but the children's names are identifiable. The will of Samuel T., dated June 25, 1923 at Wolfsville, was probated June 30, 1926 and filed in liber GES2 at folio 25 in Frederick. In the will, he specifically identifies his parents, and his wife, by her name and that of her parents. He then names nine children, although there are known to have been as many as thirteen, according to all sources, not necessarily in order:

1. Nellie M. Brandenburg, born c.1882; married John C. Palmer.
2. Sadie Ellen Brandenburg, born May 14, 1883, died September 15, 1975. Married James Ellsworth Hessong, born 1870, died 1956, son of John Thomas Hessong and Matilda Kline. They lived on a farm on Smithsburg Road near Wolfsville, and had twelve children:
   a. Ruby Matilda Hessong, born October 24, 1904. Married to Hamilton of White Hall, Maryland, and had no children.
   b. Naomi Elizabeth Hessong, born February 24, 1906.
   c. James Ellsworth Hessong, Jr., born May 4, 1908. Served in the navy during second world war, married and had a son and daughter.
   d. Ruth Sarah Hessong, born July 24, 1910. Married to Draper of Smithsburg.
   e. John Thomas Hessong, III, born January 11, 1913.
   f. Joseph Ezra Hessong, born September 10, 1915, died October 12, 1972 of tractor accident. Served in the army during second world war. Married Elizabeth V. Poffenberger. Four sons and a daughter.
   g. George M. L. Hessong, born February 26, 1918. Moved to Lebanon, Oregon. Two boys; four girls.
   h. Arthur Jacob Hessong, born March 13, 1920. Killed in action southern France, August 13, 1944.
   i. Robert Lee Hessong, born April 19, 1922. Killed in action northern France, June 12, 1944.
   j. Parker Oliver Hessong, born May 18, 1924. Served as paratrooper in second world war. Moved to Des Moines, Iowa.
   k. Charles William Hessong, born June 23, 1926, and served in Germany during second world war.
   l. Paul Andrew Hessong, born August 6, 1929.
3. Nettie L. Brandenburg, born c.1884. Married to Blain Grossnickle.

4. Sallie V. Brandenburg, married Easterday.
5. Frank C. Brandenburg, born c.1889 according to the 1920 census, who moved to Texas. In the will of his father, this child is listed as Charles F., which is apparently more correct. He is listed as Frank in the 1920 census.
6. Charles P. Brandenburg, born c.1889
7. Samuel K. Brandenburg, born September 22, 1890 and died August 28, 1919.
8. Atlee Leucien Brandenburg, born April 21, 1892 and died May 27, 1893.
9. Kelley S. Brandenburg, who moved to South Dakota.
10. Katie M. Brandenburg, married Herbat.
11. Mamie A. Brandenburg, born c.1895
12. Austin M. Brandenburg, born c.1898
13. Wilmer H. Brandenburg, born c.1901. The father's will appears to name this child Wilbur H. Brandenburg, but he is clearly Wilmer in the 1920 census.

Alvey Raymond Brandenburg
1863-1949

This son of Samuel Brandenburg and Julia Ann Catharine Grossnickle was born July 21, 1863 on his father's farm in Catoctin District of Frederick County, Maryland, and died May 9, 1949. Buried at Foxville Lutheran Church. As a young man, he went to Illinois, remaining there for a year, before returning home, where he learned carpentry, and worked at the trade for the next eight years. During that time, he purchased a home and lands at Foxville, Maryland, from Thomas C. Fox, where he planted orchards and became a shipper of large quantities of fruit to the nearby cities. He married October 21, 1889 to Estelle Ethelyn Fox, born August 9, 1866 and died June 14, 1957; daughter of Thomas C. Fox and Ruth A. Buhrman. He and Estelle appear in the 1900 census for Frederick County, with two children. In the

1920 census for the county, they are living alone. Their children were all born in Frederick County:

1. Russell F. Brandenburg, born c.1891
2. Grace Estelle Brandenburg, born September 29, 1898, died February 23, 1922.
3. Samuel Ray Brandenburg, born October 1, 1901. Married December 9, 1921 to Rae Irene Hauver, born February 11, 1901. Children:
   a. Betty Grace Brandenburg, born September 13, 1922 and married November 31, 1952 to Knowlton Lewis Burgee. Children:
      (1) Knowlton Lewis Burgee, Jr.: April 20, 1950
      (2) Brian Lee Burgee: May 28, 1952
      (3) Bruce Adrian Burgee: January 6, 1954
   b. Samuel Ray Brandenburg, Jr., born October 9, 1923 and married 1942 to Margaret Swope, born December 23, 1925. A son:
      (1) Steven Thomas Brandenburg: March 5, 1943
   c. Eugene Hauver Brandenburg, born July 26, 1925. Married Leah Belle Buhrman, and had children:
      (1) Galen Barkley Brandenburg, born September 30, 1949
      (2) Karl Brandenburg: August 23, 1951
      (3) Dawn Lee Brandenburg: September 11, 1954
      (4) Kurt Hauver Brandenburg: May 16, 1958
   d. Harold Alvin Brandenburg, born January 20, 1928. Married August 7, 1954 to Elizabeth Ann Kuhn and had children:
      (1) Harold Alvin Brandenburg, Jr., born February 11, 1957
      (2) Jeffrey Lynn Brandenburg: April 13, 1963
   e. Carolyn Yvonne Brandenburg, born October 25, 1929. Married November 7, 1947 to Robert Lee Fishack. A daughter:
      (1) Deanna Rae Fishack, born June 29, 1948

f.   Nancy Joan Brandenburg, born September 16, 1936

g.   Julia Brandenburg, born August 7, 1938

h.   Arthur Carl Brandenburg, born November 10, 1940. Married February 28, 1970 to Sonja Mae Keller.

4.   Russell T. Brandenburg.

5.   Grace G. Brandenburg, born February 23, 1922 and died April 23, 1924. Buried with her parents at Foxville.

Elmer Caleb Brandenburg
1865-1950

This son of Samuel Brandenburg and Julia Ann Catharine Grossnickle was born November 13, 1865 on his father's farm in Catoctin District of Frederick County, Maryland. He died December 15, 1950 at Hagerstown. When he was eighteen years of age, he obtained a job with Frederick Leatherman, a general merchant in Wolfsville, but after about a year and a half, began working with his brother, Cornelius Upton Brandenburg, to learn carpentry. Three years later, he went into business for himself. He apparently went to North Dakota for a time, but in 1892, bought a small farm adjoining Wolfsville. He was married November 9, 1887 to Teresa Marie Smith, born July 9, 1868 in Frederick County, died December 24, 1904, daughter of Josiah F. Smith and Ellen A. Fox. Teresa is buried at Wolfsville Lutheran Church, with a son who died young. They had children, only one of whom reached adulthood. Elmer and Teressa appeared in the 1900 census for Frederick County, with their first living child, Bertha. Teressa died December 24, 1904, and Elmer married second in 1907 to Annie Mary Bachtel, of near Hagerstown, born February 24, 1872, died October 29, 1940. Elmer and Annie appear in the 1920 census for Washington County, Maryland, living alone. The two known children were:

1.   Ross Brandenburg, born May 11, 1888, died June 7, 1889 and buried with his mother.

2. Bertha Ruth Brandenburg, born July 6, 1890, died October 17, 1918. Married March, 1907 to Otho Victor DeLawter, born September 24, 1883, died June 21, 1970, son of George Noah DeLawter (1852) and Margaret Virginia Shuff (1863). Four children. After the death of Bertha, Otho Victor was married second March 24, 1921 to Eva Catherine Schroyer in Frederick. Bertha was the mother of children, including at least these two:

   a. Evylon Grace DeLawter, born December 22, 1907. Married January 15, 1925 to Philip Anthony Rauth, born June 21, 1906, died December 14, 1962. They had children, including:

      (1) Philip Anthony Rauth, born November 23, 1925. Married June 7, 1958 Catherine Newman, and had four children:

         (a) Evylon Beatrice Rauth: July 14, 1959

         (b) Lucinda Catherine Rauth, born August 19, 1961

         (c) Leslye Louise Rauth: August 31, 1963

         (d) Amanda Joan Rauth: August 15, 1964

      (2) Ellen Louise Rauth, born April 3, 1930. Married July 10, 1954 to Bradford Moore Purcell and had children:

         (a) Margaret Ann Purcell: May 28, 1955

   b. George Woodrow DeLawter, born December 3, 1913 and died March 1, 1980 in the Canal Zone, Panama. A minister, he was married.

Chester Robert Brandenburg
1870-

This son of Samuel Brandenburg and Julia Ann Catharine Grossnickle was born June 7, 1870 on his father's farm in Catoctin District of Frederick County, Maryland. He learned carpentry but at his father's death, took over management of the family farm for the next three years. He then bought a ninety-acre farm in Hauver's District in 1902, on which he built a three-story home containing ten rooms, a bank barn, and other farm buildings. He was married May 19, 1896 at Thurmont, Maryland, to Susan Dorothy Harbaugh, born February 27, 1874, daughter of Hamilton Harbaugh and Cornelia Ann Elizabeth Pryor, among the earliest and most prominent families in Harbaugh Valley. Chester and Dorothy appear in the 1900 census for Frederick County, with no children. In the 1920 census, they are found at Smithsburg, Washington County, Maryland, with five of their children. Also in the household is the sister and mother of Susan. The sister is listed as Anna M. Harbaugh, born c.1873. However, the mother-in-law is listed as Cornelia A. Hauver, born c.1847. We can not explain the difference in last names at this point, unless her mother was married a second time. We do know, of course, that Hauver was a name associated with the area. Children, born in Frederick County:

1. Ruth M. Brandenburg, born February 14, 1896 and died at the age of four months and four days. Buried at the Wolfsville United Church of the Brethren.
2. Roscoe Hamilton Brandenburg, born October 5, 1901
3. Eva C. Brandenburg, born c.1905
4. Mildred E. Brandenburg, born c.1907
5. Samuel Rue Brandenburg, born c.1910. In the census of 1920, this child is listed as Rice S. Brandenburg. We suspect that his real name was Samuel Rice, but have no proof at this point.
6. Kenneth Chester Brandenburg, born February 3, 1911

Solomon Brandenburg
1700-
Germany
*

Wilhelm Heinrich Brandenburg
1722-
*

Aaron Brandenburg
1761-1825
*   *   *   *   *   *   *
*
*   *   Samuel Brandenburg 1784
*
*   *   Henry Adolph Brandenburg 1785
*
*   *   Mary Brandenburg 1787
*
*   *   William Brandenburg 1790
*
*   *   Jacob Brandenburg 1792
*
*   *   Susannah Brandenburg 1795
*
*   *   Nancy Anne Brandenburg 1797
*
*   *   Aaron Brandenburg 1800
*
*   *   Elizabeth Brandenburg 1800
*
*   *   Mary Brandenburg 1802
*
*   *   John Brandenburg 1804
*
*   *   Joseph Brandenburg 1806
*
*   *   Sarah Brandenburg 1808
*
*   *   Israel Brandenburg 1811

CHAPTER 3

Aaron Brandenburg
1761-1825

This son of Wilhelm Heinrich Brandenburg, (1722), as above reported, was born February 18, 1761 in Frederick County, Maryland, and died July 22, 1825 in Lebanon, Warren County, Ohio. References to Aaron and his wife Ann, or Anna, are found in the IGI records of the Mormon Church. According to the descendance charts of the Mormon Church, Aaron's wife was Ann Brandenburg, born 1766 in Pennsylvania, and died February 12, 1846 in Donnelsville, Ohio, the daughter of Samuel Brandenburg, born c.1737 in Germany, and his wife Susan Shuester, born c.1735 in Pennsylvania. There were a number of children, the first five born at Middletown, in Frederick County, the next four in Hampshire County, Virginia, and the remainder in Allegheny County, Maryland. At some point after having their family, Aaron and Ann moved to Warren County, Ohio. It should be noted that ancestral files of the Mormon Church also include a listing for one William H. Brandenburg, said there to have been born about 1758 in Germany, and the son of Solomon Brandenburg. No wife is listed for William H., but these same children appear as being his, although the records are not nearly as complete as found in the same ancestral listings for Aaron. All other records point to them being the children of Aaron Brandenburg, as here listed, and as here referenced. The children will all be first listed here, followed by details of each child in birth order:

1. Samuel Brandenburg, born March 27, 1784, died August 5, 1855, of whom more as Child 1.
2. Henry Adolph Brandenburg, born January 10, 1785, died February 27, 1859, of whom more as Child 2.

3. Mary Brandenburg, born April 12, 1787, died April 13, 1788 in Frederick County. No further information.
4. William Brandenburg, born May 4, 1790, died March 8, 1875, of whom more as Child 4.
5. Jacob Brandenburg, born August 17, 1792, of whom more as Child 5.
6. Susannah Brandenburg, born February 17, 1795, of whom more as Child 6.
7. Nancy Anne Brandenburg, born November 13, 1797, died August 20, 1827 in Warren County, Ohio. Married there December 21, 1820 to Samuel French. No further information.
8. Aaron Brandenburg, twin, born March 1, 1800. Married to Rebecca Drake. Married second to Polly. No further information.
9. Elizabeth Brandenburg, twin, born March 1, 1800, of whom more as Child 9.
10. Mary or Polly Brandenburg, born August 7, 1802, and married October 5, 1826 in Warren County, Ohio, to Henry Voorhis. No further information.
11. John Brandenburg, born March 21, 1804, of whom more as Child 11.
12. Joseph Brandenburg, born February 18, 1806, of whom more as Child 12.
13. Sarah Brandenburg, born November 3, 1808, died September 16, 1875 in Morgan County, Indiana. Married first to James Egbert, and second Deurell D. Mathews. No further information.
14. Israel Brandenburg, born April 2, 1811, died March 29, 1846 in Warren County, Ohio. Married October 21, 1838 to Charlotte Rhodes. No further information.

CHILD 1

Samuel Brandenburg
1784-

This son of Aaron Brandenburg (1761) was born March 27, 1784 at Middletown, Frederick County, Maryland, and died August 5, 1855 in Clark County, Ohio. Married January 4, 1806 in Frederick County, Maryland, to Hannah Chittester, and second November 17, 1831 to Katherine Reyborn, born April 26, 1805. He had eleven children from his first marriage, and eleven from the second, all born in Frederick County. The family apparently moved to Ohio after 1848. The children were:

1. Anna Brandenburg, born August 10, 1787, died 1808
2. Mary Brandenburg, born April 28, 1808, died 1853
3. Elizabeth Brandenburg, born June 1, 1810
4. Sarah Brandenburg, born November 17, 1812
5. Aaron Brandenburg, born November 3, 1814
6. Susannah Brandenburg, born August 14, 1816
7. Eliphalet Brandenburg, born January 15, 1818, and died May 18, 1897. Married April 2, 1871 to Lydia A. Pefley Swank, and second to Susan Steepleton. One child was born in Montgomery County, Ohio to the first marriage, and six to the second in Clear Creek Township, Huntington County, Indiana:
   a. William S. Brandenburg.
   b. Mary Brandenburg.
   c. Anthony Brandenburg.
   d. Minerva Brandenburg.
   e. Sabina Brandenburg.
   f. Elias Brandenburg.
   g. Eveline Brandenburg.
8. Samuel Brandenburg, born April 20, 1820

9. Moses Brandenburg, born March 9, 1822, died February 24, 1892. Buried in Huntington County, Indiana. Married April 28, 1843 to Mariah E. Day, born November 17, 1825; second August 24, 1862 to Carolina Longanecker, born November 27, 1843 in Huntington County; and third, May 18, 1873 to Mary Mahon, born June 24, 1824 in Utica, New York. Seven children from the first marriage, and three from the second, none from the third, born in Huntington County:

    a. Henry E. Brandenburg, born April 29, 1845. Married to Molly.
    b. Samuel E. Brandenburg, born March 18, 1847. Married to Elizabeth Belle.
    c. Amonias Brandenburg, born December 11, 1848.
    d. John Wilson Brandenburg, born May 9, 1849, and married to Sarah Jane Carmin, born March 28, 1848
    e. Mary Ellen Brandenburg, born August 7, 1852, and married to John Grossman.
    f. Joseph S. Brandenburg, born April 15, 1856. Married to Susan Brandenburg.
    g. Adam Grant Brandenburg, born March 23, 1865. Married to Sarah Forst.
    h. Dorothy A. Brandenburg, born April 25, 1868, and married to W. M. Pinney.
    i. Caroline Brandenburg, born May 23, 1872.

10. Henry Brandenburg, born December 20, 1823.
11. Pranah Brandenburg, born November 8, 1825.
12. James C. Brandenburg, born October 20, 1832, died August 8, 1833
13. Joseph R. Brandenburg, born September 27, 1833
14. Andrew R. Brandenburg, born May 8, 1835
15. William S. Brandenburg, born May 6, 1836
16. John M. Brandenburg, born November 10, 1837
17. Margaret M. Brandenburg, born August 19, 1839

18. Martha C. Brandenburg, born December 8, 1840, died August 29, 1841
19. Mathew J. Brandenburg, born February 13, 1842
20. Benjamin M. Brandenburg, born March 20, 1844
21. Eliza J. Brandenburg, born March 21, 1847
22. Katharine Brandenburg, born October 18, 1848, died February 5, 1854

CHILD 2

Henry Adolph Brandenburg
1785-1859

This son of Aaron Brandenburg (1761) was born January 10, 1785, died February 27, 1859 in Donnelsville, Clark County, Ohio. Married 1813 to Letitia Gibson.

CHILD 4

William Brandenburg
1790-1875

This son of Aaron Brandenburg (1761) was born May 4, 1790 in Hampshire County, Virginia, and died March 8, 1875 in Blanchester, Clinton County, Ohio. Married in Allegany County, Maryland, March 10, 1812 to Mary Pierson, born there October 9, 1795, and died March 17, 1878 in Clinton County, Ohio, daughter of Stephen Pierson and Ester Robinson. Children, the first one born in Allegany County, Maryland; the second in Indianola, Warren County, Iowa; and the rest in Clinton County, Ohio:
1. Delila Brandenburg, born February 10, 1813. Married January, 1831 in Warren County, Ohio, to Thomas Cole.
2. Aaron Brandenburg, born February 10, 1815, of whom more following.

3. Nancy Brandenburg, born 1818. Married June 19, 1824 to Peter Dudley. Birth date or marriage date is incorrect, but as reported in Mormon Ancestral Records.
4. Mary Ann Brandenburg, died August 15, 1837.
5. Susan Brandenburg, born 1821. Married October 8, 1842 in Clinton County, Ohio to Aaron Fordice.
6. Sarah Brandenburg, born c.1823, died August 17, 1874.
7. Elizabeth Brandenburg, born c.1829, died October 28, 1864. Married August 20, 1842 in Clinton County, Ohio to James Osborn. Again, watch the dates.
8. Lucinda Brandenburg, born 1830, died January 21, 1861. Married September 30, 1847 to William Nash.
9. Moses Brandenburg, born February 1, 1834, died September 4, 1901. Married May 22, 1855 to Rebecca A. Gallaher.
10. Morgan Brandenburg, born April 15, 1837.

Aaron Brandenburg
1815-1897

This son of William Brandenburg (1790) was born February 10, 1815, and died March 10, 1897 in Warren County, Iowa. (There is a Warren County in Ohio, Iowa and Indiana, so there can be some confusion!). Married there June 28, 1840 to Rebecca Drake. Married second March 17, 1849 to Ellen Jane Hendershot. Four children from the first marriage born in Warren County, Ohio; and twelve from the second, born in Tazewell County, Illinois:
1. John Brandenburg, born 1841
2. Mary Ann Brandenburg, born February 5, 1843. Married to Milton Brant, born February, 1845.
3. Francis Marion Brandenburg, born October 6, 1844. Married Enfield Maxwell, born June 18, 1843. They had children, born in Clayton County, Iowa:

a. William Aaron Brandenburg, born October 10, 1869. Married Altana Adaline Penfield, born July 26, 1869. Children, born in Iowa:
    (1) Lola Ethel Brandenburg, born April 28, 1894. Married Harry Kennington Leedham, born August 5, 1889.
    (2) Amy Altana Brandenburg, born April 9, 1897. Married Glen Halliday, born April 19, 1897
    (3) Francis Merrill Brandenburg: July 11, 1899.
    (4) Harold Penfield Brandenburg, born September 11, 1902.
    (5) William Aaron Brandenburg: January 26, 1910
b. Walter Edgar Brandenburg, born June 11, 1871. Married Caroline Hanchett, born May 24, 1874 at Fairbury, Nebraska. Children, the first two born in Iowa; third in Kansas:
    (1) Lucile Eleanor Brandenburg, born January 21, 1900. Married to Overton Jewel McCollum, born February 2, 1898.
    (2) Unnamed, living child.
    (3) Walter Edgar Brandenburg: January 14, 1918.
c. Amos Warner Brandenburg, born September 22, 1873. Married Minnie May Perkins, born June 16, 1878 in Fayette County, Iowa. Children, born there:
    (1) Marion Ruby Brandenburg, born February 11, 1897. Married Vera Lucille Lickess, born October 12, 1898.
    (2) Amos Lyle Brandenburg, born February 17, 1899. Married Bessie Beatrice Quitmyer, born September 19, 1901.
    (3) Leta Mae Brandenburg, born February 17, 1899. Married first Glen Fred Nus, born December 23, 1895, and second to Frank J. Bahl, born November 13, 1901.

- (4) Dortha Lavon Brandenburg, born July 10, 1910. Married Robert John Mains, born July 5, 1897 at Wells, Minnesota.
- (5) Lura Lucille Brandenburg, December 14, 1914
- (6) Finis Edgar Brandenburg: August 23, 1917.
- d. George Clinton Brandenburg, born December 8, 1878. Married Julia Elminda Swanson.
- e. Amy Luelda Brandenburg, born November 2, 1879. Married first Donald Rennie and second Henry Carmichael.
- f. Laura Ethel Brandenburg, born March 11, 1883. Married Ralph Christianson.
4. Annie Brandenburg, born April 3, 1847.
5. Zerelda Brandenburg, born November 7, 1850, and married to Artis. They had a child:
   a. Minnie Artis, born c.1869 in Illinois.
6. Clinton C. Brandenburg, born April 29, 1851. Married to Henrietta Maxwell, born April 29, 1851.
7. Lydia Ellen Brandenburg, born May 25, 1853.
8. George Brandenburg, born August 6, 1854.
9. Martha Ann Brandenburg, born November 13, 1855
10. Aaron Douglas Brandenburg, born May 24, 1859. married Matilda Maxwell, born June 18, 1860
11. James M. Brandenburg, born May 9, 1859
12. Emma Brandenburg, born May 23, 1862
13. Eva Brandenburg, born February 5, 1864
14. Luelda Brandenburg, born November 18, 1866
15. Pleasant Brandenburg, born May 12, 1869
16. Ralph Barton Brandenburg, born March 20, 1871

CHILD 5

Jacob Brandenburg
1792-

This son of Aaron Brandenburg (1761) was born August 17, 1792 in Maryland. Married to Mary Worley born February 18, 1786 in Berkley County, Virginia. Six children, born in Warren County, Ohio:
1. Prudence Ann Brandenburg, born August 27, 1817
2. Joseph Brandenburg, born June 15, 1820.
3. William Brandenburg, born c.1822
4. Samuel Brandenburg, born c.1823. Married Susan McKinney and had seven children, born in Ohio:
   a. Frank Brandenburg: February 16, 1854
   b. Mary Brandenburg: c.1858
   c. Anna Brandenburg: c.1860
   d. William Brandenburg: c.1862
   e. Ella Brandenburg: c.1865
   f. Charles Brandenburg, born October 24, 1868. Married Sarah Edith Stogden, born February 7, 1887 in Clinton County, Ohio
   g. Irene Brandenburg: c.1872
5. Eliza A. Brandenburg, born c.1823
6. Silas Brandenburg, born June 1, 1825

CHILD 6

Susannah Brandenburg
1795-

This daughter of Aaron Brandenburg (1761) was born February 17, 1795. Married January 15, 1815 in Warren County, Ohio, to Edward Drake, born c.1782 in Pennsylvania. Children, born in Warren County, Ohio:

1. Julia Ann Drake, born c.1816; married Abraham Hines, born c.1812 in Warren County.
2. Rebecca Drake, born April 3, 1819. Married to her cousin, Aaron Brandenburg (1815). Children have been reported above under his name, which see.
3. Aaron Drake, born c.1825. Married Emeline Brown.
4. Mary Drake, born c.1826. Married William Hines.
5. Peter Drake, born c.1828. Married to Mary Ann Lawler.
6. Sarah E. Drake, born c.1832. Married to Joseph C. Currier, born in Butler County, Ohio.

CHILD 9

Elizabeth Brandenburg
1800-1894

This daughter of Aaron Brandenburg (1761) was born March 1, 1800, a twin, and died September 22, 1894 in Warren County, Ohio. Married there May 18, 1822 to David S. Hopping, Sr. and had seven children. Married second James Bush and had one child. Her children were born in Warren County, Ohio:

1. Mary M. Hopping, born September 22, 1823, and married to Ezekiel R. Hopping, born November 8, 1822 in Greene County, Ohio. Children, born in Warren County:
   a. James L. Hopping, born c.1852 and married to Nancy Adaline Fudge, born February, 1856 in Delaware County, Indiana.
   b. Mary Ellen Hopping, born August 27, 1855. Married James C. Truitt, born June 8, 1851 in Delaware County, Indiana.
   c. John Hopping, born c.1857. Married to Mary Elizabeth Helm, born October, 1860 Delaware County, Indiana.

  d. Elizabeth Hopping, born c.1859. Married to Marquis A. Ekeberg, born c.1861 in Delaware County, Indiana.

  e. Albert Hopping, born July 31, 1862

  f. William Morris Hopping, born January, 1866. Married Sarah Emily Helm, born October, 1866 in Delaware County, Indiana.

2. Jane Hopping, born c.1824. Married James Bush and had a daughter:

  a. Letitia Bush.

3. Ezekiel Hopping, born c.1826

4. Sarah Ann Hopping, born c.1830

5. David S. Hopping, Jr., born September 29, 1831 and married to Margaret Thompson, born March 2, 1835 in Warren County, Ohio. Children, born there:

  a. William Horace Hopping, born July 11, 1853. Married to Sarah.

  b. Sarah Hopping, born March 28, 1855. Married to Thomas Russell Evans.

  c. Ellery Elwood Hopping, born April 23, 1857. Married Mamie Dwelly, born December 27, 1874. Married second Alice May Stokes, born December, 1859

  d. Charles Louis Hopping, born July 18, 1859. Married Florence Kaiper, born February 27, 1896, and second to Abba Bellmyer.

  e. Anna Hopping, born October 12, 1862; married to James Mitchell, born c.1856.

  f. Mary Elizabeth Hopping, born February 22, 1865.

6. Franklin Hopping, born c.1835. Married to Eliza Hopping, and had children:

  a. Eliza Hopping, born c.1861

  b. Albert John Hopping, born c.1863

7. Elizabeth Hopping, born c.1837

8. Eliza Hopping, born c.1840. Married Brant.

9. Albert M. Hopping, born February 26, 1841, and married to Adaline Carter, born March 18, 1842. Children, born in Warren County, Ohio:
   a. Gladys Hopping, born March 17, 1867
   b. Alberta Hopping, born July 13, 1868
10. Letitia B. Hopping, born c.1847. Married Samuel Stubbs and had children, born Warren County, Ohio:
   a. Edward Stubbs.
   b. Horace Stubbs.
   c. Zimrial Stubbs.
   d. Oscar Stubbs.
   e. William Stubbs.
   f. Laura Stubbs, married Keever.
   g. Alice Stubbs, married Charles Presley.

CHILD 11

John Brandenburg
1804-1864

This son of Aaron Brandenburg (1761) was born March 21, 1804, died April 16, 1864 in Lebanon, Warren County, Ohio. Married in Richland County, Ohio, September 7, 1838 to Lydia Jane Sisney, born November 6, 1822 in Ohio. Children, born in Ohio:
1. Thomas Simmon Brandenburg, born August, 1839.
2. John William Brandenburg, born November 14, 1840. Married Melissa Jane Cooper, born December 4, 1849 in Illinois. Children, the first five born at Marion County, Oregon; the last two at Klamath, Oregon:
   a. Althea Anna Brandenburg: March 31, 1869
   b. Clyde Konine Brandenburg: June 5, 1871
   c. Maude Myrtle Brandenburg: July 15, 1875

d.   Floyd Hulbert Brandenburg, born March 8, 1880. Married Helen Howard Gay, born October 13, 1875 in Colusa County, California.
e.   Grace Edith Brandenburg: May 7,1883
f.   Mabel Elson Brandenburg: February 7, 1887
g.   Earl Brandenburg: January 7, 1891
3.   George Washington Brandenburg, born c.1842
4.   Joseph Henry Brandenburg, born c.1844
5.   Martha Jane Brandenburg, born c.1846
6.   Phoebe Ann Brandenburg, born c.1848
7.   Harriet Lois Brandenburg, born c.1850

CHILD 12

Joseph Brandenburg
1806-1875

This son of Aaron Brandenburg (1761) was born February 18, 1806, and died 1875. Married to Sarah Voorhis, born September 1, 1805 in Ohio. She died in Warren County, Ohio, February 17, 1882. Children, all born there:
1.   Mary Ann Brandenburg, born March 12, 1831, and married March 12, 1851 to William Worley Shurts, born April 4, 1826 in Deerfield, Warren County, Ohio. Children, born in Lebanon, Warren County:
a.   Laura Shurts, born March 14, 1853. Married John Collins, born c.1848
b.   Sarah E. Shurts, born December 17, 1854
c.   Huldah Delise Shurts, born c.1856
d.   Henry Clay Shurts, born August 18, 1859. Married Anny Lytle.
e.   Catherine V. Shurts, born September 25, 1861 and married to Joseph Smith.
f.   Joseph B. Shurts, born 1862. Married Lena Swigart.

g. Anneta Shurts, born December 2, 1866, and married Lewis Mankor Dunn, born March 4, 1867 in Marion County, Indiana

h. William Worley Shurts, born April 18, 1869. Married Nancy J. Huffman.

i. Lewly Ardena Shurts, born October 15, 1871. Married Okey Dunn, born February 2, 1874.

j. Cora Ada Shurts, born c.1879

2. Henry E. Brandenburg, born September 29, 1832. Married Victoria Minor.

3. James Brandenburg, born August 15, 1834

4. Lawrence Brandenburg, born March 13, 1836, died March 7, 1860

5. Albert Brandenburg, born December 29, 1839

6. Caroline Brandenburg, born July 26, 1840. Married to James Hamilton.

7. Catherine Elizabeth, twin, born December 12, 1841

8. Daniel Brandenburg, twin, born December 12, 1841, an infant death.

9. Daniel Brandenburg, second use of the name, born December 6, 1843. Married Lydia Stevenson.

10. John Brandenburg, born 1845, died 1846

11. Robert Brandenburg, born October 8, 1852

Solomon Brandenburg
1700-
Germany
*

*

Wilhelm Heinrich Brandenburg
1722-
*

*

Mathias Brandenburg
1763-1818
*

*

*   *   *   *   *   *   *
*
*   * Abraham Brandenburg
*
*   * Jacob Brandenburg 1783
*
*   * Frederick Brandenburg 1788
*
*   * Henry Brandenburg 1792
*
*   * David Brandenburg 1795
*
*   * Catherine Brandenburg 1795
*
*   * Isaac Brandenburg 1797
*
*   * Daniel Brandenburg 1805

CHAPTER 4

Mathias Brandenburg
1763-1818

This son of Wilhelm Heinrich Brandenburg, as earlier reported, was one of the earlier settlers of Frederick County, Maryland. He was born c.1763 and died October 18, 1818 at the age of 55. He was a teamster, hauling merchandise to and from Baltimore. Over time, by diligent effort and hard work, he acquired a substantial property in the Jackson District of the county. He was married December 16, 1787 to Barbara Keller, born c.1769 and died February 16, 1826. She was a daughter of John Jacob Keller (1743) and Anna Maria Humbert (1747). Mathias and his wife are buried at Christ Reformed Church cemetery in Middletown. The will of Mathias was dated September 28, 1818 and probated November 10, 1818, filed in liber HS2 at folio 208, Frederick County. He names his wife, Barbara, and seven children. There appear to have been at least eight, listed here, followed by details as they may be available as to certain of the children:
1. Abraham Brandenburg, of whom nothing is known.
2. Jacob Brandenburg, not mentioned in the will, but said to be a son, of whom more as Child 2.
3. Frederick Brandenburg, born February 9, 1788, of whom more as Child 3.
4. Henry Brandenburg, born in 1792, of whom more as child 4.
5. David Brandenburg, born c.1795, of whom more as Child 5.
6. Catherine Brandenburg, born 1795, of whom more as Child 6.
7. Isaac Brandenburg, born November 28, 1797, of whom more as Child 7.

8. Daniel Brandenburg, born c.1805, of whom more as Child 8.

CHILD 2

Jacob Brandenburg
1783-1855

This son of Mathias Brandenburg (1763) is perhaps the same Jacob who is buried at Christ Reformed Church at Middletown with other members of this family. If so, he was born January 11, 1783 and died July 13, 1855. Married May 9, 1808 to Catherine Wile, born c.1785 and died January 24, 1863 at the age of 78 years, 3 months and 4 days. She is buried at Middletown Lutheran Church. Also buried there, and said to be a son of Jacob and Catherine Brandenburg, and perhaps the son of this couple, is:
1. William Lee Brandenburg, born January 1, 1826 and died October 27, 1855

CHILD 3

Frederick Brandenburg
1788-1823

This son of Mathias Brandenburg (1763) was born February 9, 1788 and died January 15, 1823. Buried at Middletown Reformed Church. He was married May 9, 1812 to Elizabeth Derr, born c.1791, died March 9, 1870, aged 79 years, 11 months and 12 days. Buried at Zion Church, Middletown, she was the daughter of Philip Derr (1750) and Barbara Koogle (1755). After the death of Frederick, she married February 18, 1824 Michael Motter, born 1790 and died May 5, 1824, a suicide by hanging. He had been first married July 2, 1810 to Catherine Keller, and was a tanner and currier.

Elizabeth then married third February 3, 1836 to Daniel Routzahn, born 1783, died 1869. Apparently no children.

CHILD 4

Henry Brandenburg
1792-1869

This son of Mathias Brandenburg and Barbara Keller was born December 12, 1792 on the family farm, two miles south of Myersville, Frederick County, Maryland, and died c.1869. After the death of their parents, he and his brother Daniel purchased the home farm, and divided it. On his portion, Henry built a substantial two-story brick dwelling, a bank barn, and other farm buildings. He was married December 23, 1819 to Mary Biser, born c.1801 and died 1859, daughter of Frederick Biser, and had five children, two of whom are buried with their parents at Christ Reformed Church at Middletown. The couple appears in the 1850 census for Frederick County with five children, including the two who are buried with them:

1. Malinda Brandenburg, born October 3, 1820, and died July 13, 1856. Buried at Middletown.
2. Elizabeth Brandenburg, born May 27, 1822 and died 1859. Buried at Middletown.
3. Mary A. Brandenburg, born c.1824. Mary was apparently never married. She appears in the 1900 census of Frederick County at the age of 76, with her sister, Harriet, at the age of 71, who was apparently also single, both still bearing the Brandenburg name.
4. Harriett Brandenburg, born July 31, 1828, died October 31, 1905. Buried at the Middletown Reformed Church
5. Eli Brandenburg, born May 15, 1830 on the family farm, and died March 23, 1911. The farm consisted of seventy-five acres of tillable land, which he purchased from the

estate after the death of his father. To the family farm, he later added twenty acres, and also purchased thirty-five acres of timber land on Catoctin Mountain. Married in Frederick County, Maryland, February 2, 1854 to Susanna Civilla Main, born June 19, 1835, died November 30, 1917. Both are buried at the Christ Reformed Church at Middletown. She was a daughter of William Main of Frederick. Eli wrote a will, dated Spetember 1, 1900 and probated April 3, 1911, filed in liber WBC2 at folio 398 in Frederick County. He names his wife, and eight of their children. The will of Susanna, dated May 23, 1912, was probated December 8, 1917, and filed in liber SD2 at folio 460 in Frederick, reading much the same as that of her husband. The family appears in the 1880 census for Frederick County, with seven of the children. In the 1900 census for the county, Eli and Susan are living alone. There were nine children, eight of whom reached maturity:

a.   Theodore McAuley Brandenburg, born August 12, 1855, died March 27, 1943. Buried at Mt. Olivet cemetery in Frederick. Married Amanda Catherine Harp, born 1857, died 1923, daughter of Josiah and Mary Harp. Theodore appears as head of household in the 1900 census for Frederick County, but his wife is there listed as Maude, born c.1855, with four children. In the 1920 census for the county, his wife is listed as Amanda, born c.1858, with one of their sons, Harry J., who appears in both census records. It appears possible that Theodore may have been married twice, first to Maude, and second to Amanda. His children included:

(1)   Guy Brandenburg, born c.1884 (census), and died 1973. This appears to be Homer Guy Brandenburg, according to the 1920 census of Hagerstown, Washington County. He is found

there with a wife, Emma, born c.1884 and one daughter:

    (a) Helen Brandenburg, born c.1903

(2)   Jennie Brandenburg, born c.1890 (census)

(3)   Harry Brandenburg, born c.1894 (census)

(4)   Josiah Brandenburg, born 1894, died 1972. Married February 19, 1924 Virginia Howard Smith, born 1902, died 1957. One daughter:

    (a) Virginia Ann Brandenburg, born August 24, 1925. Married November 29, 1947 to Thomas Eugene Walsh. Six children.

(5)   Edna Naomi Brandenburg, born 1896, died 1972. (census) Married March 17, 1939 to Percy Allen Sigler.

(6)   Jennie May Brandenburg, born January 30, 1889, died September 23, 1913. Buried at Mt. Olivet cemetery, Frederick.

b.   Marion Granville Brandenburg, born 1857, of whom more

c.   George Wilson Brandenburg of Middletown, born 1861, died 1934. Married Mary E. Kinna, born c.1860. They appear in the 1900 census of Frederick County, with two children:

(1)   Ralph L. Brandenburg, born c.1884 and died 1944. Married Grace E. Leatherman, born 1888, died 1968. They were found in the 1920 census of Hagerstown, Washington County, Maryland, with one daughter. His father and mother were living with them at the time. Their daughter was:

    (a) Hazel O. Brandenburg, born April 16, 1910. Married James Moss, born April 20, 1906.

(2)   Clay K. Brandenburg, born c.1893, died 1962. Married first Eleanor F. Stine, born 1894, died

1942. Clay and Eleanor were living in Washington County, Maryland during the census taking of 1920; there were no others in the household. Married second Ida Bragunier and had two children:

    (a) Roland Brandenburg, born May 14, 1922. Married Mary Gertrude Gaylor, born November 25, 1923. Eight children.

    (b) Hubert A. Brandenburg: March 6, 1925

d.   Calvin R. Brandenburg, born 1863, died 1935. Married Rhoda Healey, and moved to California.

e.   James C. Brandenburg, born 1868, died 1943; buried at Middletown Reformed Church, single.

f.   Edward Franklin Brandenburg, born 1870, moved to Colorado.

g.   William Washington Brandenburg, who was a merchant in Harmony, Maryland. Born 1873 and died 1953, buried at Christ Reformed Church in Middletown, with his wife. Married 1893 to Effie Mary Green, born 1870, died 1922, daughter of John W. Green and Rebecca Moser. They were found in the 1900 census for Frederick County, with four of their children, and again in the 1920 census, with four, two of whom were not in the earlier census. In 1920, Effie's father was living with them at the age of seventy-four years. Six children:

    (1) Rhoda May Brandenburg, born September 29, 1894. Married January 12, 1918 to Charles Earl Butts, born 1893, died 1960

    (2) Bessie Marie Brandenburg, born February 16, 1896; single.

    (3) Amy Viola Brandenburg, born June 6, 1897. Married June 23, 1928 to Oliver Glenn Harne, born 1895, died 1962.

(4) Edgar L. Brandenburg, born 1900, died 1928 and buried with his parents.

(5) Vinnie Frederica Brandenburg, born July 14, 1904. Married June 30, 1927 to Bernard Joseph Murphy, born March 29, 1906.

(6) Margretta Susanna Rebecca Brandenburg, born September 28, 1906

h. Clarence Main Brandenburg, born c.1875 and died April 28, 1883 at the age of 7 years, 8 months and 11 days. Buried with his parents.

i. Lewis Henry Brandenburg, born 1878, died 1961. Married Melissa Alverta Summers, born 1873, died 1975, daughter of Joshua Summers and Mary E. Leatherman. They were found without children in the 1900 census of Frederick County. In the 1920 census of the county, they had the two children listed following. Two children:

(1) Viola Virginia Brandenburg, born October 3, 1905. Married March 22, 1926 to Hubert Conrad Easterday, born September 19, 1902.

(2) Olive Beatrice Brandenburg, born January 18, 1909. Married John A. Derr, born 1910, died 1975. One daughter.

Marion Granville Brandenburg
1857-1944

This son of Eli Brandenburg was born July 11, 1857 on the home farm in Jackson District of Frederick County, and remained there working with his father until he reached the age of twenty-two. He died September 25, 1944 and is buried at Christ Reformed Church at Middletown with his wife. He was married to Laura Catherine Routzahn, born October 30, 1858 and died May 4, 1936; daughter of Noah Routzahn and Elizabeth Barbara Smith. After marriage, he farmed the P. J.

Levy farm for the next sixteen years, then for two years his father-in-law's farm, and in 1900, purchased the Thaddeus M. Biser farm, consisting of one hundred and four acres, a mile and a half south of Myersville, on the old Hagerstown Road. The census of 1900 for Frederick County lists the family, with the parents and four children. In the 1920 census for the county, the parents are listed, living alone. Four children:

1. Elmer Granville Brandenburg, born October 26, 1880, died May 20, 1957. A merchant in Hagerstown, he was married to Edith or Jennie Harp, born January 27, 1882, died 1976. They were found in the 1920 census for Hagerstown, Washington County, Maryland. Children:
   a. Albert Harp Brandenburg, born June 5, 1905. Married March 28, 1928 to Carnella Brewer, born June 5, 1905.
   b. Helen Adele Brandenburg, born 1908, died 1977
   c. Vivian May Brandenburg, born March 12, 1912
2. Carrie Lucinca Brandenburg, born November 24, 1883, died March 10, 1954. Married January 23, 1907 Franklin Peter Shank, born September 22, 1887, died April 11, 1917, son of John Jacob Shank and Clara Virginia Harp. They had children:
   a. Myree Virginia Shank, born 1907
   b. George Franklin Shank, born 1910, died 1965
   c. Margaret Catherine Shank, born 1917
3. Oscar Calvin Brandenburg, born 1886, died 1978. He married Vada Toms, born 1886 and had one son, found in the 1920 census for Frederick County:
   a. Austin T. Brandenburg, born September 5, 1918. Married Grace Eleanor Rohrer, born April 17, 1920 and had two children:
      (1) Ronald L. Brandenburg, born June 28, 1942. Married Mary Ann Pappalardo, born August 3, 1945, and had two children:

      (a) Lee Jeffrey Brandenburg, born December 27, 1972

      (b) Kerry Ann Brandenburg: April 26, 1974.

  (2)   Linda Brandenburg, born May 7, 1949. Married Fred Watkins Gregory, born January 6, 1949.

4.   Annie E. Brandenburg, born 1892, died 1928. Married Paul George DeLawder, born 1894, died 1926. They had seven children:

    a.   Earl Eugene DeLawder, born 1912

    b.   Bruce Paul DeLawder, born 1913

    c.   Katherine DeLawder, born 1915

    d.   Geneva DeLawder, born 1917

    e.   Richard Allen DeLawder, born 1921

    f.   Garland Granville DeLawder, born June 5, 1923

    g. Pauline Elizabeth DeLawder, born August 29, 1924

CHILD 5

David Brandenburg
1795-1878

This son of Mathias Brandenburg and Barbara Keller was born c.1795, and died February 10, 1878. Buried at Christ Reformed Church, Middletown, with his wife. He was married in Frederick County, October 19, 1822 to Catharine Routzahn, born c.1814, died July 10, 1889. Also one son buried there. The family appears in the 1850 census of Frederick County, with several children. There is also Mahala Brandenburg, born c.1834, listed out of order with the others, apparently not their child. The children were:

1.   Maria Brandenburg, born September 6, 1823, died August 6, 1886. Married February 2, 1846 to David William Knox, born 1820, died December 2, 1886. They had children:

a. Effie J. C. Knox.
b. Mary Knox, born 1848, died 1925
c. Sarah Knox, born 1851, died 1868
d. Charles Knox, born 1854
e. Emma Knox, born 1859
2. Eliza A. Brandenburg, born October 11, 1825, and of whom more following.
3. Catharine Brandenburg, born September 27, 1827.
4. Allen Brandenburg, born September 11, 1829, died October 1, 1842. Buried with his parents at Christ Reformed Church in Middletown.
5. Leah Ann Brandenburg, born August 21, 1831, died January 24, 1898. Married December 15, 1857 in Frederick County, Jacob Henry Flook, born August 1, 1829, died July 5, 1898, the son of John Philip Flook and Magdalena Shoemaker. Children:
a. John Flook.
b. David Flook.
c. Anna Flook, married Charles E. Minnick.
6. Ann Elizabeth Brandenburg: November 21, 1833.
7. Mahala Brandenburg, born May 9, 1836.
8. Peter Jonas Brandenburg, born June 6, 1839. Married December 21, 1863 in Frederick County to Catherine Flook, born 1836, daughter of John Philip Flook and Magdalena Shoemaker. Peter appears as head of household in the 1880 census for Frederick County, with his wife, and four children. In the 1900 census for the county, he and his wife appear alone. They had at least the four children listed:
a. Emma F. Brandenburg, born c.1866
b. Estie C. Brandenburg, born c.1868
c. Clemmie M. Brandenburg, born c.1870
d. Effie Alberta M. Brandenburg, born 1872, and died 1956.
9. David Brandenburg, Jr., born c.1841

10. Lucinda Brandenburg, born c.1843
11. Mary Ellen Brandenburg, born August 25, 1848 and died January 2, 1927. Single.

Eliza A. Brandenburg
1825-1871

This daughter of David Brandenburg (1795) and Catharine Routzahn (1814) was born October 11, 1825, and died December 8, 1871. Not included with the family in the 1850 census, having been married October 9, 1847 in Frederick County to George Levi Routzahn, born May 1, 1826, and died November 12, 1907 in Montgomery County, Ohio. They had children:

1. Carlton Routzahn, born July 10, 1848, died September 20, 1848.
2. Sarah Ellen Routzahn, born June 2, 1849, died February 6, 1850.
3. Charles David Routzahn, born February 5, 1851, died after 1920. Married Charlotte M. Linebaugh, born September, 1850. They moved to Ohio c.1870 and settled west of Dayton. Four children, the first born in Maryland, the last three in Ohio:
   a. Carrie B. Routzahn, born 1872. Married John W. Stockslager, born September 1, 1872 at Myersville, Maryland, died August 2, 1944.
   b. Walter E. Routzahn, born April 6, 1882, died 1959. Married in Montgomery County, Maryland 1908 to Edith M., born November 4, 1882, died August 11, 1973. He operated a furniture store in Farmersville, Ohio, and later became a mortician in Covington, Ohio.
   c. Elmer E. Routzahn, born May, 1886, killed in an automobile accident, November 23, 1932. Married

to Marie E., born July 14, 1888, died October, 1966. He was also a mortician. Children:

    (1)   Gerald Routzahn.

    (2)   Rosemarie Routzahn.

d.   Alma B. Routzahn, born August 1, 1891, died September 12, 1984 at New Lebanon, Ohio.

4.   Martin Luther Routzahn, born September 27, 1853, died May 4, 1892 in Montgomery County, Ohio, from injuries while felling a tree. Married Ann Cordelia Poffenberger, born April 13, 1852 near Myersville, Maryland, daughter of George J. Poffenberger (1824) and Sarah A. Doub (1831). Martin Luther had moved to Ohio before 1880, but after his death, his wife returned to Maryland, living in Hagerstown. Ann Cordelia died February 5, 1923 at her daughter's home at Hagerstown. Children:

a.   Milton Doub Routzahn, born December 26, 1880 in Ohio, died January 30, 1947 at Odenton, in Anne Arundel County, Maryland. Married Florence Brady, daughter of John Brady and Elizabeth Hopkins of Baltimore; who died August 22, 1958. Children:

    (1)   Milton Doub Routzahn, Jr.: October 25, 1917

    (2)   Jeanette Brady Routzanh, married Franzl.

    (3)   Martin Luther Routzahn, born June 3, 1925, died November, 1991. Married June 3, 1945 to Ruth Lorraine Hummer, born December 4, 1927, in Talbot County, Maryland, daughter of Roy Christopher Hummer and Helen Florence Hashhagen. Three children.

b.   Flora May Routzahn, born June 23, 1882 in Ohio, died 1948 in Baltimore. Married in Ohio to William Guy Kline, born January 1, 1882 in Frederick, Maryland, died September 12, 1932, son of Josiah Kline and Caroline Kehne. Eight children.

c.   Sarah Grace Routzahn, born May 18, 1884 in Ohio and died there July 19, 1884

d. George Markwood Routzahn, born October 14, 1888 in Ohio. Married Edna Best, and returned to Maryland after his father's death.

e. Joseph Routzahn, born 1889 in Ohio, but returned to Maryland with his mother.

5. Emma Frances Routzahn, born January 9, 1857

6. George Washington Routzahn, born May 22, 1860, died January, 1935 in Ohio. Married August 9, 1883 to Lillie Mae Routsong, born January 22, 1865 in Montgomery County, Ohio, and died there June 20, 1894, killed by lightning, the daughter of Jacob Routsong, Jr. (1840). They had children:

a. Walter Jacob Routzahn, born December 8, 1884, died August 7, 1934. Married to Hannah Catherine Stine.

b. Russell Henry Routzahn, born August 8, 1887, died February 15, 1969. Married Daisy Viola Long.

c. Grace Margaret Routzahn, born March 9, 1889, and died October 16, 1958. Married to William Arnold Barr.

d. Harold Robert Routzahn, born March 23, 1894 and died July 25, 1979. Married Ruth Marie Nicholas.

e. Beulah Katharine Routzahn, born April 12, 1896 and died September 13, 1987. Married first to Earl Franklin Sever; second to Walter George Boswell.

f. Raymond Scott Routzahn, born December 10, 1898, died August 14, 1979. Married to Melissa Frances Jones.

g. Stella Jeanette Routzah, born November, 1899, died March 22, 1919. Married to John Davis.

h. Edna Marie Routzahn, born August 18, 1901, died January 16, 1964. Married George Oliver Palmer.

7. Eliza Ann Florence Routzahn, a twin, born February 15, 1864. Married Henry W. Poff.

8. Anna Elizabeth Catherine Routzahn, a twin, born February 15, 1864, died April 14, 1864.
9. Esta May Routzahn, born August 22, 1866
10. Grant Ulysses S. Routzahn, born January 4, 1870, died July 31, 1870

CHILD 6

Catherine Brandenburg
1795-1863

This daughter of Mathias Brandenburg and Barbara Keller was born 1795, and died 1863. Married December 23, 1819 in Frederick County, to John Jacob Biser, born 1793, died 1870, son of Frederick Biser (1763) and Mary Margaret Coblentz (1765). Children:
1. Ezra Biser, born 1820. Married Eleanora Dutrow, born 1838, died 1874. At least one daughter:
   a. Emma Alice Biser, born 1862, died 1905.
2. George Washington Biser, born October 8, 1838, died April 3, 1915. Married Mary Jane Keller, born June 2, 1845, died July 24, 1908 at Keedysville, Washington County, Maryland. She was a sister of Amanda C. Keller, who married her husband's brother. Two children:
   a. Charles C. Biser.
   b. Harvey G. Biser.
3. Joshua Frederick Biser, born May 31, 1841, and died June 10, 1918 at Eakle's Mills, Washington County, Maryland. Married November 24, 1868 near Middletown to Amanda C. Keller, born August 28, 1842, died May 31, 1926. Three children:
   a. Lulu M. Biser.
   b. Wellington Frederick Biser.
   c. Edward S. Biser.

CHILD 7

Isaac Brandenburg
1797-1876

This son of Mathias Brandenburg and Barbara Keller was born died May 6, 1876 in Middletown Valley, Frederick County, Maryland. Buried at the Reformed Church with his wife, at Middletown. Married about December 21, 1820 in the city of Frederick to Catherine Youtsey, born August 5, 1792, died April 7, 1868, one of the twelve children of Michael and Christiana Youtsey. Isaac was one of the earlier settlers of Frederick County, owning a farm of one hundred and fifty-two acres, located in the Middletown Valley, which he apparently purchased prior to 1810. Isaac wrote a will, dated February 9, 1874 and probated May 22, 1876, filed in liber JRR1 at folio 42 in Frederick County. He requests that he be buried with his wife at the Reformed Church Cemetery in Middletown, and that his estate be sold and divided into six parts for distribution. He then provides that each part is to go to each of the five children then living, and that the remaining part be held in trust for the child of his daughter, Sarah Ann. The children have also been reported in *History of Frederick County, Maryland*, by T. J. C. Williams. Six children, all born in Maryland, probably near Middletown:

1. Daniel Brandenburg, born May 6, 1823, of whom more.
2. Lydia Ann Brandenburg, born August 19, 1825, and died November 14, 1921. Married Edward L. Herring, born February 15, 1817, died June 2, 1880.
3. Mary Ann Brandenburg, born May 11, 1828, died March 27, 1904 at West Lebanon, Ohio. Married February 5, 1851 to Isaiah Routzahn, born 1830, died 1893, son of Adam Routzahn and Mary Ann Poffenberger.
4. Joel Brandenburg, born July 3, 1830, and died January 24, 1877 at the age of 45 years, 6 months and 21 days.

Buried at Christ Reformed Church at Middletown. Perhaps also the same Joel who was married in Frederick County, April 23, 1857 to Melissa Hewitt.

5. Cornelia Ann Brandenburg, born October 13, 1832, died September 25, 1915. Buried at Reformed Church in Middletown, Maryland. Married Jonathan C. Main, born November 23, 1826, died September 24, 1902.

6. Sarah Ann Brandenburg, born c.1836. Married in Frederick County, November 8, 1860, to John Henry Michael. Isaac's will provides that the share to the daughter of this couple is to be held in trust by his executor, "so that John Henry Michael can not spend it" and turned over to her when she reaches maturity, or to her mother if John Henry dies first. The daughter was:

a. Flora Michael.

Daniel Brandenburg
1823-1902

This son of Isaac Brandenburg was born May 6, 1823 and died May 12, 1902 on his father's farm in the Middletown Valley of Frederick County, Maryland. He farmed the home property until his death at the age of seventy-nine years and six days. Married February 10, 1851 to Lydia A. R. Remsburg, born May 2, 1829 and died September 17, 1914 at the age of 85 years, 4 months and 15 day, daughter of Henry Remsberg and Elizabeth Coblentz. They are buried at Christ Reformed Church at Middletown. The couple appear in the 1900 census for Frederick County, living alone. His will, dated April 15, 1898, was probated May 22, 1902 and filed in liber CES1 at folio 318 in Frederick County. He left to his wife a mountain lot of 17 acres and 36 square perches, known as *Mansylvania*, and his personal property. He must have been fairly well-to-do, mentioning in his will such things as bank certificates, notes of hand, bonds and stocks. After the death of his wife, his son-in-law, Calvin R. Coblentz, and his son, Maurice C. Brandenburg, Executors, are to sell the property, and divide the proceeds equally between the children. Four children:

1. Ellen Frances Brandenburg, born 1852, died 1938. Buried Middletown Reformed Church cemetery with her husband. In her father's will, she is called Ella. Married January 20, 1873 to Martin Calvin Coblentz, born November 12, 1849, died September 29, 1914, son of Henry Coblentz (1807) and Ann Magdalena Routzahn (1816). They lived on *Rose Hill Farm*, consisting of one hundred and seventy acres in the Middletown District of Frederick County, and owned a second farm one mile to the north. They had at least seven children, three of whom died of diphtheria within a five day period:
    a. William Henry Coblentz, born 1874, died 1875
    b. Annie Remsburg Coblentz, born 1876, died 1882
    c. Victor Clayton Coblentz, born 1878, died 1882
    d. Walter Calvin Coblentz, born 1880, died 1882
    e. Albert Martin Coblentz, born 1883, died 1962
    f. Maurice Daniel Coblentz, born 1885
    g. Lizzie Adeline Coblentz, born 1888
2. Charles H. Brandenburg, who lived in Tifflin, Ohio
3. Maurice Clayton Brandenburg, born 1859 of whom more
4. Lizzie Sue Brandenburg, born 1865, died 1953. Buried at the Middletown Reformed Church with her husband. Married to Calvin R. Coblentz, born 1863, died 1929, son of Philip Coblentz (1812) and Mary Ann Kefauver (1818).

Maurice Clayton Brandenburg
1859-1952

This son of Daniel Brandenburg and Lydia A. R. Remsburg, was born May 1, 1859 on the family farm in Middletown Valley of Frederick County, Maryland, died December 6, 1952; buried with his wife at the Christ Reformed Church at Middletown. Like most of his family, he was a farmer, and acquired the farm on which his grandfather had settled more than a hundred years earlier. Married February 5, 1889 to Martha Adeline Bussard, born September 20, 1869 and died December 20, 1949, daughter of Samuel Malachi Bussard and Hannah Toms, of Middletown Valley. The family is listed in the 1900 and 1920 census returns for Frederick County, with their children. They had five children, born in Maryland:

1. Ira Clayton Brandenburg, born September 16, 1890, died September 22, 1976, single.
2. Erma Frances Brandenburg, born September 25, 1892, died November 6, 1940. Married August 9, 1917 to Marshall C. Ahalt, who died June 11, 1969. Children:
   a. Robert Marshall Ahalt, born June 24, 1918. Married to Mary Remsburg. Children:
      (1) Gregory Ahalt, born June 19, 1951
      (2) Gary Ahalt, born April 24, 1953
   b. Emory Lee Ahalt, born March 23, 1921. Married March 7, 1953 to Nellie M. Whitter.
   c. Truman Maurice Ahalt, born January 23, 1924.
3. Glenn Hoffmeier Brandenburg, born August 10, 1897, died March 25, 1868. Married December 3, 1954 to Goldye M. Nikirk, who died October 8, 1961. Her will was dated June 3, 1961 and probated October 23, 1961 in Frederick County; filed in liber TME2 at folio 62. She names several people in her will, but does not identify any of her children, although she does refer at one point to two daughters. There are granddaughters: Sandra Lee Miss; Lois Boyer; Mary Miss; and Hallie Virginia Nikirk. She also names Elmer Nikirk, Jr. and Larry Boyer, who may be the fathers of two of the grandchildren.
4. Grace Rebecca Brandenburg, born December 27, 1899 at Middletown, and died July 26, 1985. Married Novem-

ber 13, 1943 to Raymond E. Gaver, born September 13, 1892.

5. Emory Maurice Brandenburg, born January 30, 1904, died May 4, 1984 at Middletown. Married June 17, 1936 to Edna Mae Mullinix at Westminster, Carroll County. She was born November 26, 1912, died January 17, 1936. They had children:

a. Constance A. Brandenburg, born September 22, 1937. Married June 26, 1958 to Lawrence Cutsail, Jr., born May 29, 1934. A daughter:

(1) Julie Ann Cutsail, born July 22, 1965

b. Betty Jean Brandenburg, born February 11, 1940. Married August 25, 1968 to Thomas C. Black, born October 22, 1930. A son:

(1) Michael Doran Black: November 5, 1971

c. Thomas Emory Brandenburg, born March 9, 1941. Married September 18, 1965 to Christine Lantz, and had a son:

(1) Stephen Thomas Brandenburg: May 24, 1968

CHILD 8

Daniel Brandenburg
1805-1886

This son of Mathias Brandenburg and Barbara Keller was born c.1805 and died March 14, 1886. Buried at Christ Reformed Church at Middletown with his wife and other family members. Married August 27, 1832 to Susanna Smith, born June 30, 1813, died February 4, 1884, daughter of Jacob Smith. In the 1880 census for Frederick County, the elderly couple are found in the household of their son, Thomas, and listed there as father and mother. There were probably other children, but we have identified only one thus far:

1. Thomas Brandenburg, born c.1842, died 1926. Buried at the Myersville Lutheran Church with his wife. She was Anna Rebecca, born c.1841, died 1911. The couple appear again in the 1900 census of the county, with one child not listed previously. They had children, including these listed in the census of 1880 and 1900:

    a. Laura C. Brandenburg, born c.1867

    b. Millard W. Brandenburg, born February 1, 1875, died November 1, 1938. Buried at Myersville. He is listed as head of household in the 1900 census for the county, with a wife, Ada E., born c.1874, and two children:

        (1) Clarence C. Brandenburg, born c.1897

        (2) Annie R. Brandenburg, born c.1898

    c. Martin L. Brandenburg, born c.1881

Solomon Brandenburg
1700-
Germany
*

Mathias Brandenburg
1744-1806
*

*   *   *   *   *   *   *

*

*   *   Henry Brandenburg 1765

*

*   *   Joseph Brandenburg 1767

*

*   *   Elizabeth Brandenburg 1769

*

*   *   David Brandenburg 1772

*

*   *   Nancy Brandenburg 1773

*

*   *   Samuel Brandenburg 1774

*

*   *   Jonathan Brandenburg 1775

*

*   *   Solomon Brandenburg 1777

*

*   *   John Brandenburg 1779

*

*   *   Sarah Brandenburg 1781

*

*   *   Catherine Brandenburg 1785

*

*   *   Absolom Brandenburg 1786

*

*   *   Samuel Brandenburg 1786

*

*   *   Hester Brandenburg 1788

*

*   *   Ruth Brandenburg 1790

CHAPTER 5

Mathias Brandenburg
1744-1806

This son of Solomon Brandenburg (1700), was born about 1744 in Germany, and immigrated to America. Mathias died November 20, 1806 in Clark County, Kentucky. Shipping records do not indicate that he traveled with his brothers, but it does appear that he was one of the "Three Brothers" who arrived in America; the other two being Wilhelm Heinrich Brandenburg (1722), who settled in western Maryland, discussed in Chapter 1; and Alexander Henry Brandenburg, discussed in Chapter 6.

Ancestry files of the Mormon Church support the family legend that Mathias went to Kentucky to live. He was married, however, in Frederick County, Maryland, c.1764, to Hester Wolgamot, born in the county c.1744 and died September 19, 1821 in Meade County, Kentucky, in or near the village of Brandenburg, no doubt named for her husband. She was a daughter of Joseph and Catherine Wolgamot. She is named Hester Brandenburg in the will of her father, Joseph Wolgamot, which includes her mother's name as Catherine.

The couple began their married life in Frederick County, Maryland, where they lived at least until about 1769, when they moved for a short time into Hampshire County, Virginia (now part of West Virginia). They had a daughter there, and returned to Frederick County, Maryland before 1772, after which they had two children, born there. They apparently stayed in Maryland a very short time, returning to Hampshire County, where the rest of their children were born.

It would appear that most, if not all, of the children made the move to Kentucky with their parents, probably about 1800 after the last child was born. As will be seen, they had numerous descendants, in several counties of Kentucky. We will here follow some of the generations of the family; the reader who is interested in later descendants is directed to the Ancestral files of the Mormon Church, available on computer at most Family History Centers of the church. The children of Mathias and Hester were:

1. Henry Brandenburg, born c.1765, died 1838 in Meade County, Kentucky. Married c.1790 to Sarah Henrietta, born c.1770 in Virginia, and died before 1838 at or near the village of Brandenburg, Meade County, Kentucky. They had children, the first three born in Mason County, Kentucky, and the rest in Hardin County, Kentucky:

    a. Mary Brandenburg, born December 8, 1792, died October 18, 1857 in Harrison County, Indiana. Married in Meade County, Kentucky, May 9, 1825 to Philip Frakes.

    b. Solomon Preston Brandenburg, born April 12, 1794, died 1861 in Coles County, Illinois. Married September 25, 1814 in Harrison County, Indiana, to Alezan Williams, born January 3, 1798 Pennsylvania.

    c. Elizabeth Brandenburg, born 1796, died 1870 at Memphis, Scotland County, Missouri. Married in Hardin County, Kentucky, October 8, 1813 to John Rush. Married second February 1, 1834 John Crook, born January 20, 1789 in Loudon County, Virginia.

    d. Henry Emerson Brandenburg, born November 6, 1798, died May 9, 1871 in Meade County, Kentucky. Married in Indiana 1822 Henrietta A. Jenkins, born October 10, 1804 in Kentucky.

    e. Hester Brandenburg, born 1800, died 1845 Harrison County, Indiana. Married in Hardin County, Kentucky, February 28, 1818 to Samuel Thomas. Married second March, 1822 to William Harrendon.

    f. Nancy Brandenburg, born 1803, died 1883 in Coles County, Illinois. Married in Hardin County, Kentucky, February 25, 1821 to William Beavers, born July 23, 1797 in Hampshire County, Virginia.

g. Lavina Brandenburg, born 1805, died 1860 in Cape Girardeau County, Missouri. Married in Meade County, Kentucky, September 30, 1825 to John Grable. Married second c.1855 Bollinger County, Missouri, to Elihu H. Self.

h. Catherine Brandenburg, born 1807, died 1828 in Harrison County, Indiana. Married Meade County, Kentucky, January 8, 1826 to Solomon Grable.

i. Sarah Brandenburg, born 1809, died February 3, 1879 in Meade County, Kentucky. Married there June 19, 1836 to Heinrich Lenau, born c.1801 in Hamburg, Germany.

j. Susan Brandenburg, born c.1811.

k. James Calvin Brandenburg, born c.1815, died March 23, 1891 in Scotland County, Missouri. Married in Meade County, Kentucky August 20, 1839 Adaline O. Crook, born March 10, 1817 in Hardin County.

l. Martha Jane Brandenburg, born c.1817, died 1843 in Harrison County, Indiana. Married there December 22, 1839 to James Fults.

2. Joseph Brandenburg, born about 1767 in Hampshire County, Virginia, died 1864 in Owsley County, Kentucky. Married September 1, 1796 in Clark County, Kentucky to Delilah Wessa or Vasser, born c.1771 in Kentucky, daughter of Samuel and Rhoda Wessa or Vasser. She died March 20, 1856 in Owsley County and was buried in the family plot at Hiedelburg, Lee County, Kentucky. Ten children, born in Clark or Estill County, Kentucky:

a. Jonathan Brandenburg, born June 2, 1797, died December 1, 1844 in Montgomery County, Missouri. Married February 12, 1821 in Estill County to Mary L. Smith, born May 25, 1799 in South Carolina.

b. Nancy Brandenburg, born c.1799, died 1862 in Estill County, Kentucky. Married there March 1, 1825 to Joseph Blackwell.

c. Samuel Dooley Brandenburg, born c.1800. Married July 7, 1839 to Sally Brandenburg, born c.1800.

d. Joseph Brandenburg, born April 10, 1804, died November 14, 1895 in Calloway County, Kentucky. Married in Clay County, June 14, 1828 to Rhoda Hamilton, born February 10, 1810 in Estill County. Married second Mary Jane F. Gordon, born 1836 in Virginia.

e. James C. Brandenburg, born April 9, 1808, died January 14, 1896 in Clark County, Kentucky. Married in Estill County, October 11, 1837 to Nancy Thomas, born August 8, 1816 in Estill County, Kentucky. He reportedly married second September 1, 1892 to Elizabeth, born January 30, 1826 in Clay County, Kentucky.

f. Delilah Brandenburg, born January, 1811, and died c.1871 in Estill County, Kentucky. Married there July 23, 1835 to Isaac Congleton, born c.1805 in Ohio County, Kentucky.

g. Catherine Brandenburg, born c.1813, and died after 1880 in Lee County, Kentucky. Married December 27, 1835 to Archibald D. McGuire, born June 30, 1779, Fort Boonesboro, Fayette County, Kentucky.

h. Elizabeth Brandenburg, born c.1816, died after 1890

i. Hester Brandenburg, born c.1819.

j. Margaret Brandenburg, born c.1822, died November 24, 1891 in Estill County. Married there March 25, 1843 to Thomas Bowman, born c.1822 in Clay County, Kentucky.

3. Elizabeth Brandenburg, born about 1769 in Frederick County, Maryland, died before 1823 in Mason County, Kentucky. Married c.1792 in Madison County, Kentucky

to Elijah Fitzgerald, born c.1767 in Frederick County, Maryland. Children, born in Madison County:
a.   Silas Fitzgerald, born c.1792
b.   William Fitzgerald, born c.1793
c.   Mary Fitzgerald, born c.1795
d.   Henry Fitzgerald, born c.1797

4.   David Brandenburg, born July 2, 1772 Frederick County, Maryland, died October 5, 1842 in Clark County, Kentucky. Married July 25, 1795 to Agnes Morton, born December 22, 1776 in Virginia, died September 12, 1806 in Clark County, Kentucky. Five children. Married second September 7, 1825 in Virginia to Susannah Gallop, born 1785 in North Carolina, daughter of Samuel Morton and Philadelphia Gallop. Ten children. Fifteen children of David, born in Clark County, Kentucky, were:

a.   Elizabeth Brandenburg, born December 22, 1796, died June 12, 1852. Married April 6, 1815 Absalom March, born January 6, 1788 in Bourbon County, Kentucky.
b.   Hester Brandenburg, born August 22, 1798. Married February 28, 1824 to James Warren, born c.1796. Married second November 2, 1839 to David Arvin, born c.1796.
c.   Martha Brandenburg, born September 20, 1800 and died after 1860 in Boone County, Missouri. Married December 15, 1818 to John March. Married second September 17, 1854 to Absalom March in Boone County, widower of her sister, Elizabeth.
d.   Solomon Brandenburg, born 1803, died March 2, 1881. Married July 7, 1825 to Harriett Dawson. He married second May 26, 1844 to Lucetta Beasley and third in 1855 to Frances Mosley.
e.   David Brandenburg, born March 31, 1804, died after 1850. Married September 7, 1825 to Elizabeth Gallop.

f. Sarah Brandenburg, born November 2, 1809, died before 1835. Married September 8, 1825 to Willis Gallop, born 1802 in North Carolina.

g. Sanford Brandenburg, born 1811, died 1845. Married March 8, 1832 to Lucinda Stephenson.

h. Catharine Brandenburg, born December 23, 1813. Married January 8, 1833 to Peyton S. Stephenson.

i. Joseph Brandenburg, born August 26, 1815, died after 1888. Married September 25, 1837 to Sarah Gravett.

j. Eliza Brandenburg, born 1816. Married July 16, 1836 to Washington Stephenson.

k. Mariah Brandenburg, born August 11, 1817, died 1838. Married January 18, 1836 David James Pace.

l. George Washington Brandenburg, born July 7, 1819 and died 1842.

m. Jonathan Brandenburg, born May 18, 1821, died 1843. Married July 27, 1839 Elizabeth Ann Combs.

n. Susan Brandenburg, born September 4, 1823, died May 5, 1842. Married October 22, 1838 David Otho Beall.

o. James Brandenburg, born 1825, died 1833.

p. Samuel Brandenburg, born July 1, 1827, died January 29, 1886 at Milmine, in Piatt County, Illinois. Married August 20, 1854 to Adaline Haggard, born April 15, 1835 in Fayette County, Kentucky.

q. John Brandenburg, born August 13, 1830, and died 1870. Married August 9, 1849 to Mary House.

5. Nancy Brandenburg, born c.1773 in Frederick County, Maryland, died c.1845 in Woodford County, Kentucky. Married c.1793 in Mason County, Kentucky, to John Warren.

6. Samuel Brandenburg, born c.1774 in Hampshire County, Virginia, as were the rest of the children, and died c.1846 in Owsley County, Kentucky. Married c.1797 in Mason

County, Kentucky to Sarah Henson, born c.1780 in Mason County, Kentucky, died c.1872 in Dallas County, Texas. Married second in Estill County, Kentucky, July 7, 1820 to Sarah Snowden. Married third in Owsley County, Kentucky, March, 1844 to Matilda Barnes. Four children born to his first marriage; the first born in Ohio, the rest in Owsley County, Kentucky:

a.　Absalom Henson Brandenburg, born May 20, 1799 and died 1872 at Duncanville, Dallas County, Texas. Married in Estill County, Kentucky, January 24, 1819 to Nancy Ann Barker, and second 1868 in Dallas County, Texas to Permelia.

b.　John Henson Brandenburg, born March 6, 1801 and died November, 1860. Married January 19, 1834 in Kentucky to Deborah Bowman, born March 28, 1819 in Clay County, Kentucky.

c.　George Henson Brandenburg, born June 3, 1802 and died 1870. Married in Estill County August 18, 1829 to Sarah Thomas.

d.　Joseph Henson Brandenburg, born November 6, 1803, died 1847. Married in Madison County, Kentucky, March 6, 1823 to Nancy Ann Snowden, born August 15, 1802 in Fayette County, Kentucky.

7.　Jonathan Brandenburg, born c.1775, died July 16, 1854 in Harrison County, Indiana. Married October 4, 1800 in Barren County, Kentucky, to Amy Ann Jenkins, born 1783 in Pennsylvania, died after 1860 at Maukport, in Harrison County, Indiana. Children, born in Kentucky, most of whom died in Harrison County, Indiana:

a.　John Brandenburg, born March 1, 1802, and died September 16, 1865. Married in Kentucky, May 15, 1823 to Elizabeth Vertrees. Married second February 2, 1835 in Harrison County to Jane Crawford, born November 13, 1808 in Kentucky.

b.   Philip Brandenburg, born December 8, 1803, died after 1860. Married September 1, 1825 to Lydia Charley, born August 18, 1803 in Kentucky.

c.   Jane Brandenburg, born 1805. Married March 9, 1825 to Phenton Bell.

d.   Child, born c.1807

e.   Green C. Brandenburg, born 1808. Married January 17, 1834 in Harrison County, Indiana, Mariah Craig.

f.   Nancy Amanda Brandenburg, born 1810. Married February 4, 1836 in Harrison County (as were the rest of the children), to John Summers.

g.   David Brandenburg, born January 7, 1812, died September 19, 1874 in Knox County, Indiana. Married February 4, 1834 to Laura Jane Beard, born October 22, 1815 in Knox County, Indiana.

h.   Ruth Ann Brandenburg, born January 3, 1814 and died December 6, 1890. Married December 21, 1833 to Jacob Faith, born July 22, 1810 in Kentucky

i.   Joseph Brandenburg, born 1816, died 1854. Married April 14, 1843 to Sarah Ann Gwartney.

j.   Elizabeth Brandenburg, born 1818, died 1845. Married October 11, 1836 to George C. Beard.

8.   Solomon Brandenburg, born April 12, 1777, died c.1845 in Madison County, Mississippi. Married May 14, 1808 in Hardin County, Kentucky to Elizabeth Swan, born 1780 in Virginia, died September 23, 1838 at Brandenburg, Meade County, Kentucky. Her parents were John Swan and Elizabeth Van Meter. Seven children, the first six born at Brandenburg's Landing, in Hardin County; the last at or near the village of Brandenburg, in Meade County, Kentucky:

a.   Hester Brandenburg, born February 29, 1808, died October 24, 1886 in Davies County, Kentucky. Married October 8, 1820 to Burr Harrison Crutcher, born October 8, 1804 in Nelson County, Kentucky.

b. Mary Eliza Brandenburg, born 1811, died after 1860 in Ballard County, Kentucky. Married in Meade County, April 4, 1832 to Isaac Robert Sample.

c. John Swan Brandenburg, born July 1, 1812 (or February 27, 1813), died June 30, 1851 of cholera. Married January 30, 1844 to Sarah Wintersmith Wathen, born June 28, 1823 in Hardin County, died October 26, 1906, the daughter of Gabriel Wathen (1789) and his wife, Charles Seany Little (1798) of Montgomery County, Maryland. She married second November 24, 1852 to Edward H. Atwill of Meade County, Kentucky. At least three children were fathered by John Swan:

    (1) Seany Elizabeth Brandenburg, born January 2, 1845, lived one day.

    (2) Amelia A. Brandenburg, born May 13, 1846, died July 1, 1851 of cholera.

    (3) Gabriel Swan Brandenburg, born January 12, 1850, died January 29, 1878.

d. Louisiana Brandenburg, born 1816, died 1873. Married December 29, 1833 to George Calhoon.

e. David Brandenburg, born 1818, died April 21, 1848. Married in Meade County, Kentucky, October 1, 1843 to Elizabeth Fairleigh McLure.

f. Elizabeth Ann Brandenburg, born 1820, died 1887. Married in Madison County, Mississippi, October 3, 1842, to Christopher M. Dowell.

g. Thomas Solomon Independence Brandenburg, born 1822, died February 23, 1867 in Lee County, Arkansas. Married January 30, 1845 at Montgomery's Point, Desha County, Arkansas, to Theresa Montgomery, born April 19, 1830 at Montgomery's Point in Desha County, Arkansas.

9. John Brandenburg, born March, 1779, and died June 20, 1843 in Bracken County, Kentucky. Married c.1804 in

Mason County, Kentucky, to Miss Patterson, born there 1804. Married second February 10, 1813 in Fayette County, Kentucky, Catherine Cummings, born November, 1780 in Virginia. Children, born in Lewis County, Kentucky:

a. Juliana Brandenburg, born 1806. Married c.1822 to James Hughbanks.

b. Patterson C. Brandenburg, born c.1808. Married March 25, 1835 to Malinda Matthews, born October 7, 1813 in Kentucky. Married second September 22, 1861 to Hannah S. Lefton, born c.1829 in Ohio.

c. Nancy Brandenburg, born March 12, 1811, died June 30, 1852. Married March 30, 1826 to William Edward Maddox (middle name perhaps Nelson).

10. Sarah Brandenburg, born c.1781, died September 8, 1821 in Hardin County, Kentucky. Married March 25, 1800, Washington County, Kentucky, William Vertrees, born October 15, 1779 in Hardin County, Kentucky, son of Isaac Vertrees. Surname may have been spelled Ventress. Children, born in Kentucky:

a. Elizabeth Vertrees, born 1802 Washington County, died 1832 in Harrison County, Indiana. Married May 15, 1823 in Hardin County, Kentucky, to John Brandenburg, born March 1, 1802 in Kentucky, probably a cousin.

b. Isaac Vertrees, born October 25, 1802 in Hardin County.

c. Hester Vertrees, born 1805 in Hardin County. Married there February 29, 1824 to Martin Hall.

d. William Brandenburg Vertrees, born February 11, 1809 in Meade County, died July 15, 1889 near Vine Grove in Hardin County. Married March 13, 1834 to Rachel Shacklett Hayden, born March 3, 1814 at Elizabethtown, Hardin County, Kentucky.

11. Catherine Brandenburg, born c.1785, died after 1850 in Clark County, Kentucky. Married there February 12, 1808 (or December 8, 1808) to Thomas C. Green.
12. Absolom Brandenburg, born c.1786, died October, 1851 in McCracken County, Kentucky. Married August 11, 1815 in Harrison County, Indiana to Esther Frakes. He married second January 24, 1819 to Nancy Baker, and third May 4, 1838 to Susannah Wiseman. Apparently, there was only one child born to the first marriage, and several to the second; and five to the third. Records of the Mormon Church provide the names of some children, but not all of them. There may have been as many as eighteen children in all. At least the first four listed following were born in Hardin County, Kentucky, the remainder in Harrison County, Indiana. Marriages noted for several of the children apparently occurred in Harrison County, where the family must have moved about 1823. Children:
    a. Elizabeth Brandenburg, born June 25, 1816, died April 29, 1872. Married April 23, 1833 to Simeon Kingsley, born June 25, 1816 in Hardin County.
    b. Louisiana Brandenburg, born July 22, 1819, died January 4, 1899. Married to Reuben Binkley, born February 18, 1816 in Pennsylvania.
    c. Mary Brandenburg, born c.1820. Married March 3, 1839 to Thomas Hayes, born August 16, 1819 in Harrison County, Indiana.
    d. Hester Brandenburg, born c.1820. Married c.1841 to John Knapp, born c.1815 at Baden, Germany.
    e. Sarah Ann Brandenburg, born c.1823, died c.1865. Married March 8, 1841 George Edward O'Connor, born c.1805 in Ireland.
    f. Henry Brandenburg, born c.1827. Married to Lizzie.

g. Green A. Brandenburg, born c.1830, died c.1900 in Newport, Jackson County, Arkansas. Married there about 1866 to Josephine.

h. Catherine A. Brandenburg, born c.1834. Married May 28, 1859 to Henry Clay Holiday.

i. Caroline Brandenburg, born 1836.

j. David Brandenburg, born 1841 in Harrison County, Indiana, the first born to the third marriage.

k. John Brandenburg, born c.1844 in McCracken County, Kentucky, as were the rest of this group.

l. Lucy Jane Brandenburg, born c.1847.

m. Susannah Brandenburg, born c.1847.

n. Martha Ellen Brandenburg, born c.1850, and died c.1916 in Harrison County, Indiana. Married there 1871 to William J. Conrad.

13. Samuel Brandenburg, born c.1786. Married August 8, 1839 to Sally. Note that there is an earlier son of this name, who was still living and married. We do not believe that this Samuel belongs in this family, although he appears in family group sheets of the Mormon Church, as does the earlier Samuel.

14. Hester Brandenburg, born c.1788, died before 1850. Married September 30, 1826 (or October 2, 1826) in Clark County, Kentucky, to David Rene La Force.

15. Ruth Brandenburg, born c.1790, died c.1855 in Clark County, Kentucky.

Solomon Brandenburg
1700-
Germany
*

*

Alexander Henry Brandenburg
*

*

*   *   *   *   *   *   *
*
* * Barbara Brandenburg
*
* * Conrad Brandenburg
*
* * Jacob Brandenburg

CHAPTER 6

Alexander Henry Brandenburg
died 1793

As discussed in Chapter 1, Alexander Henry is believed to be a son of Solomon Brandenburg, who was born c.1700 in Germany. Alexander was probably born there as well, although the date is not now known. There is a will of Alexander Brandenburg, dated May 15, 1780, probated August 2, 1793 in Frederick County and filed in liber GM2 at folio 479. He names his three children, and the will was witnessed by George Frederick Kindley and John Kindley. There is also the will of his wife, Anne Brandenburg, dated January 29, 1794 and probated February 7, 1809, filed in liber RB1 at folio 3 in Frederick County. She names the same children, who were:

1. Barbara Brandenburg, married to Jacob Franks, born in Fayette County, Pennsylvania.
2. Conrad Brandenburg.
3. Jacob Brandenburg, said in his father's will to be the youngest of the children, and of whom more.

Jacob Brandenburg
died c.1838

Jacob, the son of Alexander Henry Brandenburg, was born in Frederick County, rather than having immigrated from Germany as has been reported elsewhere, and settled in what was then wilderness in Frederick County, establishing his home on the tract of land called *Chance*, which was owned in later years by his descendant, J. L. Baker. In the 1798 assessment of Frederick County, Jacob was listed as owning *Chance Resurveyed*, in two tracts of one hundred and eight and a quarter acres; and forty-five and a quarter acres.

Jacob died c.1839, said to have lived a long life, and was married February 13, 1787 at the Evangelical Reformed Church in Frederick to Elizabeth Rine (or Rhine or Rein), born in Frederick County, who died 1833. The will of Jacob was dated August 14, 1831 and probated March 13, 1838 in Frederick County, filed in liber GME2 at folio 296. They had children, born in New Market District of Frederick County, some of whom will be discussed in greater detail following the main listing; they are not necessarily listed in birth order:

1. William Brandenburg, who married October 18, 1822 to Rachel Purdum, and lived in Carroll County, Maryland.
2. John Brandenburg.
3. Jacob Brandenburg, who lived and died before 1831 in Montgomery County, leaving children.
4. Jesse Brandenburg, who died August 16, 1877 at Flushing, Ohio, and was buried there. Married Matilda Turner.
5. Lemuel Brandenburg, reportedly born c.1772, but more likely about 1801, and of whom more in Chapter 7.
6. Mary (Polly) Brandenburg, and of whom more as Child 6, following.
7. Mahala Brandenburg, born 1804; married Denton Watkins, and of whom more as Child 7, following.
8. Priscilla Brandenburg, born May 29, 1807, died March, 1878 and buried at Providence cemetery in Kemptown. Married December 19, 1831 to Thomas Baker.

CHILD 6

Mary Brandenburg

This daughter of Jacob Brandenburg and Elizabeth Rine was born on the family farm called *Chance*, in Frederick County, Maryland. According to the *History of Frederick County*, by T. J. C. Williams, she was married c.1808 to Edward Walker in Frederick County. He was a son of Elisha

Walker, born c.1750, and his wife Sarah King. IGI records report their marriage on December 11, 1811 in the county. Marriage records of Frederick County list the marriage of Edward Walker on December 11, 1813 to Polly Brandenburg, probably this couple. In the report by Williams, it is stated that the Brandenburg family had lived in the state for many years, with Mary being a descendant of one of three brothers who emigrated to America at an early date from Brandenburg, Germany. This may be another of the well-worn, famous "three brothers" stories as discussed in the introduction of this study. In such cases, the three brothers generally arrive together, and one goes west, south or back to the homeland, and is never heard of again. In this case, the brothers were said to be Jacob, Mathias and William. Jacob and William settled in Frederick County; Mathias went to Kentucky. That is not to say that this ancestry is not correct; only to point out that similar stories abound in numerous families and are worthy of investigation. Edward and Mary lived on a farm about two miles south of Monrovia, in the New Market District, where they had children:

1. James Walker, born c.1810
2. Reuben Walker, born 1812
3. Charlotte Walker, born March 14, 1814, died April 21, 1882. Married October 8, 1847 in Frederick County, as his second wife, to Adam Burall, born 1796, son of William Burall. Children:
   a. Jesse Marcellus Burall, born November 16, 1852 and married March 25, 1880 Delilah Sheetenhalm. In *History of Frederick County*, there is a biography of Jesse, in which it states that his grandfather William Burall was *"one of three brothers who came to America from Germany. One of the brothers settled in Virginia, one in New York or New Jersey, and one, William Burall, in Frederick County, Maryland."* The three brothers story yet again; two of

them being reported in a single family! Jesse's children were:

(1) Walter Burall; who married Ada Utz of New Market.
(2) Bessie Burall, married Clifford Thomas.
(3) Sally Burall.
(4) Irving Burall.
(5) Marshall Burall.

b. Ruth Burall, married George W. Shoemaker.
4. William Walker, born 1817
5. Jesse Walker, born March 2, 1820, of whom more
6. Sarah Walker, born 1823
7. Rhoda Walker, born 1825, married September 7, 1847 to Henry Hyatt.
8. Mary Walker, born 1827
9. Edward Walker, born 1830

Jesse Walker
1820-1869

This son of Edward Walker and Mary Brandenburg, was born March 2, 1820 on the family farm near Monrovia, Frederick County, Maryland. In 1849, he and two of his friends made their way west to the gold fields of California. Along the way, it is reported that one of the others died, and Jesse and his remaining friend preserved his body in a barrel of alcohol, and shipped it home two years later. They traveled by boat, taking six months to make the trip around Cape Horn. He failed to find the fortune he was seeking, and returned home, where he built a modest home and store at Monrovia, which he operated for a few years. He was married September 2, 1843 in Frederick County, to Jemima Moxley, born December 2, 1825 in Montgomery County, daughter of Caleb Moxley and Elizabeth Wolfe. Children:
1. Mary E. Walker, born November, 1845

2. William Norris Walker, born November 3, 1847, died December 9, 1849.
3. Jesse Clinton Walker, born March 11, 1853, and died April 28, 1883.
4. Lydia A. N. Walker, born October 23, 1856, and died June 7, 1861.
5. John Calvin Walker, born September 26, 1858, died February 8, 1915. In 1880, he became a clerk in the store of Mr. Melvin P. Wood of Monrovia. In 1889, he purchased the goods and store of Bradley T. Nicodemus at Unionville, which he operated for two years, before selling to Harry Worman, at which time he purchased the original business and real estate of Melvin P. Wood, his original employer. In 1908, he sold the entire business to his clerk, and retired. He was married in October, 1890, to Clara Bartgis, who died in December of 1891; her father having been the Mayor of the City of Frederick. He married secondly in October of 1897 to Edith M. Beachley, daughter of John D. Beachley of Middletown. He was a member of the Church of the Brethren, and had children:
   a. Louise Walker
   b. Hester Walker
6. Eleanor Jeanette Walker, born May, 1861, and married Hiram Weast.
7. Alice Catherine Walker, born January 19, 1864, and married Richard Bruce Murdoch, a merchant in Monrovia
8. Jane Rebecca Walker, born May 11, 1866; married to Henry M. Snyder, born 1864, died 1942.
9. Jemima Florence Walker, born May 19, 1869, and married William T. Mount, Jr., of Kemptown

CHILD 7

Mahala Brandenburg
1804-1884

This daughter of Jacob Brandenburg and Elizabeth Rine was born about 1804 on the family farm called *Chance*, in Frederick County, Maryland, and died c.1884. She was married January 12, 1819 to the Reverend Denton Watkins, born c.1795 and died c.1864. Various references to the family of Denton Watkins have been found in card files at the library of the Montgomery County Historical Society, and elsewhere. We have not placed him within the larger Watkins family of Montgomery County, but assume a relationship. They had children:

1. Matilda Watkins, born c.1820. Married Loren Todd.
2. Jepe Watkins, born c.1821; died at about nine months.
3. Priscilla Watkins, born about 1824, and married Robert Farnsworth.
4. Edward Taylor Watkins, married and had children, including:
    a. Clarence E. Watkins, who had children:
        (1) Lois Allene Watkins, born December 27, 1915
        (2) Dorothy Watkins, born September 22, 1917 and married to William Newton.
        (3) Kenneth Watkins.
        (4) Marjorie Nell Watkins, born either January 12 or March, 1922. Married to Kenneth Rupp.
    b. William Henry Watkins, born January 25, 1867, of whom more following.
    c. George Washington Watkins, born June 24, 1869 and died 1945. Married three times: first to Dora Waldron; second November 26, 1900 to Bertha Gunther; third in 1927 to Anna Hart. Children:

        (1)   George Victor Watkins, born July 17, 1904, and married to Frances.

        (2)   Winifred Lenore Watkins, born November 26, 1906 and married to Cochran.

        (3)   Herbert Taylor Watkins, born December 7, 1910

        (4)   William Edward Watkins, born August 3, 1916 and married to Mary.

    d.   Stella Florence Watkins, born September 9, 1872, died October 10, 1954. Married James Ira Sellers.

    e.   Mary Winifred Watkins, born September 29, 1876, died November 23, 1963. Married George Washington Jones.

5.   Miranda Watkins, born April 6, 1828. Married twice: first to George McVey and second to Jesse Miracle.

6.   Mary Watkins, born 1830. Married to Jacob Farnsworth.

7.   McKendree Watkins, born c.1833

8.   Milton B. Watkins, born c.1845. Married to Rachel A. Miracle. Children, including:

    a.   Wannie Blanche Watkins, born 1879. Married to Allen Whetstone.

9.   Hamilton Watkins, born February 18, 1847, died January 12, 1937, and had children:

    a.   Ernest Watkins, who had children:

        (1)   Lawrence Watkins, born 1893, an infant death

        (2)   Opal Watkins, born July 15, 1907

    b.   Jesse Watkins, born May 1, 1872. He had children:

        (1)   Joyce Watkins.

        (2)   Merhle Watkins, born October 10, 1896 and died October 19, 1971.

        (3)   Paul Watkins.

        (4)   Ralph Watkins.

    c.   Hattie Watkins, born August 13, 1873, died July 5, 1956. Married to Reese Ingle. These may be their children:

(1)   Iva Ingle, born May 24, 1891

(2)   Lawrence Ingle, born 1893, an infant death

(3)   Vera Ingle, born May 24, 1895, and married to McGavern.

d.   Laura Blanche Watkins, born September 3, 1884; died May 21, 1963. Married May 22, 1907 to John Roscoe Lieurance.

e.   Edward Evan Watkins, born May 10, 1906, and died July 24, 1965. Married 1929 to Vera Dempsey. Children:

(1)   Dorothy Watkins, who married Pierce.

(2)   Harold Watkins, who had children:

(a) Jack Watkins.

(b) Kenneth Watkins.

(c) Norma Watkins.

f.   Inza Isidore Watkins, married twice: first to Will Branaman, and second to Summer Crumpacker.

g.   Pearl Watkins, married May 9, 1906 to Elbert L. Maxedon.

10. Evan R. Watkins, who had children:

a.   William T. Watkins, born 1863

b.   Harriet Watkins, a twin born 1874. Married Rhodes.

c.   Harry Watkins, a twin, born 1874

Solomon Brandenburg
1700-
Germany
*

Alexander Henry Brandenburg
*

Jacob Brandenburg
*

Lemuel Brandenburg
1801

*   *   *   *   *   *   *

*   *   Jesse B. Brandenburg 1824
*

*   *   Ezra Brandenburg 1826
*

*   *   Emily Brandenburg 1827
*

*   *   Elizabeth Brandenburg 1828
*

*   *   William R. Brandenburg 1829
*

*

*   *   Lucinda Brandenburg 1832
*

*   *   Emanuel Brandenburg 1833
*

*   *   Hepzibah Brandenburg 1835
*

*   *   Charlotte Brandenburg 1837
*

*   *   Lemuel Brandenburg 1838
*

*   *   Matilda Brandenburg 1840
*

*   *   George E. L. H. Brandenburg 1842
*

*   *   Sarah Louisa Brandenburg 1843
*

*   *   Garrison McLain Brandenburg 1845
*

*   *   Mary Manzella Brandenburg 1849

CHAPTER 7

Lemuel Brandenburg
1801-1871

Son of Jacob Brandenburg and Elizabeth Rine, Lemuel was born May 23, 1801 in the New Market District of Frederick County, Maryland, on the family farm known as *Chance* and died February 3, 1871. Buried at Providence cemetery at Kemptown, Maryland. Married March 31, 1824 to Charlotte Kindley, born September 6, 1804, and died January 6, 1887 at the age of 82 years and 4 days; daughter of William Kindley (1770) and Rachel Basford. Lemuel lived on a farm in Frederick County, where their children were born. Some reports list Lemuel with a middle initial of "M". Lemuel died February 8, 1871 and Charlotte died January 6, 1887. The will of Lemuel was written January 18, 1870 and probated February 28, 1871, filed in liber SGC1 at folio 130 in Frederick County. He names his wife, and appoints his sons Jesse and Ezra as Executors. The principal legacy was his farm of two hundred and twenty-one acres, left to his two sons, Garrison and Emanuel. By document filed the same day, Ezra renounces his right to administer the estate. The children, several of whom will be treated in detail following the main listing, were:

1. Jesse B. Brandenburg, born June 16, 1824, died April 6, 1896, of whom more as Child 1.
2. Ezra Brandenburg, born January 28, 1826, died June 20, 1887. Buried at Kemptown Church. Married first to Miss Wortman, and secondly January 11, 1858 to Margaret E. Wenner, born c.1835, died August 26, 1892, and buried with her husband. Some research of others report his first wife as a Miss Wortman, but she is most likely Mary Austen Waltman, who was born November 11, 1827 in

Albemarle County, Virginia, and died January 16, 1853, the daughter of M. H. Waltman, as reported in *Names in Stone* Volume 1, by Jacob Mehrling Holdcraft. Frederick County marriage records report the marriage of Ezra and May Waltman as March 27, 1852. There was at least a son, an infant death:

    a.   William H. Brandenburg, born January 8, 1862 and died July 2, 1862.

3.   Emily Brandenburg, born April 5, 1827, of whom more as Child 3.

4.   Elizabeth Brandenburg, born May 12, 1828, died April 15, 1915. Married November 27, 1847 to John Boyer, and lived in Baltimore.

5.   William R. Brandenburg, born November 15, 1829, of whom more as Child 5.

6.   Ann Priscilla Brandenburg, born February 11, 1831, and of whom more in Chapter 8.

7.   Lucinda Brandenburg, born June 12, 1832. Married December 27, 1855 to John William Browning, and lived in Montgomery County. They had children, mentioned in the will of Lemuel:

    a.   Cybil Browning.

    b.   Mary Browning.

    c.   Millicent Browning.

8.   Emanuel Brandenburg, born November 20, 1833, died November 4, 1901 at Johnsville, in Frederick County. Married December 8, 1863 to Elizabeth Anna Johnson, born c.1843 and died October 5, 1933 at the age of 90 years, 4 months and 22 days. On cemetery records, her name is shown as Annie E., as it is in the 1880 census. Both are buried at Johnsville Methodist Church. One child is buried at Kemptown Methodist Church; there were others. The couple appear in the 1880 census for Frederick County, with five children, and in the 1900 census for the county with just one. Annie E. appears (as

a widow) in the 1920 census for the county, with one daughter in the household, who is married, with one son. She was Cora, listed following. The children included:

a. Ella May Brandenburg, born c.1861, died July 27, 1883 at the age of 9 years, 7 months and 22 days.

b. Stewart Johnson Brandenburg, born September 20, 1865, died 1935. Married to Sarah C., born 1861 and died 1945. Both buried at Union cemetery, at Pipe Creek. They appear in the 1900 and 1920 census for Carroll County, with one child:

    (1)   Wilbur Brandenburg, born c.1897

c. Samuel Edward Brandenburg, born January 27, 1868, died 1936. Buried at Mountain View, Union Bridge, Maryland. His wife is buried there also; she was Capitola E., born 1862, died 1951. There is one daughter buried with them. There were other children, found with their parents in the 1900 census for Frederick County. In the 1920 census for Carroll County, Samuel and his wife are shown with four of their children. They were parents of, at least:

    (1)   Walter L. Brandenburg, born c.1896

    (2)   Helen M. Brandenburg, born c.1898

    (3)   William E. Brandenburg, born c.1900

    (1)   Anna E. Brandenburg, born c.1901, died October 23, 1911, aged 10 years, 8 months and 19 days.

    (5)   Carroll T. Brandenburg, born c.1905

d. Addie D. Brandenburg, born c.1870

e. Cora E. Brandenburg, born c.1872. Married Edward A. Warner, born c.1872, and had at least one son. As mentioned above, the couple were living with the mother of Cora in 1920. Their son was:

    (1)   Ralph A. Warner, born c.1913

f. Ella May Brandenburg, born c.1874

9. Hepzibah Brandenburg, born April 24, 1835. Married January 25, 1853 to Greenberry W. Baker, and lived in New Market District of Frederick County.
10. Charlotte Brandenburg, born February 20, 1837, died January 22, 1889. Buried at Kemptown Methodist Church. Married April 9, 1859 Andrew Jackson Lease, and lived in New Market District
11. Lemuel Brandenburg, born June 12, 1838; died young
12. Matilda Brandenburg, born February 7, 1840. Married February 13, 1862 to John H. Bell and died in Montgomery County. Buried at Kemptown Methodist Church.
13. George E. L. H. Brandenburg, born December 11, 1842 and died as an infant.
14. Sarah Louisa Brandenburg, born February 4, 1843, of whom more as Child 14.
15. Garrison McLain Brandenburg, born April 16, 1845, of whom more as Child 15.
16. Mary Manzella Brandenburg, born March 4, 1849. She was married December 7, 1867 to Jonathan Jacobs, and lived in Gaithersburg, in Montgomery County, Maryland.

CHILD 1

Jesse B. Brandenburg
1824-1896

This son of Lemuel Brandenburg and Charlotte Kindley was born June 16, 1824 and died April 6, 1896 in Montgomery County, Maryland. Married December 30, 1847 to Sarah Rebecca Purdum, born January 29, 1829 and died November 10, 1911 at Kemptown, daughter of John Lewis Purdum (1798) and Jemima King (1805). Jesse and his wife are buried at Kemptown Methodist Church, with at least one of their daughters. They appear in the 1880 census of Frederick

County, with five of their children. Children, all said to have been born in Montgomery County:

1. Charlotte Lavinia Brandenburg, born 1851, died 1887. Married Basil Francis Buxton, born 1843 and died 1927 at Kemptown, son of Brook Buxton and Kitty Mullinix. At least two daughters:

    a. Emma Rose Buxton, born August 21, 1874, died June, 1957. Married November 7, 1894 to William Eldridge Watkins, born 1867 and died April 1, 1943, son of Caleb H. Watkins (1806) and Sarah J. Lovejoy (1809). William and his wife are buried at Montgomery Chapel, Claggettsville, Maryland. His will, dated May 23, 1924, was probated May 12, 1950 and filed in will book WCC 49 at folio 166, Montgomery County. They had children:

        (1) Myra Lavinia Watkins, born February 16, 1896, died 1987. Married December 28, 1915 at the parsonage in Kemptown Emory Cross Woodfield, born June 17, 1889, died December 9, 1934, son of Thomas Griffith Woodfield (1856) and Emma Cassandra Boyer (1868), and had children:

            (a) Eldridge Woodfield.
            (b) Rose Woodfield.
            (c) George Woodfield.

        (2) Nellie Mae Watkins, born July 4, 1897 and married Mullinix.

        (3) Albert Dewey Watkins, born January 28, 1899, died 1969. Buried at Forest Oak cemetery in Gaithersburg. Married Helen Mobley, who predeceased him.

        (4) Cora Elaine Watkins, born March 1, 1901 and married Solomon.

        (5) Anna Louise Watkins, born February 16, 1903 and married Shoemaker.

b. Helen E. Buxton, born March 2, 1880, and of whom more following.

2. Wilhemina Anna Brandenburg, born October 30, 1859, and died December 16, 1905. Married October 6, 1881 in Frederick County to Jesse William Moxley, born October 6, 1855 and died August 23, 1934, son of Risdon Moxley. Buried at Kemptown. They had eight children:

a. Ernest Walter Moxley, born April 30, 1882, died September 12, 1973; married Mary Margaret Clay

b. Lester Moxley, born July 26, 1886, died December 8, 1969. Married June 6, 1909 to Lottie May Burdette.

c. Allison Moxley, born May 26, 1888, died March 19, 1952. Married October 30, 1912 to Margaret Gertrude Shoemaker.

d. Lillie May Moxley, born June 30, 1890, died May 9, 1957. Married Milton Nash.

e. Stillbirth Moxley, son.

f. Jesse Herman Moxley, born June 5, 1893, died July 15, 1943; buried Prospect cemetery, Mt Airy, Maryland. Married December 2, 1914 to Mary Catherine Condon.

g. Elvira Moxley, born March 9, 1896, died October 1, 1986; buried St. Peter's Catholic cemetery at Libertytown. Married Edward Joseph Noonan.

h. Vivy Moxley, born November 17, 1900, and died October 15, 1903; buried at Kemptown.

3. Bradley Jefferson Brandenburg, born about 1863, and of whom more.

4. Mary Roberta Brandenburg, born November 7, 1865. Married Tobias Calvin Watkins, born c.1865 and died 1954 at Kemptown; the son of Caleb H. Watkins (1806) and Sarah J. Lovejoy (1809). Tobias and Mary had at least five children:

a. Grover Sim Watkins, born May 14, 1892

b. Oakley Massarene Watkins, born February 3, 1895. The name is spelled Oaksly on church record cards of the library of Montgomery County Historical Society in Rockville, but Oakley in the 1900 census.

c. Infant Watkins, born May 10, 1897; died June 1, 1897.

d. Virgie I. Watkins, born c.1899

e. Infant Watkins, born August 24, 1900; died October 4, 1900.

5. Ezra Stewart Brandenburg, born June 24, 1868, died January 28, 1936 at Fort Crockett, Texas. His cemetery record indicates that he served as a corporal in the 52nd Artillery during the first world war. Buried at Kemptown Methodist Church. He was a Marine Band musician, and was married April 11, 1889 in Frederick County, Maryland, to Tillie M. Renn, born c.1871 in the county, and died February 1, 1950 in Carroll County; buried at Mt. Airy, daughter of M. Luther Renn. Several church records, reporting the birth of their children, list her name as Lillie, which appears to be correct. They appear in the 1900 census for Montgomery County, with five of their children. Other records tend to indicate that the children were born in Frederick County. However, in the 1920 census for Mt. Airy, in Carroll County, Tillie appears as head of household, apparently while her husband was away in Marine service, with what appears to be the three youngest children. Their children included:

a. Windsor M. Brandenburg, born c.1890, died 1950 to 1954, probably in Baltimore.

b. Osca Pearl Brandenburg, born January 31, 1892; married September 18, 1913 to Raymond Watkins, born March 10, 1885, died September 12, 1962, son of Thomas Ellsworth Watkins (1862) and Rosa Medora Moxley (1865). Raymond was associated for a number of years with Peoples Lumber Supply Company, a family owned business. Later, he purchased the family farm on Kemptown Road, where some of his descendants still live. His will, dated April 11, 1956, was probated November 13, 1962 and filed in will book VMB 155, at folio 598, in the county. They had children:

(1)   Lois Virginia Watkins, born November 19, 1914; married June 17, 1934 to Francis Hahn and divorced without children. Married second in 1946 to James L. Bolger, born July 21, 1903, died November 27, 1989. No children; she lived in Miami, Florida.

(2)   Janice Pearl Watkins, born March 21, 1917; married April 6, 1937 at Montgomery Methodist Church to Raymond Carl Lewis, of Kemptown, Maryland. He was born January 7, 1915, died March 24, 1972, without children.

(3)   Margaret Rae Watkins, born December 13, 1919, and died March 20, 1982 in Miami, Florida. Buried at the Providence Cemetery in Kemptown, Maryland. Married December 12, 1942 to Seth Edward Bishop, and had at least one son, followed by divorce:

(a)   Ray Edward Bishop; December 28, 1949

(4)   Thomas Ellsworth Watkins, born May 9, 1922, and married December 31, 1946 Marjorie May Miles. Lived at Kemptown, divorced, no children.

c.   Earl D. Brandenburg, born June 20, 1893, and died August 22, 1965 at a Veteran's hospital in Howard County. Married to Elizabeth, and had children:

(1)   Frances Brandenburg, married Sutherland.

(2)   Shirley Brandenburg, married Murray.

d.   Hanson Ezra Brandenburg, born March 4, 1895, died September 6, 1954 at Perry Point Veterans

Hospital; buried at Kemptown or Mt. Airy; single. In the 1900 census, this child is listed as Ezra H., but what we list here appears correct.

e. Sellman Jesse Brandenburg, born c.1898, died May 4, 1963 at Peculiar, Missouri; buried at Mt. Airy. Married Marian Kuhn. This is perhaps the individual reported in Church records as Jesse S. Brandenburg, born March 9, 1898 (reversing the given names). In the 1900 census, his name is also shown as Jesse S.; he is listed only as Sellman in the 1920 census. His obituary states that he had five grandchildren, and names one son. There is a young girl also buried at Mt. Airy, who is perhaps a daughter, records stating that she was the daughter of S. J. and M. L. Brandenburg. She is included here:

   (1) Elizabeth C. Brandenburg, born November 6, 1925, died August 2, 1926.

   (2) Leroy Brandenburg.

6. Lucy Beatrice Brandenburg, born about 1871, died 1932. Married July 3, 1895 in Frederick County, to John Thomas Mullinix, son of Robert Mullinix and Evelyn Baker. They had children:

a. Clyta Beatrice Mullinix; married December 24, 1914 to Joseph Leslie Woodfield, born March 4, 1891, and died July 3, 1949, son of Thomas Griffith Woodfield (1856) and Emma Cassandra Boyer (1868). Children:

   (1) Willard Woodfield.

   (2) Beatrice Woodfield.

   (3) Dorothy Woodfield.

   (4) Vincent Woodfield.

b. Leslie Mullinix.

c. Aubrey Mullinix.

d. Genevieve Mullinix.

e. Dorothy Mullinix, married Leslie King.

7.   Sybell R. Brandenburg, born January 7, 1873, and died March 15, 1873; buried at Kemptown.

Helen E. Buxton
1880-1961

This daughter of Basil Francis Buxton (1843) and Charlotte Lavinia Brandenburg (1851) was born March 2, 1880 and died January 16, 1961. Married December 28, 1897 to Sylvester Watkins, born December 7, 1869 and died November 2, 1950; son of Jeremiah Columbus Watkins (1841) and Ann Wilson Moxley (1847). Children:

1.   Rudy Edward Watkins, born August 13, 1898, died October 7, 1982. Married Delma Viola Mullineaux, born 1893, died 1966, the daughter of Eldridge Mullineaux and Rosene E. Merson. Another report (cemetery record) states that the wife of Rudy was Delma Viola Buxton, born 1893, died 1966, the daughter of Upton Buxton and Jane Wolf. After the death of Delma, Rudy Edward married second Hazel Viola Hall, who had been previously married and was from Kansas. Two children born to his first marriage:

   a.   Betty Lee Watkins, born September 22, 1924. Married Clayton Otis Smith of New Market, born June 10, 1913, had two children, and was divorced. Married second Eric Leopold Van Glabeke, born September 28, 1924. Clayton married second Joyce Anne Norwood, born September 9, 1938 (or 1934). The two children of Betty Lee Watkins from her first marriage were:

      (1)   Gerald Edward Smith, born September 10, 1947.

      (2)   Sharon Lee Smith, born May 8, 1951. Married to Merhle Wayne Warfield, born December 15, 1950, and had children:

       (a)   Jason Edward Warfield; April 8, 1979

       (b)   Kristin Leeann Warfield; July 26, 1984

  b.   Rudell Edward Watkins, born April 29, 1932. Married June 14, 1952 to Norma Lee Lewis, born November 7, 1932, daughter of Eugene Francis Lewis (1910) and Linda Amelia Bennett (1913). Two children:

      (1)   Bruce Edward Watkins, born March 5, 1957.

      (2)   Debra Lee Watkins, born February 27, 1958. Married February 11, 1978 to Gary Ray Estapinal, born January 15, 1955; divorced. One son:

         (a)   Justin Ray Estapinal, born November 11, 1983

2.   Norman Sylvester Watkins, born December 17, 1900 and died February 9, 1986. Buried at Laytonsville Methodist Church cemetery. Married July 27, 1929 to Ethel Hilda Mount, born July 17, 1911, daughter of Wilfred Edgar Mount and Nona Augusta Burns. Three children:

  a.   Mary Jean Watkins, born January 17, 1931. Married March 30, 1967 Homer W. Akridge, born March 10, 1929. No children reported.

  b.   Shirley Lee Watkins, born August 26, 1933, died August 2, 1984. Married March 8, 1952 to Donald Eugene Butt, and had children:

      (1)   Donald Eugene Butt, Jr., born June 30, 1955. Married July 18, 1979 to Ann Kelly Willard.

      (2)   Mark Timothy Butt, born December 8, 1958. Married August 21, 1982 to Susan Marie Holz, born June 12, 1959, daughter of Dr. Richard G. Holz of Frederick; children:

         (a)   Kathleen Lee Butt; February 21, 1984

         (b)   Jacob Watkins Butt, born March 14, 1987

  c.   Barbara Ann Watkins, born September 5, 1938. Married August 27, 1954 to Bedford Ashley Dodson, born March 29, 1936, and had a son. Barbara Ann married second on June 8, 1968 to Charles Junior Reed, born September 28, 1940. Her one child was:

    (1)   Norman Bedford Dodson, born December 31, 1954. Married Shirley October 24, 1981; a son:

        (a) Adam Charles Dodson, born May 3, 1983

3.   Addie Watkins, born December 5, 1902. Married to Gary U. Stull, born September 27, 1899, died April, 1954. They had nine children:

  a.   Eloise Stull, born February 5, 1923. Married Sterling McQuay and had children:

    (1)   Jane McQuay.

    (2)   Jean McQuay, married Warnick; children:

        (a) Susan Warnick.

        (b) Gail Warnick.

    (3)   Sterling McQuay, Jr.

    (4)   Terri Lynn McQuay, married Pickett, and had children:

        (1) Bruce Pickett.

        (2) Bridgett Lynn Pickett, born c.1988

    (5)   Kelly McQuay.

  b.   Gary U. Stull, Jr., born March 15, 1927. Married Marion and no children reported.

  c.   Miriam Stull, born April 26, 1928. Married to Norman Shipley and had children:

    (1)   Robin Shipley, married Graham.

  d.   Charles Stull, born March 30, 1929, married and had four children:

    (1)   Deborah Stull, married Myers; children:

        (a) Ericka Myers.

        (b) Nicole Myers.

        (c) Tiffany Myers.

    (2)   Charles Stull, Jr.

        (3)   Pamela Stull, married Graham.

        (4)   Brian Keith Stull, died 1988

   e.   Mary Stull, born June 22, 1930. Married Kenneth Haines and had children:

        (1)   Sharon Haines, who marrried Robinson and had children:

            (a) Jessica Robinson.

            (b) Brian Robinson.

        (2)   Michael Haines, married and had children:

            (a) Nathaniel Haines.

            (b) Camrell Haines.

        (3)   Bonnie Haines, married McEvoy.

   f.   Dorothy Stull, born October 13, 1931. Married George Long.

   g.   Stanley Stull, born July 4, 1934; married Shirley, and had a daughter:

        (1)   Bonnie Stull.

   h.   Lois Stull, born July 17, 1938. Married Richard Ford.

   i.   George Stull, born June 30, 1940. Married Jo Ann and had a son:

        (1)   Michael Stull.

4.   Anna Reba Watkins, born January 2, 1908. Married January 28, 1942 in Frederick, John Wesley Thompson, born October 26, 1900, died August 29, 1965. No children reported.

5.   Lester Basil Watkins, born April 3, 1910, died November 14, 1968. Married Ruth Evelyn Swartzbaugh, born July 21, 1914, died November 20, 1984. Buried at Montgomery Chapel. Children:

   a.   Lois Evelyn Watkins, born August 24, 1931, married January 27, 1951 to Walter Lee Cline, born August 18, 1926, son of Carl Albert Cline (1898) and Esther Leith Moxley (1898). They had children:

        (1)   Michael Lee Cline, born June 30, 1951

(2)   Robin Lynne Cline, born November 9, 1954

b.   Mildred Colleen Watkins, born January 12, 1933. Married first to Ronald Max McPherson and second on December 22, 1979 to Charles Peter Schuettler, born February 20, 1919. Children from her first marriage:

(1)   Stephen Duane McPherson; July 29, 1956

(2)   Ronald Max McPherson, Jr., born April 7, 1959. Married December 7, 1984 to Cynthia Thompson, who was previously married to Granahan. She was born February 28, 1958. One child:

(a)   Matthew Ronald McPherson, born September 16, 1985.

6.   Lucy Marian Watkins, born June 16, 1914. Married to John Roland Swartzbaugh, born July 9, 1908, and had children:

a.   Doris Elaine Swartzbaugh, born April 11, 1931. Married George Raymond Sauble, Jr.; children:

(1)   George Roland Sauble, born January 26, 1950. Married Kathy Sue Adamson, born August 16, 1950, and had children:

(a)   Kristin Anne Sauble, born June 26, 1976

(b)   Janis Elaine Sauble, born April 14, 1979

(2)   Scott Randal Sauble, born December 17, 1954. Married to Sharon Kosenski, and had children:

(a)   Scott Randal Sauble, II, born November 8, 1983

(b)   Justin Raymond Sauble, born October 17, 1985

b.   Betty Swartzbaugh, born April 23, 1938, died April 14, 1990. Married Fred Dioquino and had children:

(1) Timothy Dean Dioquino, born May 20, 1958. An officer in the Coast Guard, he married Judith Lynn Ott, born March 23, 1958.

(2) Teresa Rene' Dioquino, born November 29, 1960. She was a deputy sheriff in Pinellas Park, Florida.

7. Robert Watkins, an infant death at five months.

8. Helen Elizabeth Watkins, born June 26, 1917. Married November 28, 1936 to Herbert Gervis Miller, born December 21, 1914, and had seven children:

a. Joyce Ann Miller, born August 18, 1937. Married November 10, 1956 to Allen Bliss, born March 18, 1932, and had a daughter:

(1) Dawn Bliss, born February 25, 1958. Married to Michael Montlenone and had one child. Married second September 5, 1985 to Glenn Michael Miller, born December 19, 1958. Her child was:

(a) Dawn Bliss (Montlenone) Miller, who was born January 25, 1979.

b. Elsie Miller, born October 2, 1938. Married first Dale Thomas Clickner, born November 25, 1930; and second on June 13, 1983 to George Hogan. Children from first marriage only:

(1) Dale Thomas Clickner, Jr. born February 10, 1960 and married August 9, 1986 to Christina Polansky, born November 23, 1962.

(2) James Andrew Clickner; September 7, 1961

c. Helen G. Miller, born October 5, 1941. Married April 22, 1958 to Robert Jessie Rawles, born March 28, 1935, and had children:

(1) William Douglas Rawles, born June 14, 1960 and married January 29, 1980 to La Brenda Ashley, born August 12, 1961; children:

        (a) Jennifer Hope Rawles, born November 23, 1981

        (b) Marci Ann Rawles: May 23, 1984

    (2)   Robert Cleon Rawles, born February 19, 1964. Married December 9, 1985 to Tiffany Swartout, born May 28, 1966; children:

        (a) Jessica Rawles, born February 2, 1989

    (3)   Carl Rawles, born May 6, 1966. Married June 28, 1968 to Carla Ingram, and had children:

        (a) Cody Allen Rawles; January 28, 1986

d.   Mary Miller, born August 28, 1943. Married first Zollars who died, and second June 24, 1986 to Larry Simmons, born July 12, 1946. They lived in Louisiana; no children.

e.   Herbert Allen Miller, born December 30, 1945. Married May 16, 1968 to Melva Gerhart, born August 28, 1948 and had two children:

    (1)   Patricia Ann Miller, born January 2, 1971 and died January 8, 1971.

    (2)   David Allen Miller, born October 17, 1982

f.   Beverly Jo Miller, born March 14, 1947. Married to Frederick Miller, born November 16, 1933; divorced after two children:

    (1)   Michael Allen Miller, born January 25, 1967.

    (2)   Glenn Scott Miller, born October 6, 1974

g.   William David Miller, born January 25, 1950. Married August 3, 1974 to Beverly Lowe, born October 14, 1947. She had two children by a prior marriage.

9.   Alvin Rudell Watkins, born January 17, 1921 and married August 30, 1945 to Maizie H. Haines, born April 12, 1925, the daughter of Walter Edward Haines (1890), and Rosie Smith (1895). Children:

a.   Alvin Rudell Watkins, Jr., born November 20, 1946. Married July 24, 1971 to Ruby L. Wisner, born May

1, 1953, the daughter of Paul and Mildred Wisner of Frederick. Three children.

b. Glenda Eileen Watkins, born July 5, 1950. Married February 14, 1978 David Devilbiss. No children.

c. Bernard Lee Watkins; March 3, 1960.

Bradley Jefferson Brandenburg
1863-1945

This son of Jesse B. Brandenburg (1824) and Sarah Rebecca Purdum (1829) was born c.1863 and died November 10, 1945. Married first December 26, 1888 to Valerie Eveline Hyatt, born November 22, 1867 and died 1921 at Kemptown, daughter of Eli Hyatt, III (1837), and Georgianna Lewis (1840). Both are buried at the Kemptown Methodist Church. Married second Nicie V. Lee. They appear in the 1900 census for Frederick County, with four of their children. Also in the household is the mother of Bradley, and Louis N. Brandenburg, his nephew, born c.1880. Bradley's will, dated October 31, 1938, was probated December 3, 1945 and filed in liber RLL2 at folio 195 in Frederick records. He names his second wife, and makes his son, B. Claytus Brandenburg Executor. He then names several of his children. Seven children born to his first marriage:

1. Jessie Fay Brandenburg, born January 6, 1892 and of whom more following.

2. George Floyd Brandenburg, born August 21, 1893 and died August 8, 1920. Buried at the Kemptown Methodist Church. Married December 26, 1914 to Katherine Elizabeth Williams, born May 2, 1895, died March 1, 1968, and was buried at Kemptown with her husband. She was the daughter of Downey Williams and Frances Elizabeth Bolton. At least two sons:

a. Bradley Monroe Brandenburg, born January 15, 1916. Married July 9, 1938 to Shirley Laura Harryman, born August 16, 1920, of Baltimore. Two children. After her husband's death, Shirley married second James B. Foreman, who died November, 1985. Children:

(1) Roma Lee Brandenburg, born February 25, 1939. Married Donald Edward Posner born December 24, 1937, son of Benjamin Posner and Elizabeth Hannon. Two children:

    (a) Terri Dawne Posner, born August 6, 1962. Married May 19, 1984 August Joseph Stitzel.

    (b) Julie Lynn Posner; August 4, 1965.

(2) Dawn Shirley Brandenburg, born April 6, 1942. Married David Forbes Blanche, a son of Thomas and Nan Blanche, from Scotland. Three children:

    (a) Greg Thomas Blanche; May 7, 1965

    (b) Gary David Blanche: January 3, 1968

    (c) Glen Bradley Blanche, born December 30, 1971

b. Malcolm L. Brandenburg.

3. Bradley Claytus Brandenburg, born January 26, 1895, died February 24, 1972. Married March 12, 1919 to Leah Marie Williams, born October 7, 1893, died December 7, 1969, daughter of Downey Williams and Elizabeth Bolton. Children:

a. Bradley Carlton Brandenburg, born December 5, 1920, died July 25, 1995. He was the founder of Brandenburg Paving Co., and an employee of Browning Construction Co. He was married to Audree Virginia Mullinix, born May 23, 1923, daughter of Granville Roland Mullinix and Ethel Duvall. No children.

b. Constance Marie Brandenburg, born January 14, 1924. Married March 3, 1945 to John Russell Glaze, born September 18, 1922, son of Basil Russell Glaze (1887) and Bertie May King (1886). Two daughters:

(1)   Judith Marie Glaze, born May 16, 1947, died August 18, 1988; buried at Clarksburg United Methodist. Married June 5, 1966 to Allen Roosevelt Hawse, born January 9, 1946, son of William Hawse and Mary Ellen Keith. Two children:

    (a)   Beverly Michelle Hawse, born November 18, 1968. Married October 8, 1988 to Terence L. Wright, born July 19, 1967, son of Elward Wright.

    (b)   Michael Allen Hawse: August 2, 1974.

(2)   Cathie May Glaze, born March 23, 1952. Married September 23, 1973 Henry Clark Warfield, born October 5, 1942, son of John O. Warfield and Louise Hoffman. A daughter:

    (a)   Julie Marie Warfield: September 2, 1981.

c.   Ruth Valerie Brandenburg, born January 11, 1926. Married June 11, 1949 to Richard Franklin Brown, born February 10, 1923, son of Benjamin Franklin Brown and Rosie Valinda Brown. One child:

(1)   Patricia Ann Brown, born December 15, 1957. Married September 22, 1979 to Fred Benny Pridemore, Jr., born October 18, 1956, son of Fred Benny Pridemore, Sr. and Shirley Thompson. No children.

d.   Lloyd Claytus Brandenburg. Church records report the birth of Floyd Clayton Brandenburg on May 22, 1934, son of Bradley and Leah. But, the obituary of his brother reports the name as Lloyd, which appears to be correct. Married October 10, 1954 to Marlene Yvonne Watkins, born July 24, 1936, daughter of James Russell Watkins (1908) and Mildred Elizabeth Stanley (1909). Five children:

(1) Sharon Kay Brandenburg, born July 26, 1957. Married May 16, 1981 to Ronald Wayne Murphy, born April 5, 1955, son of Eugene Francis Murphy and Irma Lucille Rhoderick of Ijamsville, Maryland.

(2) Debora Jean Brandenburg, born May 5, 1959. Married John Walter and divorced. She has one daughter:

    (a) Leah Marlene Brandenburg, born January 14, 1983

(3) David Lloyd Brandenburg, born November 1, 1960. Married October 18, 1980 to Theresa Ann Evans, born August 6, 1961, daughter of D. Ray Evans and Carole Ann Winebrenner of Mt. Airy. Two daughters:

    (a) Angela Ann Brandenburg, born June 17, 1983 at Frederick.

    (b) Bethany Yvette Brandenburg, born December 10, 1984 at Frederick.

(4) Mark Alan Brandenburg, born June 17, 1963. Married January 17, 1987 Deborah Gail Helsel, born March 18, 1964, the daughter of James A. Helsel and Rosemary Compton. Two children:

    (a) Ryan Mark Brandenburg: July 23, 1987.

    (b) Michelle Elizabeth Brandenburg born July 12, 1989

(5) Robert Matthew Brandenburg, born October 3, 1976 at Frederick.

4. Maysie Nadine Brandenburg, born November 18, 1897, died August 13, 1989. Married June 1, 1921 to Lester Steele Watkins, born June 23, 1895, died March 19, 1966; son of Joseph Grant Watkins (1866) and Nettie F. Beall (1872). Buried in the cemetery of Bethesda United Methodist Church at Browningsville. Children:

a. Eloise Nadine Watkins, born September 11, 1925 and died September 29, 1925.
b. Lester Edsel Watkins, born October 21, 1927, and married October 15, 1949 Peggy Woodfield, born April 3, 1928, daughter of William Robert Woodfield and Grace Rogers. They had children:
   (1) Steven Edsel Watkins, born July 16, 1952 and married June 28, 1974 to Shirley Tucker, born January 16, 1952, of Annapolis, daughter of Joseph Lester Tucker and Josephine Benning. One child.
   (2) Dennis Wayne Watkins, born June 2, 1955 and married October 2, 1982 Tania Moxley, born January 22, 1962. Two children.
5. Fairy Brandenburg, born March 2, 1903; married to Lester William Burdette, son of Luther Melvin Burdette (1875). She was married second April, 1957 to Clay E. Ward, born 1901, died 1960. Children:
a. Carolyn Fay Burdette, born May 25, 1934. Married January 28, 1955 to Donald Wilford Bell, born March 17, 1934. Three children:
   (1) Michael Donald Bell, born July 22, 1956. Married July 12, 1978 to Susan Elizabeth Long, born May 15, 1960. Three children:
      (a) Cory Michael Bell: April 3, 1981
      (b) Stacy Lorraine Bell: June 27, 1983
      (c) Leslie Ann Bell: May 10, 1988
   (2) Gary Wayne Bell, born May 3, 1960
   (3) Pattie Lynn Bell, born October 6, 1962. Married March 21, 1987 to George Palmer Wood, III.
b. Rosalie Nadine Burdette, born July 10, 1938. Married May 19, 1965 to William Harvey Rittase, born August 4, 1934, of Littlestown, Pennsylvania. Two children:

(1) Jacque Nadine Ritasse: June 19, 1967.

(2) Jeffrey Scott Ritasse: January 29, 1969

6. Evelyn Crothers Brandenburg, born November 5, 1907. Married Lester Baker Riggs, born November 24, 1903, died April 21, 1973; buried at Kemptown. Two children:

a. Jesse Lee Riggs, born January 2, 1925. Married October 18, 1946 Mary Catharine Hilton, born August 23, 1928, daughter of Ray Hilton (1893) and Iva M. Watkins (1897). Jesse Lee was a farmer, buying the family farm in 1949. Three children:

(1) Charles Larry Riggs, born December 1, 1948. Married in 1972 to Patricia Kirchgassner of Silver Spring, daughter of George and Marjorie Kirchgassner. Two children, and divorced. Larry was married second to Judy Williams Hylan, born December 30, 1948, who had two children from a prior marriage. Larry's two children were:

(a) Andrew Hilton Riggs, born December 13, 1973

(b) Carolyn Patricia Riggs: March 19, 1975.

(2) James Brian Riggs, born September 10, 1950. Married in 1971 to Linda Ann Driskill, born April 12, 1953, daughter of Jack and Mary Driskill. It is of passing interest to the author to recall that it was this Jack Driskill, a barber, who gave his first haircut to my son about 1960. Two children:

(a) James Brian Riggs, Jr.: March 6, 1972.

(b) Jessica Christine Riggs, born November 6, 1975.

(3) Julie Marie Riggs, born August 8, 1957. Married September 18, 1976 to C. Wayne Frum, son of Reverend and Mrs. Charles Frum of West Virginia. Divorced after one child:

(a) Kelly Marie Frum: April 20, 1979
- b. Almeda Riggs, born August 23, 1931. Married November 19, 1949 to William Wesley Geisler, born November 14, 1927, son of James Wesley Geisler (1896) and Martha Sophia Brandenburg (1888). Four children:
  - (1) Gary Lee Geisler, born November 3, 1952. Married June 7, 1980 Vicki Marie Boone, born June 7, 1953, a daughter of Charles and Jean Boone of Mt. Pleasant, Maryland. Gary and Vicki drive tractor-trailer trucks together. One child:
    - (a) Amy Marie Geisler, born September 14, 1982, and lived two days.
  - (2) Donna Kay Geisler, born October 1, 1956
  - (3) Carole Jean Geisler, born November 27, 1961
  - (4) Lori Ann Geisler, born May 7, 1963
7. Merhl Hyatt Brandenburg, born August 26, 1910, died January 9, 1980. Married Ethel L. Justice, born February 15, 1915, died December 4, 1986. Mehrl was a conservationist with the State of Maryland. His obituary states that he was survived by one son, nine foster children, fifteen foster grandchildren, and two foster great grandchildren. His son was:
- a. Bradley Thomas Brandenburg: November 11, 1937.

Jessie Fay Brandenburg
1892-1963

This daughter of Bradley Jefferson Brandenburg (1863) and Valerie Eveline Hyatt (1867) was born January 6, 1892 and died September 27, 1963. Married at her home near Kemptown, December 25, 1909 to Asa Hull Watkins, born February 12, 1887 and died January 13, 1967; son of Thomas Ellsworth Watkins (1862) and Rosa Medora Moxley (1865).

Asa Hull Watkins was associated with People's Lumber Supply Company and a founder of Hamilton Homes, Inc., builders in Frederick and Hagerstown. Jessie Fay and Asa Hull had children:

1. Rose Eveline Watkins, born September 18, 1915. Married December 30, 1939 to William James Kiefer, born September 16, 1914, died November 29, 1965 in a tractor accident. After his death, Rose married second Richard Albert Mott, born February 8, 1917. Two children were born to her first marriage:
   a. Patricia Dale Kiefer, born September 3, 1943
   b. William James Kiefer, Jr., born July 2, 1947 and died April 7, 1973 in a highway accident. He left one child:
      (1) Diana Kiefer, born c.1970, living in England with her mother, whom her father met while in service.
2. Bradley Ellsworth Watkins, born June 24, 1918 and died July 6, 1981. Married Margaret Virginia Stauffer, born January 11, 1920, of Frederick, Maryland. Two children:
   a. Sally Fay Watkins, born September 22, 1939 and married Ronald A. Lennox, born October 14, 1936 and were divorced in 1987, after three children:
      (1) Valerie Ann Lennox, born March 19, 1963 and married September 28, 1986, to Douglas Alan Dailey.
      (2) Laura Beth Lennox, born April 17, 1968
      (3) Ronald Watkins Lennox; August 27, 1972
   b. Bradley Ellsworth Watkins, born September 29, 1947. Married Marsha Lynn Cantrell, born November 28, 1946, the daughter of Verdin Smith Cantrell and Drucilla Iona Mitchell of Salisbury, Maryland. One child:
      (1) Bradley Mitchell Watkins; November 16, 1974

3. Jessie Nadine Watkins, born January 29, 1921. Married Donald Edward Grigsby, born June 16, 1918, and died August 27, 1977. They had two children:
   a. Don Ellsworth Grigsby, born December 28, 1942. Married Beverly Ann Nelson, daughter of William C. Nelson of Frederick. Don owned and operated Great Eastern Concrete, Inc. in Frederick. They have two children:
      (1) Don Ellsworth Grigsby, Jr.; March 20, 1964
      (2) Heather Lea Grigsby; July 10, 1973
   b. Christopher Hull Grigsby, born April 23, 1949 and died September 12, 1980. Married Deborah Ann Magers, daughter of Howard Magers. They were divorced after one child. He married second Vickie and had a son. His two children were:
      (1) Heidi Grigsby, born May 28, 1972
      (2) Shane Grigsby, born November 6, 1973

CHILD 3

Emily Brandenburg
1827-

This daughter of Lemuel Brandenburg (1801) and Charlotte Kindley (1804) was born April 5, 1827. Married January 12, 1850 to Rufus King Purdum, born June 5, 1827, and died November 23, 1905 at Appomattox, Virginia, to which they had relocated about 1869. He was a son of John Lewis Purdum (1798) and Jemima King (1805). Children, based largely on census records:

1. John Fillmore Purdum, born January 31, 1851 Frederick County, Maryland; died March 24, 1935 in Appomattox County, Virginia, where he is buried. Married January 21, 1873 to Laura Richard Hewitt, born May 1, 1855 in Bedford County, Virginia, and died July 10, 1917 at Ap-

pomattox, Virginia; daughter of George Hewitt (1815) and Rebecca Leftwich (1815). A daughter:

    a.   Laura Purdum, born at Appomattox, Virginia, August 20, 1879, and died February 27, 1971 in East Orange, New Jersey. Married October 11, 1898 to Charles Cawthorn.

2.   Samuel (or Lemuel) W. Purdum, born c.1853. Married c.1874 to Margaret.
3.   Jemima Purdum, born c.1855
4.   Anna O. Purdum, born c.1858
5.   Edward E. Purdum, born c.1860
6.   Virginia L. Purdum, born c.1862
7.   Cornelia G. Purdum, born c.1864; died October 8, 1865 at New Market, Virginia.
8.   William Reich Purdum, born May 24, 1866 near New Market, Virginia.
9.   Emma L. Purdum, born c.1869 at Appomattox, Virginia.

CHILD 5

William R. Brandenburg
1829-

This son of Lemuel Brandenburg (1801) and Charlotte Kindley (1804) was born November 15, 1829. He married November 27, 1856 to Sarah E. Mullineaux, born c.1837. The couple appears in the 1860 census for Damascus with two children. In the 1880 census, they again appear, with six of their children. One daughter is buried with them at Kemptown Methodist Church, and there were other children:

1.   Alura Brandenburg, born c.1858
2.   Sarah E. Brandenburg, born c.1860
3.   Oliver Jordan Brandenburg, baptized June 8, 1862. He is the same Oliver J. Brandenburg who was born September 23, 1861 and died May 27, 1942. Buried at Damas-

cus Methodist Church. His wife is also buried there; she was Susie L., born October 27, 1860 and died December 21, 1904. The stone carries another name, which is apparently the second wife of Oliver. She was Carrie C. Reiblich, born February 6, 1882 and died October 29, 1970. The obituary of their son Tilghman names his parents. Oliver appears as head of household in the 1900 census for Frederick County, with his wife, three of their children, and his sister, Annie G. living with them. In the 1920 census for Montgomery County, Oliver and Carrie are listed with their youngest known child. The will of Oliver was dated January 4, 1938 and probated June 9, 1942; filed in liber HGC 40 at folio 357 in Montgomery County, Maryland. Strangely, it is the earliest recorded Brandenburg will that I was able to find in the county. He names his wife and four sons: The children were:

a. William Asbury Brandenburg, born December 16, 1887, died June 16, 1963 at his home in Damascus, Maryland. His will, dated September 27, 1951, was probated July 17, 1963 and filed in liber VMB 165 at folio 436 in Montgomery County. It names his five children. Buried with his wife at the Damascus Methodist Church. Married to Bessie May Burdette, born September 14, 1891, died March 30, 1951, daughter of Nathan J. Burdette (1842) and Rispa Ann Lewis (1844). They appear in the 1920 census of Damascus, with some of the children. Children:

   (1) Annie Lauretta Brandenburg, born April 27, 1914, and of whom more.
   (2) William Arnold Brandenburg, born c.1917
   (3) Marjorie A. Brandenburg, born c.1919, as she appears in the 1920 census with her parents. In her father's will, she is called Marjorie Boyer Campbell. Married Edward Campbell.

(4) Emma Grace Brandenburg, who married Albert Molesworth.

(5) Jeremiah Elsworth Brandenburg, born January 22, 1925. Married May 19, 1948 Mary Mildred Linthicum, born May 9, 1930, daughter of Purdum Burdette Linthicum (1906) and Edna Wilson Hyatt (1905). No children.

b. Elsie V. Brandenburg, born c.1891, married to Gue. Abstracts of the *Sentinel* newspaper also report the marriage of Elsie Brandenburg, daughter of Mr. and Mrs. Oliver Brandenburg, to Jesse Brandenburg, during the last week of August, 1907, in Baltimore. Perhaps second marriage for Elsie.

c. Roy O. W. Brandenburg, born March 7, 1898, died March 7, 1949. Buried Damascus Methodist Churh. He may be the same Roy O. Brandenburg who was married to Edna P., who died February 5, 1981. In the will of his father, it was stated that his brother, William A., was named as Trustee to care for the inheritance of Roy, which in the case of his death, would pass to his daughter. The estate of Edna P. was settled without probate in Montgomery County, in which her two daughters are named:

(1) Betty Estelle Brandenburg, born July 23, 1929 at Damascus. Married there February 10, 1951 to Edward Middleton Brown, born February 29, 1928 at Purdum, son of Willard Harrison Brown (1888) and Sarah Elizabeth King (1888). One son:

(a) Glenwood Middleton Brown, born January 11, 1952 Olney, Maryland. Married August 30, 1974 to Barbara Duvall, and had a son:

1. Jeffry Brown: November 19, 1984

(2) Dorothy Brandenburg, married Duvall.

d. Tilghman J. Brandenburg, born c.1910 and died June 11, 1993. He was a police officer for twenty-eight years, and was survived by his wife, Margaret Scheel, and a daughter, and two granddaughters. Margaret Scheel was born August 22, 1913 in Mt. Airy, and died March 27, 1994 at Shady Grove Hospital; the daughter of George H. Scheel and Olive Nicholson. His daughter was:

   (1) Nancy Kay Brandenburg, married Easterday, and had children. According to her mother's obituary, she was apparently married second to Paul Black. Her children were:

   (a) Sandra Kay Easterday.

   (b) Anita Easterday, who was married to George Koon or Coon.

   (c) Robert Franklin Easterday, who died before 1993, apparently, according to the obituary of his grandmother. He had at least one son:

   1. Jordon Alan Easterday.

4. Charlotte E. Brandenburg, born c.1864

5. Andrew J. Brandenburg, born October 3, 1866, and died November 29, 1935. Married November 4, 1889 in Montgomery County to Carrie G. Watkins, born August 19, 1871, died November 19, 1925 at Mt. Airy. Andrew is head of household in the 1900 census for Wolfsville, with his wife, and three children. In the 1920 census for Mt. Airy, Frederick County, they are listed with four children. They were parents of:

a. Raymond R. Brandenburg, born c.1891

b. Della M. Brandenburg, born c.1893

c. Blanche E. Brandenburg, born December 16, 1897 and died November 19, 1930 at Mt. Airy.

d. Edith M. Brandenburg, born c.1905

e. Hilda E. Brandenburg, born c.1909

6. William B. Brandenburg, born c.1870. This is perhaps William Bromwell Brandenburg, born November 24, 1869 and died April 4, 1932; buried Montgomery Chapel cemetery at Claggettsville. Married January 31, 1893 in Montgomery County, Maryland, Minnie E. Watkins, born November 20, 1876, died September 7, 1910, daughter of Fillmore C. Watkins (1852) and Louisa E. Lyddard (1858). Buried with her husband. There is a family listed in the 1900 census of Montgomery County, which appears to be this one. The census lists the parents and three children, all ages matching individuals from other sources. The children included:

a. Susan L. Brandenburg, born c.1894, according to the census of 1900.

b. Lola May Brandenburg, born August 29, 1895. Listed in the census, and married to Justice.

c. William Dewey Brandenburg, born c.1899

d. Pearl Estella Brandenburg, born October 29, 1901. Married to Layton.

e. Claude Fillmore Brandenburg, born January 19, 1903 in Damascus, died August 13, 1979. Married to Velma Winifred Watkins, born born October 22, 1906, and died May 6, 1986, daughter of Milton Watkins (1873) and Dora E. Phebus (1877). She is buried at Marvin Chapel cemetery in Mt. Airy, and was first married December 22, 1925 to Raymond J. Spurrier, born August 6, 1897, died August 15, 1939. Claude had been previously married to Mary Angeline Spurrier), born 1902, died May 23, 1934, sister of Raymond J., by whom he had four children. She was buried at Damascus Methodist Church. The children were:

(1) Lorraine Brandenburg, married Earl Lee Watkins and had two children.

> (2) Rodney S. Brandenburg, born 1924, died 1940. Buried with his mother at the Damascus Methodist Church cemetery.
>
> (3) Mary Naomi Brandenburg, married first to Donald Moxley and second to Robert McIntosh.
>
> (4) Evelyn Louise Brandenburg; married first to John Shellhorse and had three children. Married second to Rocco Los Calzo.

f. Alvin Brandenburg. This may well be Alton P. Brandenburg, born 1904, died 1968, who is buried with his parents at Montgomery Chapel cemetery at Claggettsville. With him is his wife, Mary A., born 1889, died 1974.

7.. Florence C. Brandenburg, born November 28, 1872 and died November 1, 1880.

8. Annie G. Brandenburg, born c.1879.

Annie Lauretta Brandenburg
1914-

This daughter of William A. and Bessie M. Brandenburg was born April 27, 1914. Married September 2, 1936 to Gilmore Edward Hurley, born August 16, 1913, son of Harry Gilmore Hurley (1885) and Bessie Vierna Warthen (1886).

For those readers who may be interested in the Hurley ancestry (including that of the author), it should be pointed out that there are at least three different groupings of that family in Montgomery County. The Damascus Hurleys, of which these here discussed are a part, are descended from Michael Hurley, born September 29, 1811 in Castletown Parish, Kinaugh, County Cork, Ireland. He immigrated to America in the middle 1800s. The author is descended from one Daniel Hurley, who arrived in Talbot County, Maryland, during 1676, having sailed from the port of Bristol as an indentured servant. The Hurley families who lived in the vicinity of Clarksburg were also descended from Daniel, but are now not to be found, except in early records and cemeteries. Those Hurleys who lived near Rockville were perhaps also descended from Daniel, but not yet proven.

In any case, six children were born to Gilmore and Annie Lauretta:

1. Alfred Ellsworth Hurley, born June 27, 1937. Married June 17, 1960 to Ruth Elaine Brown, born May 29, 1942, daughter of Harold and Margaret Brown of Mt. Airy. Four children:
   a. Bruce Edward Hurley, born November 17, 1960
   b. Ronald Lee Hurley, born April 1, 1962
   c. Connie Elaine Hurley, born July 18, 1966. Married March 24, 1984 to John Allan Quickel, born July 17, 1962. One child:
      (1) Matthew Allan Quickel, born July 13, 1984
   d. David Allen Hurley, born February 21, 1968
2. Robert Gilmore Hurley, born February 13, 1940. He owns three electronic shops in Virginia. Married first to Georgia Sidler of Damascus and divorced after three children. Married second August 25, 1979 to Elizabeth Dasher Stacy, who had a son by a former marriage. The three children of Robert were:
   a. Timothy Robert Hurley, born June 11, 1966
   b. Dorothy Lauretta Hurley, born December 20, 1967
   c. James Anthony Hurley, born January 14, 1969
3. Lauretta Ann Hurley, born November 11, 1941. Married August 2, 1958 to Gilbert Dean Ashley, born December 30, 1939. Two children:
   a. Theresa Ann Ashley, born February 17, 1959. First married Michael A. Burdette, and had one son. She married second December 31, 1982 to David Lee Tracey, born December 1, 1961. They had a daughter. Her two children were:

    (1)   Michael A. Burdette, Jr.: September 29, 1976

    (2)   Jessica Lynn Tracey, born October 5, 1984

  b. Michael Todd Ashley, born February 5, 1962. Married January 12, 1985 to Susan Regina Miller.

4. Harold Edward Hurley, born May 3, 1943. Married and had two sons. Married second May 19, 1979 to Kimberly Ellen West, born April 21, 1960, a teacher's aide for Montgomery County. They had two children. His four children were:

  a. Jeffrey Wayne Hurley, born October 22, 1967

  b. Gregory Scott Hurley, born May 16, 1970

  c. Dawn Michelle Hurley, born April 23, 1980.

  d. Gina Ree Hurley, born February 13, 1982

5. Kathleen Ruth Hurley, born January 21, 1945. Married Donald Wayne Grigg; both are school teachers. Three children:

  a. Robert Henry Grigg, born April 2, 1970

  b. Kelly Dawn Grigg, born August 21, 1975

  c. Jody Owen Grigg, born July 13, 1978

6. William Arthur Hurley, born September 2, 1949. Married May 20, 1970 to Beverly Jean Drewry, born October 9, 1950 of Poplar Springs, Maryland. She was originally from Eagle Rock, near Roanoke, Virginia. Two children:

  a. Karie Ann Hurley, born November 24, 1973

  b. William Michael Hurley, born July 22, 1977

CHILD 14

Sarah Louisa Brandenburg
1843-1917

This daughter of Lemuel Brandenburg and Charlotte Kindley was born February 4, 1843 in Frederick County, and died April 8, 1917. Married April 25, 1861 to Luther Henry Harrison Browning, born March 11, 1840 and died January

26, 1908 at his home in New Market District of Frederick County. He was the son of Luther Martin Browning (1810) and Harriet Ann King (1807). Like his father, he was a blacksmith and a farmer, occasionally mended clocks, and was known to practice a bit of medicine. They had children:

1. Harrison McGill Browning, born February 9, 1862; a machinist, who lived in Baltimore. Married to Mary Virginia Young, the daughter of Mrs. Sarah F. Young, and had two children:
   a. Earl Harrison Browning.
   b. Marie Elmer Browning.
2. Melville Newton Browning, born January 12, 1864
3. Lina M. Browning, born February 2, 1866; married Jackson Clay, and had five children:
   a. Linda Clay.
   b. Carol Clay.
   c. Sterling Clay.
   d. Mabel Clay.
   e. Thelma Clay.
4. Harriett Charlotte Browning, born c.1868, died 1934. Married to Franklin E. Spurrier and had four children:
   a. Clarence Spurrier.
   b. Stella Spurrier.
   c. Everett Spurrier.
   d. Margaret Spurrier.
5. Luther L. Browning, born March 14, 1869; married to Ida Barton. Lived in Baltimore and had three children:
   a. Holly Browning.
   b. Lawrence Browning.
   c. Agnes Browning.
6. Elizabeth Browning, born December 2, 1871
7. James Monroe Browning, born August 1, 1873, and died December 1, 1948. Married to Nannie L. Thompson and had two children, one of whom was:
   a. Algie Browning.

8. Eldridge M. Browning, born September 20, 1875, died September 3, 1947. Lived in Mt. Airy; married Annie R. Trout. One child:
   a. Layman Browning.
9. Rosella May Browning, born December 29, 1877. Lived near Frederick; married to Lewis White and had three children:
   a. Lillian White.
   b. Paul White.
   c. Murr White.
10. Agnes Matilda Browning, born May 3, 1880, died September 11, 1949. Married to Titus E. Brown in Montgomery County
11. Hepzi Edith Browning, born February 26, 1882. Married Nathan Clagett.
12. Raymond Atlas Browning, born December 10, 1884. Married Della Fleming.

CHILD 15

Garrison McLain Brandenburg
1845-1927

This son of Lemuel Brandenburg and Charlotte Kindley was born April 16, 1845 on his parents' farm in Frederick County, Maryland, and died November 22, 1927. Buried at Kemptown Methodist Church cemetery. He worked on the farm with his father, and inherited the property, known as the *Sarah and Elizabeth Farm*. In 1866, he married Mary E. Norwood, the daughter of Belt M. Norwood (1813) and Sarah Ann Day (1814). She was born June 14, 1844 and died March 19, 1928. Buried with her husband, as are several of their children. Garrison and his wife appear in the 1880 and 1900 census for Frederick County, with children. (The 1890 census for Maryland and many other states does not exist.) In the 1920 census, Garrison and his wife appear in Mt. Airy, Carroll County, Maryland, with one daughter, Lillie, still living with them. His will was dated April 9, 1925 in Carroll County, and probated June 12, 1928 in Frederick County, Maryland, filed in liber GES2 at folio 394 in the latter county. There, he named his wife, and only four living children, as well as the son of a deceased daughter. He left a small bequest to Providence Methodist Church at Kemptown, in trust, for maintenance of the burial ground where his parents are buried. They had children, born on the home farm:

1. Oscar Morgan Brandenburg, born June 27, 1868 and died 1937. Married Mary J. (Mollie) Baker, born 1869 and died 1952, and lived at Kemptown, where they are buried at the Methodist Church. Two children:
   a. Goldie Brandenburg.
   b. Ray Brandenburg.
2. Matilda May Brandenburg, born October 20, 1869, who married James W. Burdette of Gaithersburg, who was an Executor of the will of her father. No children.
3. Lemuel Reece Brandenburg, born November 15, 1870 and died 1926. Buried at Kemptown Methodist Church. Married Lillia Tribby, and lived at Baltimore.
4. Eunice Estella Brandenburg, born June 16, 1872. Married William Norwood, born 1862. Buried in Providence Church cemetery at Kemptown. Lived in Montgomery County, and had children:
   a. Fay Norwood; married, but no children.
   b. Mabel Norwood, married to Darby, and was quite specifically excluded from her grandfather's will. At least one son:
      (1) Windsor D. Darby.
   c. Norval Lester Norwood, born October 12, 1891 at Damascus, died September 30, 1953. Married Sarah Elizabeth Bowman, born March 27, 1906 at Shaefersville. Nine children:

(1) Doris Adabelle Norwood, born April 20, 1925 and died April 13, 1972. Married Paul B. Clay and had children:
  (a) Thomas Glen Clay.
  (b) Paul Dale Clay.
  (c) Barry Clay.
  (d) Bonnie Lou Clay.
(2) Julian Garrison Norwood: October 14, 1930. Married and had children, born at Mobile, Alabama:
  (a) Julian Garrison Norwood, Jr.
  (b) Rebecca Norwood.
  (c) Michael Norwood.
(3) Joyce Anne Norwood, born September 9, 1938 (of 1934) and married June 11, 1960 to Clayton Otis Smith, born in Frederick, June 10, 1913, his second wife. He was a cattle dealer; no children reported.
(4) Allan Wayne Norwood, born August 24, 1937 and married May 19, 1962 to Patricia Ann Topper, born in Frederick August 25, 1940. Two children, born Frederick:
  (a) Cynthia Kay Norwood: October 29, 1962
  (b) Angie Beth Norwood: May 26, 1967
(5) Beverly Lee Norwood, born November 17, 1938. Married September 29, 1962 to Shelby Jean Shifflett, born at Elkton, Virginia, March 23, 1941. Three children:
  (a) Deborah Lynn Norwood, born Frederick, June 9, 1963
  (b) Tammy Sue Norwood, born January 24, 1968 at Westminster, Maryland.
  (c) Lisa Michelle Norwood, born November 25, 1971 at Westminster.

(6) Carolyn Yvonne Norwood, born March 26, 1943. Married June 10, 1961 John Melvin Masser, born September 15, 1938. Children, born at Frederick, Maryland:
    (a) Renee Dawn Masser: August 12, 1961
    (b) Teresa Lynn Masser: April 29, 1964

(7) Darryl Everett Norwood, born May 10, 1945. Married April 12, 1969 to Janet Mae Porter, born April 12, 1949. Lived in Gaithersburg with one son:
    (a) Brent Everett Norwood, born December 16, 1971 at Frederick.

(8) Sharon Lynn Norwood, born December 28, 1946. Married December 31, 1964 John Carl Sidler, born July 6, 1946 at LaPlata, Maryland. A daughter, born at Frederick:
    (a) Jennifer Cheryl Sidler: July 5, 1971.

(9) Constance Sue Dawn Norwood, born April 6, 1948. Married October 21, 1967 to Ronnie Gene Allen, born October 17, 1948 at Richwood, West Virginia. One son, at Frederick:
    (a) Mark Randall Allen: June 4, 1968

d. Garrison Norwood, born November 8, 1896, died January 16, 1949. Married Evaleen.

e. Ella Norwood.

5. Effie Clearfield Brandenburg, born February 12, 1877 and died August 8, 1910. Buried at Kemptown.

6. Lillie Brandenburg, born c.1877, according to the 1920 census of Carroll County, where she appears with her parents, listed as a daughter. That is the only record of this child that we have found.

7. Anna Myrtle Brandenburg, born October 29, 1878 and died August 23, 1921. Buried at Kemptown.

8. Maulty D. Brandenburg, born c.1881 and died July 24, 1882 at the age of 8 months and 24 days. Buried with her parents at Kemptown.
9. Cleveland LeRoy Brandenburg, born November 27, 1882 and died September 21, 1903. Buried Kemptown.
10. Norma Oleanda Brandenburg, born March 5, 1884 and died January 25, 1918. She was married July 7, 1913 to William Andrew Baker, born August 28, 1880 at Poplar Springs, and died May 28, 1942. He was a teacher, and the son of John T. Baker (1851) and Caroline Virginia Mullinix (1854). Norma was the second of his three wives, and they had one child:
    a. Rudelle Brandenburg Baker, born January 4, 1914 near Damascus. Married June 28, 1943 Sarah L. Chain, born July 7, 1918 at Mt. Olive, Mississippi. A daughter:
        (1) Susan L. Baker, born November 5, 1954 at Miami, Florida.
11. Kerby Brandenburg, born November 28, 1888, and died April 7, 1889; buried at Kemptown.

Solomon Brandenburg
1700-
Germany
*

*

Alexander Henry Brandenburg
*

*

Jacob Brandenburg
*

*

Lemuel Brandenburg
1801
*

*

Ann Priscilla Brandenburg
1831

*   *   *   *   *   *   *

*

* * Titus Granville Day 1850

*

* * Lattimer W. Day 1852

*

* * Addison Singleton Day 1856

*

* * Altona Bovincia Clintinchia Day 1857

*

* * Preston Clairsville Day 1859

*

* * Harriet Emma Day 1863

*

* * James Start Day 1865

*

* * Laura Arvilla Day 1867

*

* * Langdon Storrs Day 1871

*

* * Nora May Day 1875

CHAPTER 8

Ann Priscilla Brandenburg
1831-1915

This daughter of Lemuel Brandenburg and Charlotte Kindley was born February 11, 1831 and died October 10, 1915 in Frederick County. Married there October 23, 1849 to Rufus King Day, born May 13, 1827 at Kings Valley, in Montgomery County, Maryland, and died December 1, 1902 in Frederick, Maryland; buried at Bethesda United Methodist Church at Browningsville. He was the son of Luther Day and Harriet Ann King (1807). Rufus King Day and Ann Priscilla Brandenburg had children, born either in Frederick or Montgomery County, Maryland. Each child will be treated separately following the main listing, with the exception of the fourth child, who remained single, and the last one, who died young. The children were:

1. Titus Granville Day, born September 16, 1850.
2. Lattimer W. Day, born c.1852.
3. Addison Singleton Day, born January 8, 1856.
4. Altona Bovincia Clintinchia Day, born October 22, 1857 and died November 19, 1934. She died single, remaining at home to care for her invalid mother. Buried Bethesda Methodist Church cemetery at Kemptown.
5. Preston Clairsville Day, born October 21, 1859.
6. Harriet Emma Day, born c.1863 at Kemptown.
7. James Start Day, born c.1865 near Kemptown.
8. Laura Arvilla Day, born July 11, 1867, of whom more.
9. Langdon Storrs Day, born c.1871.
10. Nora May Day, born August 14, 1875; died March 26, 1879.

CHILD 1

Titus Granville Day
1850-1931

This son of Rufus King Day (1827) and Ann Priscilla Brandenburg (1831) was born September 16, 1850, and died November 23, 1931. A schoolteacher, he was married October 16, 1885 to Laura Dorcas Watkins, born February 22, 1858, died September 20, 1940. No children.

CHILD 2

Lattimer W. Day
1852-1935

This son of Rufus King Day (1827) and Ann Priscilla Brandenburg (1831) died 1935. A farmer near Kemptown, he married after November 12, 1878 to Venia W. Browning, born 1857, died 1933; buried Providence cemetery at Kemptown. Three children:
1. Venia Wynonia Day.
2. Ira Eugene Day, born c.1880 near Kemptown, Maryland, and of whom more.
3. Melissa B. Day, born c.1883. Married John Watkins, born 1881, died 1960. Two children:
   a. J. Latimer Watkins, married Mary. No children.
   b. Roland Watkins, married Ruth.

Ira Eugene Day
1880-1955

This son of Lattimer W. Day (1852) and Venia W. Browning (1857) was born c.1880 near Kemptown, Maryland, and died April 10, 1955. He was a farmer in the Richmond, Virginia, area. Married December 19, 1903 to Sallie Caskie Lester, born there December 9, 1882, died 1963; buried Doswell, Virginia. Eight children, first three born at Kemptown, the rest at Doswell, Virginia:

1. Janice June Louise Day, born June 5, 1904, and married October 14, 1921 to Carl Paul Pflugradt, born March 11, 1900. Children:
    a. Evelyn Damaris Pflugradt, born September 19, 1922 at Richmond, Virginia. Married April 5, 1941 Joseph Bernard Collier, born September 16, 1921, died December 29, 1970 and had children:
        (1) Beverly Diane Collier, born October 20, 1944 at Richmond, Virginia. Married June 10, 1961 to Howard Sterling Mann, born March 25, 1942. Two children and divorced. Married second August 21, 1971 Eddie Steven Rusak, born August 7, 1924. Her two children were:
            (a) Deborah Leigh Mann, born July 28, 1962
            (b) Howard Sterling Mann: January 11, 1965
        (2) Janice Gayle Collier, born April 19, 1946. Married July 25, 1964 Wesley Earl Smith, born October 9, 1942. Two children and divorced February 16, 1968. Married second August 14, 1971 Kenneth Howell Boyle, born February 9, 1934. Children from the first marriage only:
            (a) Wesley Earl Smith, Jr.: July 30, 1965
            (b) Lisa Gayle Smith, born December 6, 1966
        (3) Jayne Blair Collier, born September 21, 1953, and married June 22, 1974 Terry Crew, born March 4, 1957.
    b. William John Roger Pflugradt, born August 7, 1924. Married August 21, 1948 Margaret Earle Johnston, born April 26, 1926. Live in Virginia; have children:
        (1) Bruce Alan Pflugradt: October 3, 1954

      (2)   Susan Elaine Pflugradt: July 18, 1965

    c.   Gretchen Anne Pflugradt, born August 6, 1926. Married April 10, 1944 Warren George Harding, born September 10, 1923. Live in Virginia and have children:

      (1)   Paul Jeffrey Harding, born March 30, 1946

      (2)   David Michael Harding: June 2, 1950

2.   Claude Randolph Day, born October 21, 1906 and died October 23, 1973; buried Forest Lawn cemetery at Richmond, Virginia. Married June 20, 1933 to Alberta Mae Mehl, born November 20, 1907. No children.

3.   Thelma Lester Day, born August 27, 1910, and married December 2, 1932 Raymond Charles Traylor, born November 9, 1902. Lived at Mechanicsville, Virginia, and had children:

    a.   Pauline Fay Traylor, born January 18, 1944. Married July 3, 1969 Richard Daniel Paine, born July 30, 1941. One son:

      (1)   Richard Daniel Paine, Jr.

    b.   Forrest Raymond Paul Traylor, born February 18, 1947. Married January 2, 1969 Marilyn Paige Wilkinson, born May 30, 1948. One son:

      (1)   Shawn Paul Traylor; September 10, 1969

4.   Clara Lavinia Day, born March 1, 1913. She was a registered nurse, and married March 27, 1936 to Julian Leigh Richardson; divorced 1938. Married second November 30, 1940 to Gene Richard Davies; one child and divorced. Clara was married third in 1954 to Herbert Loving; divorced 1956. Married fourth to Walter Lewicki, who died August 12, 1958. Married fifth November 5, 1960 to Claude Swenson Chandler and divorced April, 1964. Her child was:

    a.   Shirley Jean Davies, born July 21, 1943. Married June 29, 1962 Lloyd Michael Mounce, born October 13, 1942. Lived Oneonta, New York, with children:

      (1)   James Robert Mounce, born June 30, 1964

      (2)   Tammara Lynn Mounce; August 7, 1967

5. Robert Adrian Day, born November 4, 1915. Married February 5, 1938 Althah Ernestine Latham, born January 8, 1918. Children:

a. Barbara Loretta Day, born July 4, 1939. Married August 17, 1959 Patrick L. Wright, born March 13, 1940, and had children:

      (1)   Robert Ashby Wright: August 7, 1961

      (2)   David Patrick Wright: November 25, 1967

      (3)   Thomas Wright: September 25, 1968

b. Roberta Angela Day, born February 19, 1944. Married August 4, 1962 Shelton Lamar Brunson, born November 27, 1938. Children:

      (1)   Eugene Lamar Brunson, born June 27, 1965

      (2)   Angela Elizabeth Brunson December 26, 1969

6. Margaret Antonia Day, born June 21, 1918. Married November 22, 1938 Thomas Otway Snead, born December 18, 1917, died November, 1962; one child. She married second July 18, 1946 to John Wallace Pecawicz, born August 23, 1915; Major, USA retired. They had two children. The three children of Margaret were:

a. Judith Loraine Snead, born September 2, 1939 Richmond and married October 4, 1958 Alan G. Blewett, born February 2, 1931 at Minneapolis, Minnesota. Live in Florida, and have children:

      (1)   Carla Elaine Blewett, born January 3, 1960

      (2)   Ronald Rush Blewett, born October 21, 1961

b. Brenda Inez Pecawicz, born March 14, 1949, at Richmond.

c. Alan Eugene Pecawicz, born July 27, 1950 at Frankfurt, Germany.

7. Emil Rodney Day, born August 12, 1921. Married first to Lillian Penny and divorced. Married second Septem-

ber 16, 1946 to Opal, and divorced after two children. Remarried Lillian. His children were:
   a.   Susan Day, adopted.
   b.   Karen Day, born January 14, 1957
   c.   Scott Ronald Day, born August 14, 1958
8.   Leroy Edward Day, born January 1, 1927. Married May 18, 1947 Mary Elizabeth Hornbuckle, born September 3, 1925. Children:
   a.   David Franklin Day, born January 13, 1949, married to Ingrid Korth and lived in Hawaii
   b.   Jean Shirley Day, born August 3, 1951. Married July 27, 1974 to Allen Cary.
   c.   Michael Philip Day, born May 15, 1957

CHILD 3

Addison Singleton Day
1856-1929

This son of Rufus King Day (1827) and Ann Priscilla Brandenburg (1831) was born January 8, 1856, and died December 19, 1929. A farmer in Frederick County, Maryland, he married Laura Washington Beall, born in Montgomery County, January 9, 1859, died March 2, 1936. Buried at Bethesda Methodist Church at Browningsville. Four children:
1.   Harrison Edward Day, born January 6, 1888 in Frederick County, died 1920. Single.
2.   Daisy May Day, born November 18, 1891, died April 26, 1968. Married to her cousin, Murray Otis Day, born September 29, 1888 in Montgomery County, died April 26, 1968. Two children:
   a.   Laura Ann Day, born May 19, 1915. Married June 21, 1938 to Jesse Downey Day, Jr., born June 30, 1914 near Mt. Airy, Frederick County. He was a

farmer, raising beef cattle; she was an elementary teacher. Two sons:
- (1) David Ellis Day, born January 4, 1943
- (2) Douglas Edsel Day, born July 11, 1945

b. Ruth Edna Day, born November 20, 1918; married April 17, 1940 to Henry Cornelius Krantz, Jr., born September 15, 1917 in Frederick County. They had children:
- (1) Kenneth Edward Krantz: October 10, 1941
- (2) Beverly Kaye Krantz: January 8, 1947

3. Annie Griffith Day, born August 18, 1896, died February 8, 1905.

4. Rufus Addison Day, born February 21, 1901 in Frederick County, died June 19, 1932; buried at Providence Church in Kemptown. Married to Myrtle Day, born September 7, 1901, and had children:

a. Rufus Addison Day, Jr. Married Mary Jane Pryor; no children.

b. William Emory Day, married Helen Willier and had a son:
- (1) Howard Michael Day, born June 24, 1948 at Baltimore. Married April 4, 1966 to Cheryl Jeanne Harrison, born August 30, 1948. They live in Baltimore; two children, first born at Olney; second at Baltimore:
  - (a) Gregory Robert Day: November 27, 1966
  - (b) Joelle Denise Day: April 27, 1971

CHILD 5

Preston Clairsville Day
1859-1931

This son of Rufus King Day (1827) and Ann Priscilla Brandenburg (1831) was born October 21, 1859, and died

October 21, 1931. A pharmacist in Washington, D. C., he was married after June 14, 1887 to Roberta Grant Purdum, born September 17, 1865, died January 12, 1903, daughter of William Henry Harrison Purdum (1841) and Mary E. Lewis (1843). Buried at Bethesda Methodist Church at Kemptown. Three children:

1. Harold Lewis Day, born November 7, 1888, died September 13, 1968. A pharmacist who operated his father's store after his death, he was married November 28, 1914 to Julia Wrightman Denham, born September 3, 1885, died January 17, 1969. A daughter:
   a. Virginia Lee Day, born July 14, 1918. Married June 10, 1939 to Theodore W. Chase, Jr., born December 13, 1914. Divorced after children, and later married Will Browning Kern. Her children:
      (1) Theodore W. Chase, III, born May 8, 1940 at Schenectady, New York, and married Marilyn R. Moore, born at Baltimore.
      (2) Julia Ann Chase, born October 31, 1941 at Columbus, Georgia. Married to Richard M. King, born in Baltimore. Children:
         (a) Douglas M. King: September 10, 1963
         (b) Holly Ann King: December 28, 1965
      (3) Philip Scott Chase, born August 20, 1953
2. Wilfred Preston Day, born July 13, 1890, a pharmacist. He married Lucille Hill, born January 1, 1904 Marietta, Ohio. No children.
3. Ralph King Day, born September 6, 1897, died August 23, 1858. Buried at Rose Hill cemetery, Oklahoma City, Oklahoma. Married to Dell Pemberton Slaughter, born October 20, 1892 at Woods Hole, Massachusetts. They had no children.

CHILD 6

Harriet Emma Day
1863-1949

This daughter of Rufus King Day (1827) and Ann Priscilla Brandenburg (1831) was born c.1863 at Kemptown, and died October 29, 1949. Married February 16, 1887 to James Oliver Barnes, born April 2, 1860, died January 11, 1939. A farmer, buried at the Bethesda Methodist Church cemetery near Browningsville, Maryland. Two children:

1. Herbert Day Barnes, born March 6, 1891, died April 7, 1958. Married July 29, 1916 to Rosa May Lewis, born January 9, 1896; died September 21, 1968. Like many of the family members, she is buried at Bethesda Methodist Church cemetery, Browningsville, Maryland. Children:
   a. Dorothy Pauline Barnes, born December 4, 1917. Married June 19, 1935 to George Franklin Burdette, born September 2, 1912, died May 31, 1970, and buried at Damacus Methodist cemetery. Children:
      (1) James Larry Burdette, born April 2, 1936, died February 13, 1974
      (2) Dinah Elaine Burdette, born March 21, 1947 at Frederick. Married October 14, 1967 Larry Wayne Mullinix, born July 14, 1948. Live at Damascus and have a child:
         (a) Tammy Dawn Mullinix: July 28, 1974
   b. Anna Louise Barnes, born March 23, 1920, and married October 11, 1940 to Brandon Woodrow Duvall, born March 4, 1913 near Damascus. He was a Maryland State Policeman. Children, all born at Frederick:
      (1) Jerry Brandon Duvall, born March 19, 1943, and married January 9, 1971 to Karen Ann Rosapepe, born November 9, 1945 at Young-

stown, Ohio. He is professor of economics at Montgomery College.

(2) Jeannette Louise Duvall, born July 27, 1944, and married July 15, 1966 Meredith Hall MacKusick, III, born August 8, 1940 in Chicago. A daughter:

    (a) Elizabeth Ann MacKusick, born December 24, 1974 at Washington, D. C.

(3) Herbert Sherwood Duvall, born December 12, 1945. Married September 22, 1967 Sandra Lynn Eagle, born November 1, 1944 at Galesville, Illinois. Two children:

    (a) Christopher Brandon Duvall, born January 9, 1969

    (b) Alice Louise Duvall: October 14, 1971

c. Vivian Bernice Barnes, born July 23, 1923, and married December 10, 1941 to Charles Hanford Browning, born December 7, 1921. Children:

(1) Charles Hanford Browning, Jr., born July 13, 1943 and married June 20, 1964 to Patricia Lee Barnes, born October 14, 1945 at Frederick. President of Browning Construction Company; three children:

    (a) Charles Hanford Browning, III, born July 8, 1967

    (b) Duane Edward Browning, born November 23, 1968

    (c) Aaron Robert Browning, born May 27, 1974

(2) Nancy Rosalie Browning, born October 21, 1945. Married July 5, 1970 Ormus Durrett Bennett, born June 19, 1946 at Cumberland, Maryland. Children:

    (a) Belinda Berniece Bennett, born February 26, 1971

        (b) Clifton Wayne Bennett: July 31, 1972

d.   Mazie Emma Barnes, born November 8, 1926, and married July 12, 1947 to Albert Francis Rebert, born October 11, 1916 at Pottstown, Pennsylvania. They had children:

    (1)   Nelson Wayne Rebert, born July 2, 1952.

    (2)   Debra Louise Rebert, born March 22, 1954. Married July 14, 1974 to Robert Francis Davis, born August 17, 1954 at Olney, Maryland. Child:

        (a) Kathryn Debra Davis: January 29, 1975

    (3)   Dennis Alan Rebert: September 19, 1958

2.   Raymond Oliver Barnes, born June 11, 1893. Married to Lula Norene Day, born April 12, 1899, died October 1, 1966. They had children:

a.   Marion Evangeline Barnes, born May 5, 1917. Married June 15, 1938 to John William Lawson, born September 21, 1912, died November 3, 1969. They had three children, and she married second February 14, 1973 to Dwight Talmadge Walker, born 1903. Her children were:

    (1)   Sylvia Elaine Lawson, born August 5, 1939 and died June 10, 1943

    (2)   Dianne Cecil Lawson, born February 4, 1941

    (3)   John William Randolph Lawson, born May 19, 1950

b.   James Raymond Hamilton Barnes, born May 31, 1927. Married Mary McClairy, and had a child. He married second Pat Brashears. The child was:

    (1)   Jamie Luanne Barnes, married April 29, 1973 to Gordon Alan Chertoff.

c.   Eleanor Irene Virginia Barnes, born October 9, 1934. Married June 3, 1960 David J. Sessa, born March 3, 1938 at Hackensack, New Jersey, and had children:

(1)   Brian David Sessa, born April 5, 1963
(2)   Valerie Irene Sessa; August 20, 1964
(3)   Kenneth Gregory Sessa; August 4, 1969
(4)   Jennifer Danielle Sessa; April 11, 1972

CHILD 7

James Start Day
1865-1949

This son of Rufus King Day (1827) and Ann Priscilla Brandenburg (1831) was born c.1865 near Kemptown, Maryland, and died November 9, 1949. He was a farmer, and was married December 26, 1894 to Laura Helen Davis, born November 5, 1874, died February 14, 1942 and buried at Bethesda Methodist Church, at Browningsville. Twelve children, born near Browningsville:

1.   Rufus Wilson Day, born November 2, 1895, died December 30, 1918, single.
2.   Ethel Virginia Day, born August 2, 1897, died January 8, 1939. Married November, 1916 Samuel Wesley Walker, born December 10, 1892, died July 18, 1951. Buried at the Bethesda Methodist Church, Browningsville. Their descendants are discussed in her husband's section.
3.   James Sellman Day, born July 6, 1899, died June 21, 1924. Married November 19, 1919 to Jessie Marie Purdum, born July 12, 1900, daughter of Rufus Elsworth Purdum (1869) and Alice Sardinia Baker (1867). Jessie Marie and James Sellman Day had two children, born at Pleasant Grove. She was married second to R. Leslie Davis, born c.1891 and died 1948, son of R. Lee Davis and Cora Layton. They had one daughter. The children of James Sellman Day were:

a. Laura Helen Day, born October 3, 1920. Married February 15, 1939 to George Josiah Stup, born July 23, 1917 at Burtonsville, and had children:

(1) George Larry Stup, born November 13, 1939. Married June 29, 1969 Judy Ann MacIntyre, born July 31, 1946 at Baltimore. Two children, born at Frederick:
  (a) Lauren Davis Stup: August 9, 1973
  (b) Joel Lynn Stup, born March 18, 1975

(2) Linda Jeanne Stup, born October 29, 1940. Married June 26, 1965 to Robert Easterday Broadrup, born October 17, 1940 Frederick. He is a dentist; three children, born Frederick:
  (a) Elizabeth Easterday Broadrup, born March 20, 1968
  (b) Robert Livingston Broadrup, born June 27, 1970
  (c) Garrett Cade Broadrup: August 29, 1974

(3) Darryl Leslie Stup, born July 22, 1943, and married May 2, 1970 to Judy Mae Roberts, born April 13, 1947 at Frederick. No children

(4) Alison Elizabeth Stup, born March 15, 1949. A registered nurse, she married July 27, 1974 Gary Wayne Stitley, born May 30, 1944 at Catoctin Furnace, Maryland. No children.

(5) Stephen Jay Stup, born July 31, 1951. Married February 3, 1973 to Sharon Ann Musial, born September 27, 1952 at Bethesda. A child:
  (a) Corey Stephen Stup: May 24, 1973

b. Alice Marie Day, born August 11, 1922. Married February 12, 1950 Clifford Hefner, born June 12, 1922 Lewisburg, West Virginia; no children.

4. Clarence Emory Day, born January 25, 1901, and died September 23, 1901

5. Anna Lucille Day, born July 16, 1902, died 1979. Married December 27, 1924 to Rudell Leroy Brandenburg, born December 4, 1905 near Kemptown, died April 10, 1960. They had children:

a. Betty Elaine Brandenburg, born July 25, 1925 and married June 1, 1943 to Earl Edward Dixon, born May 11, 1920 Frederick. Church records at the Historical Society list her name as Betty Claire Brandenburg. Children, born Frederick County:

   (1) Bernard Leroy Dixon: February 11, 1945
   (2) Janice Elaine Dixon: October 3, 1946. Married March 2, 1963 to Dewey Douglas Tibbs, born August 22, 1943 in Virginia. Children, born in Frederick:
      (a) Jacqueline Elaine Tibbs: August 12, 1963
      (b) Dewey Douglas Tibbs, Jr.: April 9, 1965
      (c) Joanne Marie Tibbs: July 22, 1966
   (3) Linda Louise Dixon, born December 15, 1947 and married December 23, 1966 to Donald Wayne Linton born August 22, 1948 at Frederick. One child; divorced. She married second October 19, 1974 to Clarence John Shull, III, born January 31, 1947 at Frederick. Her child was:
      (a) Don Wayne Linton: December 29, 1966

b. Mary Helen Brandenburg, born August 5, 1926. Married August 30, 1947 Earle Lynwood Browning, born February 28, 1924. Children:

   (1) Marlene Carol Browning, born June 18, 1950 and died June 11, 1972
   (2) Lynette Adele Browning, born June 18, 1950, married December 20, 1972 Edward Leroy Sellers, born April 30, 1948 in Virginia. A daughter:
      (a) Cresent Carol Sellers: July 14, 1973

  (3) Gary Martin Browning; April 26, 1952.

c. Robert Leroy Brandenburg, born November 11, 1927; died November 17, 1927

d. Charlotte Virginia Brandenburg, born March 15, 1929. Married December 3, 1954 to Paul Burlin Rosencrantz, born at Stockdale, Pennsylvania, November 27, 1922. No children.

e. James Oscar Brandenburg, born January 17, 1933. Married June 28, 1956 to Mary Ann Walker, born February 6, 1936 at Mt. Airy. Children:
  (1) Barbara Lynn Brandenburg: April 23, 1958
  (2) Nancy Lee Brandenburg: December 24, 1962
  (3) James Michael Brandenburg: July 9, 1966
  (4) Randy Lee Brandenburg: November 25, 1969

f. Shirley Ann Brandenburg, born June 16, 1934, and married December 4, 1951 to Charles William Emswiler, born December 24, 1925 at Timberville, Virginia. Live at Kemptown and have children:
  (1) Larry Wayne Emswiler: January 30, 1953
  (2) Donald Lee Emswiler: January 30, 1954

g. Rosalie Brandenburg, born June 15, 1936. Married October 19, 1951 to Marvin W. Hubble, born June 1, 1932 at Nebo, Virginia. They live at Monrovia: children:
  (1) Robert Lee Hubble, born April 27, 1952
  (2) Kevin Richard Hubble: September 15, 1957
  (3) Keith Allen Hubble, born July 12, 1959
  (4) Brenda Lee Hubble; December 23, 1961

h. Franklin Rudell Brandenburg, born November 28, 1940. Married November 25, 1959 to Carolyn Maye White, born February 15, 1942 at Sandy Spring, Maryland. Lived at Kemptown; children:
  (1) Ricky Franklin Brandenburg, born November 12, 1960
  (2) Sherri Ann Brandenburg: September 21, 1963

        (3)   Jeffrey Keith Brandenburg: October 11, 1966

6. Murray Davis Day, born May 20, 1904. Married December 26, 1925 to Lois Elaine Burdette, born August 18, 1906. Children:

  a. James Murray Day, born November 3, 1926, and married July 23, 1947 Betty Marie Beall, born December 8, 1926 at Browningsville. Children:

     (1)   Brenda Jean Day, born August 20, 1948. Married September 13, 1969 Robert Osborne Drisch, born June 13, 1946 at Dickerson. Daughter:

        (a) Christy Lynn Drisch: January 23, 1973

     (2)   Gary Wayne Day, born October 22, 1952. Married July 6, 1974 Wanda Kaye Shiers, born November 10, 1956 at Olney.

     (3)   Joan Marie Day, born January 5, 1954. Married September 5, 1973 to Roy Stanley, born June 29, 1953 at Olney.

  b. Kenneth Lee Day, born May 26, 1930. Married March 31, 1950 to Rowena Jane Lee. Children:

     (1)   Kenneth Berkely Day, born December 6, 1964 at Bethesda, Maryland

     (2)   Sherri Lee Day, born March 5, 1968

  c. Carroll Davis Day, born July 31, 1944. Married January 9, 1965 to Jessie Darlene Kaufman, born October 22, 1946 Gaithersburg. Children, born Bethesda, Maryland:

     (1)   Carol Ann Day, born January 10, 1968

     (2)   Patricia Ann Day; September 13, 1971

7. Raymond Fout Day, born April 26, 1906. Married December 25, 1928 to Annie Sophronia McElfresh, born February 11, 1906 near Browningsville. Children:

  a. Dorothy Jean Day, born October 16, 1929, and married July 30, 1948 to Willis Webster Beall, born

September 7, 1927, son of Barry Beall and Edith Burdette. Live near Clarksburg and have children:

(1) Mark Willis Beall, born December 19, 1950, and married January 11, 1973 to Pamela Ann Mandy, born at Birmingham, Alabama.

(2) Melanie Ann Beall, born June 10, 1953. Married June 9, 1973 Jeffrey Thomas Valcourt, born October 5, 1953 at Coronado, California.

(3) Wendy Jeanine Beall, born March 17, 1959 at Olney, Maryland

b. Raymond Harold Day, born December 12, 1930. Married January 27, 1951 Shirley Ann Woodfield, born January 9, 1931 at Galesville, Maryland. Children, born at Annapolis:

(1) Judith Elaine Day, born March 13, 1953. Married June 10, 1972 David Lee Loftice, born April 8, 1952 in Virginia. Daughter:

(a) Amanda Leigh Loftice: June 20, 1974

(2) Cheryl Ann Day; December 14, 1954

(3) Cindy Lou Day, born May 18, 1957

c. Barbara Ann Day, born July 30, 1938. Married December 20, 1958 Ralph Eugene Kemp, born October 17, 1938 in Frederick County. Children, born there:

(1) Michael Allen Kemp, born July 20, 1959

(2) Julie Renee Kemp; December 11, 1960

(3) Janiele Anita Kemp; December 24, 1962

8. Kelsel Williams Day, born October 2, 1907. His birth has also been reported as May 20, 1904. Married December 21, 1929 to Mildred Jane Burdette, born June 12, 1910 near Damascus, daughter of Claude H. Brudette (1872) and Sarah Rebecca Boyer (1874). Six children:

a. Kelsel Williams Day, Jr., born March 15, 1931. Married August 24, 1951 Elizabeth Ann Lockard, born December 22, 1931 at Eldersburg. Children:

      (1)   Gayle Marie Day, born August 27, 1953 at Anchorage, Alaska. Married June 25, 1971 Larry Hood.

      (2)   Kevin Scott Day, born August 22, 1955

  b.   Evelyn Jane Day, born March 26, 1933 and died March 11, 1934

  c.   Maxwell Latimer Day, born March 4, 1935, and married to Shirley Ann Crum, born June 23, 1935 at Frederick. Children, born at Olney, Maryland:

      (1)   Alan Christopher Day; August 14, 1962

      (2)   Brian Keith Day; December 13, 1968

  d.   Basil Boyer Day, born July 15, 1936. Married June 9, 1957 to Sally Jo Eisenbeis, born October 10, 1937 at Williamsport, Pennsylvania. Her name has also been reported as Eisenberg. Children:

      (1)   Basil Boyer Day, Jr., born January 14, 1958 at Olney, Maryland

      (2)   Polly Jo Day, born November 16, 1964 at Frederick, Maryland

  e.   Janet Louise Day, born November 23, 1937, and married December 14, 1957 to Austin Delmar Rippeon, born December 11, 1932 at Frederick. Children, born at Frederick:

      (1)   Austin Delmar Rippeon, Jr.: August 11, 1958

      (2)   Wesley Pierre DeVoe Rippeon: June 25, 1960

      (3)   Hope Dayon Rippeon: November 23, 1974

  f.   John Marvin Day, born May 5, 1951. Married October 6, 1973 to Amanda Lou Helwig, born October 10, 1951 at Hanover, Pennsylvania.

9.   Helen Mildred Day, born June 8, 1909. Married October 20, 1927 in Frederick to Carl Oscar Mullican, born June 22, 1906 near Lewisdale, Maryland, died 1978; son of Oscar Thomas Mullican (1886). Children:

  a.   Oscar Ray Mullican, born September 13, 1928 in Lewisdale, Montgomery County, Maryland, and

married September 11, 1954 in Frederick to Olive Elizabeth Rice, born June 12, 1937. Children, born at Lewisdale, in Montgomery County:
(1) Danny Lee Mullican, born May 26, 1959
(2) David Scot Mullican, born April 26, 1960
(3) Dennis Ray Mullican; March 10, 1965

b. Robert Day Mullican, born August 6, 1932 at Lewisdale; married March 22, 1952 Delores Ann Burdette, born August 17, 1934; twins, born at Olney, Montgomery County:
(1) Deborah Lynn Mullican, born 1952; married to S. Darron Long, son of Irvin Long and Betty Burdette.
(2) Marcia Ann Mullican, born 1952; married May 19, 1972 in Damascus to James Stephen Robertson, son of Robert L. Robertson.

c. Carroll Lee Mullican, born May 21, 1943 in Lewisdale and died that same day

10. Effie Madeline Day, born January 14, 1912. Married December 25, 1929 Raymond Merson Moxley, born March 6, 1909 near Kemptown. They had children:
a. Gloria Alvin Moxley, born December 20, 1930; married September 2, 1948 Merhle Basil Warfield, born February 26, 1927 at Etchison. Children:
(1) Merhle Wayne Warfield, born December 15, 1950. Married June 19, 1971 to Sharon Lee Smith, born May 8, 1951 at Damascus. They had children:
(a) Jason Edward Warfield; April 8, 1979
(b) Kristin Leeann Warfield; July 26, 1984
(2) Raymond Curtis Warfield: January 20, 1952
b. Leonard Wayne Moxley, born December 28, 1941. Married September 10, 1960 Alfrieda Mae Duvall, born June 23, 1940. Children:
(1) Kevin Harold Moxley: November 5, 1961

        (2)   Kristen Leon Moxley: July 28, 1964

        (3)   Kelly Wayne Moxley: July 8, 1969

   c.   Donna Jeanne Moxley, born April 13, 1948, and married December 20, 1969 Arthur Howard Isaacs born April 6, 1948 at Thurmont. Children:

        (1)   Aaron Jeffrey Isaacs, born June 6, 1972 at Hialeah, Florida

        (2)   Chad Jeremy Isaacs, born December 31, 1974 near Damascus, Maryland

11. Richard Marvin Day, born May 24, 1913. Married December 24, 1942 to Lillian Blanche Brown, born April 10, 1918 at Purdum, the daughter of Richard Jefferson Brown (1867). No children.

12. Hanford Perry Day, born January 28, 1916. Married December 24, 1938 to Marie Allen Chick, born September 18, 1921 near Clarksburg. Children:

   a.   Robert Perry Day, born July 26, 1940. Married July 12, 1959 Rosia Mary Green, born October 11, 1942 near Mt. Airy. Children:

        (1)   Terry Ann Day, born March 7, 1960

        (2)   Douglas Robert Day; October 23, 1961

        (3)   Michael Allen Day, born July 10, 1964

   b.   Evelyn Louise Day, born April 7, 1943. Married May 9, 1962 Wayne Sellman Watkins, born May 15, 1938 near Lewisdale. Children:

        (1)   Catherine Marie Watkins; June 15, 1963

        (2)   Patricia Lynn Watkins; August 12, 1967

   c.   Doris Jane Day, born March 16, 1946. Married January 19, 1967 to Alexander Paul Watkins, born January 26, 1938 at Mineola, New York. They had no children.

CHILD 8

Laura Arvilla Day
1867-1943

This daughter of Rufus King Day (1827) and Ann Priscilla Brandenburg (1831), was born July 11, 1867 at Browningsville, and died January 23, 1943. Married on December 24, 1890 to William Alfred Baker Walker, born November 1, 1867 and died August 8, 1947. He was the son of George Washington Wesley Walker and Rachel Browning Purdum Walker. In 1907, William and Laura, said to be of Frederick County, Maryland, executed a mortgage, recorded in Liber 195 at folio 356 in the Land Records of Montgomery County, Maryland. She died January 27, 1943, and in her will is said to be of Frederick County, although the will was probated in Montgomery. She names her husband, and their two sons, who were Executors. An inventory of the real property is included in the probate, and included one third interest in a farm of 154 acres, 2 roods and 20 perhces in Frederick County; and two parcels located partly in Frederick, Montgomery and Howard Counties, one containing 25 acres and the other, 10 acres. They had twelve children, all born at Ridgeville, Maryland:

1. Blanche Willard Walker, born January 19, 1892; died August 8, 1926. Married November 21, 1924 Ernest Ehrenberg, born August 15, 1891 at Ludington, Michigan; died September 13, 1966. No children.
2. Esther May Walker, born March 28, 1893; married May 28, 1921 to William A. Taylor, born at Inwood, Long Island, New York. Children, born at Mt. Airy, Maryland:
    a. Theodore Paul Ernest Taylor, born September 3, 1930; married to Marian Davis Faunce.
    b. Jessie Laura Taylor, born November 24, 1932; married on September 5, 1953 to William Maxwell Tees

Hanklin, a clergyman, born September 30, 1929 at Upland, Pennsylvania, and had children:

(1) Judith Ann Hanklin, born August 22, 1954; married January 27, 1973 Mark A. Light, born at Lebanon, Pennsylvania. One son:

(a) Andrew Mark, born December 11, 1973.

(2) William Maxwell Tees Hanklin, II, born July 15, 1956

3. Daughter Walker, born January 8, 1895; died July 3, 1895

4. Bessie Pauline Walker, born August 4, 1897; died March 7, 1916

5. William Paul Walker, born August 7, 1898 at Ridgeville, Maryland. He was an educator and a scientist; and a professor at the University of Maryland. Married May 6, 1938 to Frances Myers, born at New Windsor July 17, 1907, and died July 14, 1973. At least one child:

a. William F. Walker, born December 23, 1942 at Takoma Park, Maryland.

6. Wesley Day Walker, born September 29, 1900, and died May 29, 1901.

7. Rufus Wesley Walker, born April 2, 1902; died February 5, 1903.

8. Dwight Talmadge Walker, born August 23, 1903 at Ridgeville, Maryland, and married August 23, 1925 to Ruth Davis, born February 22, 1904 at Linwood, Carroll County, Maryland; died January 22, 1972. They had five children, and he was married second February 14, 1973 to Marion Evangeline Barnes. The children were:

a. Dwight Talmadge Walker, Jr., born April 8, 1929

b. June Wanita Walker, born March 23, 1932; married June 10, 1955 to Charles Franklin Beck, II, born March 14, 1929 at Mt. Airy, Maryland, and had children:

(1) Charles Franklin Beck, III; October 1, 1964

(2)   Beth Luella Beck, born March 26, 1969
c.   Wava Jane Walker, born September 13, 1934; married December 23, 1952 to George Evert Emswiler, born December 13, 1931 at Timberville, Virginia, and had children:
(1)   David Leroy Emswiler, born August 9, 1953
(2)   Rodney Gordon Emswiler; December 2, 1954
(3)   Wanda Sue Emswiler; November 17, 1956
(4)   Kirk Walker Emswiler, born August 7, 1959
d.   Mary Ann Walker, born February 6, 1936 at Mt. Airy, Maryland. Married June 28, 1956 to James Oscar Brandenburg, born January 17, 1933. They had four children:
(1)   Barbara Lynn Brandenburg; April 23, 1958
(2)   Nancy Lee Brandenburg; December 24, 1962
(3)   James Michael Brandenburg; July 9, 1966
(4)   Randy Lee Brandenburg; November 25, 1969
e.   William Richard Walker, born June 28, 1940. Married August 1, 1969 to Christa Sikken, born September 29, 1946 at Norden, West Germany.
9.   Ernest Artman Walker, born August 29, 1904 at Ridgeville, Maryland; married August 28, 1929 to Irene Elizabeth Baker, born December 17, 1905 at Niagara Falls, New York, and had one child:
a.   Elizabeth Ann Walker, born April 21, 1944 Washington, D. C . Married June 14, 1989 John Arthur Gill, born May 4, 1925 Dubuque, Iowa. One son:
(1)   David Ernest Gill, born December 17, 1970 at Madison, Wisconsin.
10.   Wilfred Taft Walker, a twin, born May 21, 1908; died August 2, 1908.
11.   Wilbur Bryan Walker, a twin, born May 21, 1908; died August 5, 1908.
12.   Willing Wendell Walker, born July 9, 1910; married August 6, 1964 to Mary Vandevort Nicklas, born Novem-

ber 20, 1910 at Pittsburg, Pennsylvania; died April 13, 1977. Buried at the Bethesda United Methodist Church cemetery near the village of Browningsville, with numerous other family members. No children.

CHILD 9

Langdon Storrs Day
1871-1954

This son of Rufus King Day (1827) and Ann Priscilla Brandenburg (1831) was born c.1871, and died July 2, 1954. He was a pharmacist in the city of Washington, and was married November, 1896 to Maude Ozella Day, born February 16, 1871 at Browningsville, died February 4, 1924. They had three infant deaths, and one surviving child. He was married second September 2, 1924 to Sadie Elizabeth Gue, born February 18, 1901 at Laytonsville, and had a son. His two children were:

1. Ivah May Day, born September 3, 1901. Married June 14, 1923 Trago Winter Lloyd, born December 30, 1893 at Inwood, West Virginia. He was a Methodist minister, and they had children:
    a. Carroll Langdon Lloyd, born January 19, 1925 at Martinsburg, West Virginia. Married October 31, 1952 Phyllis Barnes, born September 5, 1928 at Lisbon, Maryland. No children.
    b. Jeanne Winifred Lloyd, born July 1, 1930 at Frederick, Maryland. Married August 22, 1953 to Harry Nevin Keller, born May 13, 1925 at Millheim, Pennsylvania. Children, born in New Jersey:
        (1) Anne Margaret Keller: February 24, 1957
        (2) Paul Nevin Keller, born March 5, 1959
        (3) Joyce Helen Keller, born July 11, 1961

2. Quentin Langdon Day, born October 17, 1926. Married July 30, 1961 to Ruth Virginia Woodfield, born July 26, 1942 near Claggettsville. Children, the first and third born at Frederick; the second at Sandy Spring, Maryland:
   a. Larry Langdon Day, born December 5, 1962
   b. Joseph Loren Day, born February 3, 1965
   c. Lisa Carol Day, born July 20, 1967

CHAPTER 9

Brandenburgs of Baltimore County, Maryland

Baltimore County is close enough to Frederick, Carroll, Montgomery and Howard, that some of the family members found their way to that county as well. Those that have not been identified within the framework of chapters 1 thru 8 will be presented here for further reference.

Lawrence Brandenburg
1892-

Lawrence is found as head of household in the 1920 census for Baltimore County, born c.1892. His wife is listed as Mary E., born c.1897, and there are three children:
1. Lawrence Brandenburg, born c.1915
2. Edward F. Brandenburg, born c.1916
3. Robert J. Brandenburg, born c.1918

Levi Brandenburg
1863-

Levi is head of household in the 1900 census for Baltimore County, born c.1863. His wife, Agnes, was born c.1868, and there were three children listed. They appear again in the 1920 census for the county with the youngest child found in 1900, and one additional. They had at least four children, and perhaps more:
1. Bessie Brandenburg, born c.1889
2. Raymond Brandenburg, born c.1895. In the 1920 census there is a Raymond L. Brandenburg, born c.1895, perhaps this one. His wife was Mary G., born c.1897 in West Virginia. There were two children:

a.   John R. Brandenburg, born c.1917

b.   Pearl A. Brandenburg, born c.1919

3.   Gertrude Brandenburg, born c.1899

4.   Leroy Brandenburg, born c.1903

Arthur A. Brandenburg
1886-

Listed as head of household in the 1920 census for Baltimore County, Maryland, Arthur was born c.1886. His wife was Nancy J., born c.1890 in Virginia, and there were two children listed:

1.   Hazel Brandenburg, born c.1911

2.   Arthur Brandenburg, born c.1919

John Brandenburg
1885-

John is listed in the 1920 census for Baltimore County, born c.1885. His wife is Bertie, born c.1884 in Pennsylvania and there are three children:

1.   Everett Brandenburg, born c.1907

2.   Lillian Brandenburg, born c.1909

3.   Helen Brandenburg, born c.1918

James W. Brandenburg
1887-

Found in the 1920 census for Baltimore County, John was born c.1887. His wife was Edna M., born c.1890, and they had one child listed with them:

1.   Murrill P. Brandenburg, born c.1915

J. B. Brandenburg
1875-

This individual is listed only by his initials in the 1920 census for Baltimore County, born c.1875. His wife is Ida M., born c.1878, and there were two children:
1.   Clifford B. Brandenburg, born c.1905
2.   Calvin G. Brandenburg, born c.1902

CHAPTER 10

Brandenburgs of Carroll County, Maryland

As mentioned in earlier chapters, family members have been located primarily in Frederick County, Maryland, with a major movement into Montgomery County. However, several members of the family have been identified in neighboring Howard and Carroll Counties, where they adjoin Frederick and Montgomery. Many of them have been identified in the main chapters of the text, a few have not. They will be presented here for further reference.

Joseph J. Brandenburg
1845-

This individual is found as head of household in the 1880 and 1900 census for Carroll County, Maryland, born c.1845. In both cases, he is listed solely by his initials, J. J., but in the birth report of one of his daughters, Joseph J. appears. His wife was Mary Jane, born c.1846. The children, based on the census records, included:

1. Lula M. Brandenburg, born c.1872
2. Franklin J. Brandenburg, born c.1875. This is perhaps the same individual found in the 1920 census of the county, listed there as Frank J., with the proper age. He has a wife, Effie C., born c.1887, and four children:
   a. A daughter, which appears to be Thelma, born c.1909, although the microfilm was difficult to read.
   b. Frank J. Brandenburg, born c.1911
   c. Robert J. Brandenburg, born c.1912
   d. Lillian E. Brandenburg, born c.1916
3. William M. Brandenburg, born c.1877

4. Jesse R. Brandenburg, born c.1879. In the 1900 census for the county, this child is listed as Robert J.
5. Mary M. C. Brandenburg, born c.1884
6. Florence Brandenburg, born May 25, 1886.

Joshua P. Brandenburg
1843-

This individual appears as head of household in the 1880 census for Carroll County, Maryland, listed only as J. P., born c.1843. His wife is Lydia J., born c.1850, and they have four children listed. They appear again in the 1900 census with his full first name, a middle initial for his wife, and six children, including two of those listed in 1880. The children were:
1. William L. Brandenburg, born c.1872
2. Joshua B. Brandenburg, born c.1874
3. Etta M. Brandenburg, born c.1877
4. Ernest R. Brandenburg, born c.1879
5. Arminta A. Brandenburg, born c.1881
6. Eva Brandenburg, born c.1884
7. Leah L. Brandenburg, born c.1887
8. Daniel Brandenburg, born c.1890

Elias Brandenburg
1837-1892

This individual and his family were found in *Ancestral Colonial Families, Genealogy of The Welsh and Hyatt Families of Maryland and Their Kin*, by Luther W. Welsh, 1982, Independence, Missouri. Elias was born April 16, 1837 and died April 8, 1892, apparently in Maryland. Married to Martha Welsh, born March 4, 1837, died October 3, 1916, daughter of Philip Welsh and Roxana Wilson. The family appears in the census of 1880 for Carroll County, Maryland, although there Elias is said to have been born c.1830. In the

1900 census for Carroll County, Martha is listed at the age of sixty-four, apparently a widow. With her is her son, Joseph, listed following. The children included:

1. Levi H. Brandenburg, born c.1859
2. Ellea M. Brandenburg, born c.1861
3. James E. Brandenburg, born c.1864. This is probably the same James E. found in the 1920 census of Carroll County, there listed as being born c.1866. His wife is Susan A., born c.1874, and there are four children in the household:
   a. James R. Brandenburg, born c.1900
   b. Maisie A. Brandenburg, born c.1904
   c. Alice A. Brandenburg, born c.1907
   d. Edith E. Brandenburg, born c.1910
4. Lemuel F. Brandenburg, born June 23, 1871, died January 31, 1925. Married Margaret Conoway, born c.1876. They appear in the 1900 census for Baltimore County, with two children. Also in the household is Lemuel's brother, John Thomas. The family is also found in the 1920 census of the county, with more of the children, who included at least:
   a. Carl S. Brandenburg, born c.1898 who died young.
   b. Nelson E. Brandenburg, born c.1899
   c. Cora P. Brandenburg, born c.1901. Married Carroll Crawford, and had a daughter:
      (1) Margaret Crawford.
   d. Walter V. Brandenburg, born c.1910
   e. Lysle Brandenburg, born c.1913
5. Martha Elizabeth Brandenburg, born October 11, 1872. Married Charles Grimes and had four children:
   a. Albert Grimes, married Edith Harris. Two children:
      (1) Donald Grimes.
      (2) Ray Grimes.
   b. Marvin Grimes.
   c. May Grimes.

    d.   Pearl Grimes, married Tyson Gosnell.
6.   Joseph Hayes Brandenburg, born April 11, 1876. Married Cora Conoway; no children. They appear together in the 1920 census for Carroll County.
7.   John Thomas Brandenburg, born December 31, 1878. Married Mary Ritter; no children.

Jesse W. Brandenburg
1838-1879

His parentage is not known, but Jesse was born December 19, 1838 and died January 9, 1879. He was married to Mary Catherine Prugh, born December 27, 1848 and died November 2, 1916, daughter of David Prugh and Caroline Beasman. They are buried at Eldersburg Methodist Church, in Carroll County, Maryland. At least two children:
1.   O. Shriver Brandenburg.
2.   W. Clinton Brandenburg.

Elizabeth Brandenburg
1833-1908

Her parents are not identified in Mormon Church files, but Elizabeth was born January 14, 1833 in Howard County, Maryland, and died April 19, 1908 in Carroll County. She was married September 1, 1855 in Howard County to William Sellman, born August 12, 1832 in Anne Arundel County, and died July 29, 1899 near Berrett, Carroll County, Maryland. He was the son of Walter Sellman and Elizabeth Shipley. Children, born in Maryland:
1.   William Chapman Sellman, born 1856. Married March 21, 1881 to Emma C. Dorsey.
2.   Matilda B. Sellman, born 1857. Married to Henry Cook.
3.   Rachel Sellman, born 1859. Married to Benjamin Brown.

4. Walter Sellman, born December 22, 1860, died April 4, 1917. Married to Helen LeGourd.
5. Joseph Sellman, born January 9, 1863, died November 7, 1892.
6. Ninasau Sellman, born January 28, 1866, died March 18, 1904. Married February 27, 1884 to Burgess Hughes.
7. Joshua Sellman, born 1868.
8. Lawman Sellman, born May 7, 1869, died January 15, 1920 at Ontario, California. Married at San Bernadino, California, May 4, 1912 to Minerva Anna Spelts.
9. Frank C. Sellman, born September 17, 1872 and died September 18, 1885.
10. Marshall H. Sellman, born 1873; married Anna.
11. May Sellman, born 1875; married Houser.

Jacob Brandenburg
1832-

Jacob appears as head of household in the 1880 census of Carroll County, Maryland, born c.1832. His wife is listed as Martha L., born c.1838, and they have eight children. In the 1900 census for the county, they again appear, this time with four children, two of them having been born since the earlier census return. The children included:
1. Dorsey W. Brandenburg, born c.1859. He appears as the head of household in the 1900 census for Carroll County with his wife, Virginia T., born c.1869, and five children. She appears in the 1920 census for the county, perhaps widowed, with two of her children. They included:
   a. J. Andrew Brandenburg, born c.1889. This is perhaps the same individual who is listed in the 1920 census for Carroll County as Andrew J. Brandenburg, born c.1890, with wife, Lula G., born c.1894, and one small daughter:
      (1) Lula G. Brandenburg, born c.1917

   b.   E. Mary Brandenburg, born c.1892

   c.   Elsie U. Brandenburg, born c.1895

   d.   William Brandenburg, born c.1897

   e.   Dorsey Brandenburg, born c.1900

2.   Jesse T. Brandenburg, born c.1861

3.   Rachel E. Brandenburg, born c.1864

4.   Mary M. Brandenburg, born c.1867

5.   Anna M. Brandenburg, born c.1869

6.   Jacob E. Brandenburg, born c.1873

7.   Elizabeth Brandenburg, born c.1875

8.   George E. Brandenburg, born c.1877. George appears in the 1920 census of the Carroll County, with his sister Anna (above).

9.   Berniece E. Brandenburg, born c.1881

10. John M. Brandenburg, born c.1885

Margaret Brandenburg
1849-

Margaret appears in the household of Ralph David at the age of just thirty-one (born c.1849) in the 1880 census of Carroll County and was perhaps a widow, with three young children. We do not know her maiden name nor that of her husband, although Ralph David may have been her father. The children were:

1.   David S. Brandenburg, born c.1872

2.   Willie B. Brandenburg, born c.1874

3.   Jesse D. Brandenburg, born c.1878

CHAPTER 11

Brandenburgs of Frederick County, Maryland

As mentioned early in the study, the principal families were found in Frederick County, Maryland, with some of their descendants moving into the neighboring counties of Montgomery, Carroll, Howard and Baltimore. We had also found a number of references to Brandenburg families still in Frederick County, who have not been placed within the basic farmework of the larger groups under discussion.

Robert Franklin Brandenburg

At this point, we know of Robert Franklin only through the will of his wife. She was Nellie Rhoda, who wrote her will May 21, 1966 and recorded it in liber TME6 at folio 261 in Frederick County, although the will has not been probated as of 1997. She names her husband there, and three children:
1. Maxine V. Brandenburg, married Youkins.
2. Wayne L. Brandenburg.
3. Gloria Lee Brandenburg, married to Rhea.

Peter Brandenburg
1812-1877

Peter's parents have not yet been identified, but he was born c.1812 in Frederick County, Maryland, and died May 28, 1877 at the age of sixty-five years, four months and fourteen days. Buried Burkettsville Union cemetery. He was married in the county, January 23, 1836 to Hannah M. Gaver, born c.1817, died June 19, 1877 at the age of sixty years, six months and six days. Buried with her husband. The will of Peter, dated May 28, 1877, was probated in the county June

19, 1877 and filed in liber JRR1 at folio 179. He leaves his entire estate to his wife, Hannah, and named his son as the Executor. The son was:

1. Amos W. Brandenburg. Probably the same Amos W. who was born March 12, 1845 and died January 22, 1898. Buried at Burkettsville, Frederick County, Maryland. His wife was Alice Salome, born December 24, 1845 and died June 27, 1921, also buried there. They appear in the census of 1880 for the county with three children. She appears as a widow in the 1920 census, with two of her daughters. The children were:

    a. Charles P. Brandenburg, born c.1874. This may be the same Charles Brandenburg who is found in the 1920 census for Howard County, born c.1873. He there has a wife, Mary, born c.1871, and they have five children:

        (1) Mildred Brandenburg, born c.1901
        (2) Amos Brandenburg, born c.1902, and perhaps named for his grandfather.
        (3) Marjorie Brandenburg, born c.1904
        (4) Donald Brandenburg, born c.1907
        (5) Charles P. Brandenburg, Jr., born c.1912. The census specifies Jr., but lists the first name only as Charles.

    b. Harry L. Brandenburg, born c.1876
    c. Hannah B. Brandenburg, born c.1879
    d. Margaret E. Brandenburg, born c.1884

John David Brandenburg
1827-1900

We do not yet know the parents of John David, but he was born c.1827 in Frederick County, Maryland, and died December 26, 1900. Married August 19, 1862 to Amanda Toms, born 1848 and died February 15, 1920. They appear in the 1880 census for Frederick County, with four of their children, and in the 1900 census of the county, with more of their family. The children included, at least:

1. William Hanson Brandenburg, born c.1863, of whom more following.
2. Albert Brandenburg, born c.1866
3. Mary E. Brandenburg, born c.1870
4. John Wesley Brandenburg, born c.1872, died 1939. Married August 25, 1896 to Ada Alice Harshman, born 1875, died 1936, daughter of Cornelius Harshman and Claretta Virginia Hoover (1853). Buried Wolfsville Lutheran Church. They were living in the household of his father and mother during the census of 1900, with three children. They are found also in the 1920 census, with four children. At that time, his mother, Amanda, is also living with them, at the age of seventy-two. They were the parents of, at least:
   a. Henning R. Brandenburg, born c.1897
   b. Annie P. Brandenburg, born c.1900, died August 15, 1902. Buried at Ellerton Church of the Brethren.
   c. Archie Merhle Brandenburg, born c.1902, of whom more following
   d. Maude Brandenburg, born c.1906
   e. Etta Brandenburg, born c.1908
   f. Ray Brandenburg, born c.1911
   g. Amanda Brandenburg, born January 13, 1911, and married to Arthur Franklin Kline, born 1910, died 1962.
5. Charles F. Brandenburg, born c.1885

Archie Merhle Brandenburg
1902- 1987

This son of John Wesley Brandenburg (1872) is found mentioned in the obituary of his wife. He was born August 14, 1902 and died September 7, 1987. Married December 4,

1929 to Louisa Catherine Bussard, born August 11, 1906, died June 20, 1995. She was a daughter of Charles Franklin Bussard and Mary Ellen Cartee. The children were:

1. Charles Brandenburg, married Mary Margaret.
2. Lorraine Mae Brandenburg, born June 7, 1935. Married March 6, 1954 to Jay Benjamine Strite. Children:
   a. Beverly Marie Strite, born November 5, 1956
   b. Jay Benjamin Strite, Jr., born September 21, 1958
   c. Thomas Alan Strite, born January 24, 1962
3. Richard Lee Brandenburg, born June 18, 1938. Married June 18, 1959 to Evelyn Elaine Ahalt, born August 8, 1941, daughter of Charles Clifford Ahalt and Evelyn Glendora Routzahn (1916). Children:
   a. Joyce Elaine Brandenburg, born April 24, 1960
   b. Brenda Lee Brandenburg, born September 4, 1962

William Hanson Brandenburg
1863-1953

This individual was a son of John David Brandenburg (1827). Based on the obituary of one of his sons (Arthur W.) we can identify at least part of this family. According to cemetery records, William was born September 27, 1863, died December 14, 1953. Mormon Church records state that his mother was Amanda Toms (1848), but do not list his father. Buried at Wolfsville Lutheran Church with his wife. William was married to Rohann Pryor, born July 27, 1867, died October 20, 1944, daughter of Samuel Pryor and Louise Kline. They appear in the 1900 census of Washington County, Maryland, with five of their children. In the 1920 census, they are found in Frederick County, with three children, only one of whom was listed in 1900. Eight children, one of whom was an infant death, all born at Wolfsville:

1. Oscar Albert Brandenburg, born June 21, 1889, died November 13, 1975 at Hagerstown. Married June 3,

1916 at Keedysville, Maryland, to Sarah Ellen DeLawter, born September 22, 1892, daughter of George Noah DeLawter (1852) and Margaret V. Shuff (1863). The couple appears in the 1920 census for Frederick County, with their first-born son. Six children:

a. Hoye Elwood Brandenburg, born March 16, 1917. Married 1939 to Mary Elizabeth Fair, born December 21, 1919. Married second October 19, 1966 to Oneita Grace Wolf, born December 11, 1919. He had children:

(1) Anita Kay Brandenburg, born May 8, 1943. Married August 29, 1961 Richard Lee Harshman, born March 5, 1941 and had children:

(a) Sue Ellen Harshman, born April 11, 1962

(b) Richard Lee Harshman, II, born January 7, 1965.

(c) Anne Marie Harshman, born September 3, 1966.

(2) Sue Fair Brandenburg, born August 1, 1945. Married October 26, 1963 Howard Gaspin.

b. Eleanor Virginia Brandenburg, born September 13, 1920. Married April 26, 1940 to Reverend Charles Basil Grossnickle. Children:

(1) Dale Eugene Grossnickle, born August, 1971

(2) Carol Ann Grossnickle, born April 24, 1944. Married June 16, 1962 to Merhl Glenn Harne and had three children:

(a) Danny Lee Harne: December 12, 1962

(b) Brenda Lynn Harne: October 24, 1964

(c) Jeffrey Glenn Harne: October 17, 1966

c. Isabel Brandenburg, born September 11, 1922, and married January 31, 1946 to Charles Ralph Yingling, born February 13, 1915. Children:

(1) Kathy Lynn Yingling: June 23, 1956

(2) Karen Lea Yingling: August 25, 1961

d. Joyce Ellen Brandenburg, born November 19, 1923. Married August 28, 1946 to James K. Davis, and had children:
   (1) Jama Cheri Davis, born November 19, 1954
   (2) James Kent Davis, born June 6, 1955
e. George Nevin Brandenburg, born August 11, 1925. Married three times: Deloris Weddle, divorced; Pauline Monahan, died April 3, 1962; and Paige Dorsey. Two children:
   (1) JoAnne Brandenburg.
   (2) David Brandenburg.
f. Sarah Jane Brandenburg, born February 6, 1937. Married August 11, 1957 to Carroll Zimmerman and had children:
   (1) Anita Kay Zimmerman: February 23, 1960
   (2) Dean Ashley Zimmerman: October 4, 1961

2. Flora Edith Brandenburg, born April 16, 1890 in Frederick County, Maryland, died there March 20, 1959. Married there September 4, 1917 to Ralph Emerson Morgan, born March 12, 1889 in Frederick County and died there June 12, 1966, son of Irving Recher Morgan and Ida Mary Ellen Smith. At least these children:

a. Ralph William Morgan, born May 22, 1918. Married August 16, 1938 to Charlotte Mae Baer, born October 25, 1921, and had children:
   (1) Joyce Jean Morgan, born April 9, 1940. Married December 26, 1960 Gail Thomas Guyton, born March 2, 1940, and had children:
      (a) Bradley Charles Guyton, born February 14, 1962
      (b) Sharon Lea Guyton, born April 29, 1964
      (c) Darrell Thomas Guyton: June 30, 1965
   (2) Gloria Ann Morgan, born October 26, 1943. Married July 24, 1964 Bryan Joseph Moore, born February 13, 1941, and had children:

(a) Bryan Joseph Moore, II: March 5, 1970
b. Paul Irving Morgan, born December 5, 1921. Married August 7, 1943 to Vera Naomi Kline, born August 9, 1924. A son:
   (1) Dwight Irving Morgan, born January 28, 1945 and married May 9, 1966 to Ann Routzahn, born May 7, 1946. Children:
      (a) Ann Morgan: August 11, 1967
      (b) Kimberly Sue Morgan: June 28, 1970
   (2) Judy Floretta Morgan, born November 11, 1949. Married March 23, 1969 to Harold Francis Routzahn, born June 2, 1949, son of Paul Austin Routzahn (1914) and Marianna Jane Brandenburg (1916), and had children:
      (a) Chad Paul Routzahn: February 2, 1972
      (b) Wesley Davis Routzahn: April 9, 1978
      (c) Shannon Morgan Routzahn born May 20, 1982
   (3) Cindy Lou Morgan, born August 1, 1956
c. Ruth Rohann Morgan, born May 11, 1924. Married April 24, 1943 to Grayson Josephus Michael, born July 6, 1921.
3. Amanda Louise Brandenburg, born March 8, 1892, died September 4, 1963. Married January 21, 1914 Raymond Leslie Smith, born April 11, 1885, and died February 6, 1966. They had children:
   a. Ralph William Smith, born May 12, 1917. Married December 23, 1939 to Ruth Adelaide Leatherman, born May 31, 1916. They had a son:
      (1) Edward Ralph Smith, born March 25, 1942. Married August 2, 1963 to Deanna Sue Flook, born April 5, 1946, and had children:
         (a) Dennis Edward Smith: February 25, 1942
         (b) Debra Dee Smith: September 23, 1967

b. Ellen E. Smith, born May 21, 1926, died January 31, 1929.

4. Carrie Edna Brandenburg, born c.1898. Married to Leatherman.

5. Hazel C. Brandenburg, born c.1900

6. Ivy M. Brandenburg, born c.1896, died June 22, 1897 at age one year, five months and twenty-one days. Buried at Wolfsville Lutheran cemetery with her parents.

7. Eva I. Brandenburg, born c.1904; married to Palmer.

8. Arthur W. Brandenburg, born June 11, 1910 and married to Florence G. Kline. Her middle name was perhaps Geraldine. A cemetery record of a child who died young, lists Arthur W. and Geraldine as parents. Children:

   a. Arthur R. Brandenburg, born January 10, 1933 and died August 20, 1933. Wolfsville Lutheran Church.

   b. Leah R. Brandenburg, married to Wilbur E. Martin of Middletown.

   c. Grace E. Brandenburg, married to James J. Garver of Mt. Airy.

   d. Carol A. Brandenburg, married to Franklin W. Norris of Middletown.

   e. Virginia L. Brandenburg, married to Jerry L. Axline of Woodsboro.

   f. Paul E. Brandenburg, married to Christine.

   g. Harold W. Brandenburg, married to Linda L.

   h. Charles A. Brandenburg, married to Wanda L. This is perhaps Charles Austin Brandenburg, who was born March 16, 1932 and was killed in action in the Korean War, September 3, 1950

William Howard Taft Brandenburg
1908-1980

This individual was born May 25, 1908 and died December 23, 1980. Married June, 1934 to Helen Gertrude Shoemaker, born August 29, 1909, died April 1, 1991. Both are buried in Rocky Springs cemetery, Frederick, Maryland. They had two children:

1. Richard Taft Brandenburg, born August 26, 1935. First married October 17, 1958 to Doris Jane Shuff, and had a child; then divorced. Married second February 12, 1972 to Nancy Virginia Moats, born August 6, 1946, and had two more children. His children were:
    a. Debra Lynn Brandenburg, born October 24, 1960. Married John Dreisonstok and had two children:
        (1) John Dustin Dreisonstok: March 27, 1981
        (2) Daniel Jacob Dreisonstok: December 9, 1986
    b. Steven Taft Brandenburg, born January 5, 1973 and adopted.
    c. Brian Taft Brandenburg, born April 20, 1974, died 1977 of cancer.
2. Sandra Jane Brandenburg, born May 29, 1944. Married Jerome Ferdinand Norland, born January 24, 1942, and lived in Kalamazoo, Michigan. Two children:
    a. Derek Alan Norland: October 8, 1967
    b. Leif Andrew Norland: September 1, 1970

Rudolph Brandenburg
1924-

Rudolph (which may not be his proper given name) was born December 27, 1924 in Frederick County, and married October 14, 1944 to Evelyn Earlene Ropp, born September 11, 1926. They had children:

1. Gary Wayne Brandenburg, born October 16, 1948, and married August 18, 1967 to Donna Jean Plunkard, born April 9, 1948. A daughter:
    a. Kristi Lynn Brandenburg: April 27, 1970
2. Teri Brandenburg, born September 5, 1954

Margaret Brandenburg
1835-

At this point, we do not know the maiden name of this individual, nor that of her husband. She appears as head of household in the 1880 census for Frederick County, Maryland born c.1835, with three children:
1. Cora W. Brandenburg, born c.1860
2. Charles W. Brandenburg, born c.1865
3. Walter G. Brandenburg, born c.1872

Charles Brandenburg
1873-

Charles appears in the 1900 census for Frederick County born c.1873. His wife was Emma M., born c.1873, and they had two small children:
1. Paul D. Brandenburg, born c.1898
2. Mildred D. Brandenburg, born c.1899

Oscar Brandenburg
1888-

Oscar is listed in the 1920 census for Frederick County, born c.1888. His wife is Mary J., born c.1889. One son:
1. Leroy Brandenburg, born c.1906

CHAPTER 12

Brandenburgs of Howard County, Maryland

As mentioned in earlier chapters, family members have been located primarily in Frederick County, Maryland, with a major movement into Montgomery County. However, several members of the family have been identified in neighboring Howard and Carroll Counties, where they adjoin Frederick and Montgomery. Many of them have been identified in the main chapters of the text, a few have not. Those found in Howard County, and not otherwise identified, will be presented here for further reference.

Jesse L. Brandenburg
1857-

Jesse was found in the 1900 census for Howard County, born c.1857, with a wife, Florence E., born c.1864. There were four children in the household. The 1920 census for the county includes the couple, with one more son, for a total of five identified children. There were perhaps others:
1. Carrie Brandenburg, born c.1884
2. William Brandenburg, born c.1886
3. Gertrude Brandenburg, born c.1890
4. Beulah Brandenburg, born c.1892
5. Carl L. Brandenburg, born c.1906

George Brandenburg
1806-

George appears as head of household in the 1900 census of Howard County, at the age of eighty-four, born c.1806. He has a sister living with him, Sarah E. Brandenburg, born c.1821. There is also one of his daughters still at home, perhaps caring for her aged father. She was:

1. Sarah E. Brandenburg, born December 25, 1843, died November 27, 1922. Buried at Mt. Carmel Church in Montgomery County, Maryland.

James Brandenburg
1861-

James is found in the 1900 census for Howard County, born c.1861. His wife is Amelia, born c.1874, and they have one son living with them. He was:

1. James R. Brandenburg, born c.1900

Stephen Brandenburg
1861-

Not otherwise identified, Stephen appears as head of household in the 1900 census for Howard County, born c.1861. His wife Maggie was born c.1865 and they then had four small children. In the 1920 census for Baltimore County, his wife is called Margaret, and they have six children living in the household:

1. Emily Brandenburg, born c.1894. Shown as Amelia in the 1920 census.
2. Ethel Brandenburg, born c.1896
3. Maude Brandenburg, born c.1898
4. Leo Brandenburg, born c.1899
5. Isabella Brandenburg, born c.1904
6. Victor Brandenburg, born c.1906

George Brandenburg
1816-1904

George was born February 14, 1816 and died June 16, 1904. Buried with his two wives. He was first married on February 3, 1841 in Howard County to Sarah Isaacs, born c.1820, died September 26, 1848, daughter of Joseph and Patience Isaacs. His second wife was Sarah Ann Anderson, born c.1832, died January 10, 1864, daughter of Stephen and Mary Ann Anderson. No children yet found.

CHAPTER 13

Brandenburgs of Montgomery County, Maryland

A few members of the family have been found in Montgomery County, but not yet placed within the larger groups under discussion. They are mentioned here for further reference and study.

Millson F. Brandenburg

Millson was married September 1, 1923 to Ruth Estelle Fulks, born November 30, 1900, died February 10, 1982, daughter of Thomas Iraneus Fulks (1870) and Fannie Lois Williams (1876). They apparently had no children. Millson had at least a sister, Mrs. Jerry McCarty. The will of Ruth Estelle was dated October 27, 1960 and probated in Montgomery County. Her husband was not mentioned and had apparently predeceased his wife; she left her estate to several nieces and nephews, and her brother and sister, all named in the estate papers.

Arnold Brandenburg
1916-1994

Arnold was born c.1916 near Damascus, Maryland, and died October 22, 1994 at his home in Largo, Florida, where he was living in retirement. Survived by wife, Beatrice, three sisters, one brother, six grandchildren, and three children:
1. Georgia Mae Brandenburg, born December 20, 1938 at Browningsville. Married to Bass.
2. Mack Brandenburg.
3. Carol Brandenburg, married to Saunders.

James William Brandenburg
died 1960

The will of this family member was written July 7, 1960 and probated September 14, 1960; filed in liber VMB 127 at folio 608 in Montgomery County, Maryland. The records show that he died August 5, 1960, leaving a wife, two sons and a sister. His wife was Leilah Thomas Brandenburg, and he named as his Executrix, his sister, Hazel B. Kyber. The two sons were:

1. James William Brandenburg, III (suggesting that testator was in fact James William, Jr.). Will records of Montgomery County contain the settlement of estate of Helen Marie Brandenburg, who died March 4, 1987. She left a will, although it was written prior to the birth of her second son, and prior to the death of her first husband, who was named Doland. At the time of her death, she and James William were estranged, and he renounced claim to her estate, leaving it to be divided between her two sons of the first marriage.

2. Harold Thomas Brandenburg. There is a will, dated March 6, 1969, not yet probated, filed in liber TME9 at folio 575 in Frederick County records. It is that of one Gussie Arnold Brandenburg, who names her husband as being Harold T. Brandenburg, perhaps this individual. If so, they had at least two children:
   a. Diana Brandenburg, married David Werner.
   b. Harold T. Brandenburg, Jr.

George W. Brandenburg
1856-

According to the census of 1900 for Montgomery County, where George appears as head of household, he was born c.1856. He was married November 29, 1881 to Sarah F.

Brown at Mt. Carmel Church in Montgomery. At the time, he was said to be of Howard County. He appears as head of household in the 1900 census of Montgomery, born c.1856, with his wife, Sarah F., born c.1855, and four children. Also in his household is Achsah Groomes, born c.1852, said to be his sister. The children were:

1. George F. Brandenburg, born c.1883
2. Arthur F. Brandenburg, born c.1884.
3. Sarah D. Brandenburg, born c.1886
4. Mary C. Brandenburg, born c.1888

Rufus Brandenburg
1898-

Rufus is head of household in the 1920 census for Montgomery County, Maryland, born c.1898. His wife is Lola, born c.1898, and at that time, they had two children:

1. Rufus Brandenburg, born c.1916
2. William A. Brandenburg, born c.1917

CHAPTER 14

Miscellaneous Brandenburg Family Members

In the first eight chapters of our study, we have discussed the principal families found in the early history of Frederick County, where most of the family apparently lived, with some movement back and forth into neighboring Montgomery, Howard, Baltimore and Carroll Counties. In chapters 9 thru 13, we have included some of those found in those neighboring counties, but not yet identified. In early records of the Mormon Church, particularly the International Genealogical Index (the IGI), and in other records, we have found several other family groups who should be mentioned here.

Roy G. Brandenburg
1890-

Roy was found in the 1920 census for Washington County, Maryland, born c.1890. His wife was Lela M., born c.1885, and there were three children:
1. Rudolph L. Brandenburg, born c.1907
2. Louise S. Brandenburg, born c.1911
3. Jeanette Brandenburg, born c.1915

S. Brandenburg
1886-

In the 1920 census for Washington County, Maryland, there is a listing in which the first name of the head of household is almost impossible to read. It appears to be Saris G. Brandenburg, but we have been unable to identify him further. His wife is Annie, born c.1888, and there are children:
1. Freda M. Brandenburg, born c.1909

2. Gladys P. Brandenburg, born c.1912
3. Katherine M. Brandenburg, born c.1915
4. Kenneth L. Brandenburg, born c.1915
5. Sarah R. Brandenburg, born c.1917
6. Max A. Brandenburg, born c.1920

A number of bits of information have been found which can best be described as "one-liners" relating to individuals bearing the Brandenburg name. All individuals in the left column bear that surname.

Individual	Information
Absolom	Md Fred. Co. 03/30/1826 Mary Fout.
Amanda C.	Born 02/10/1857, died 06/03/1923. Bur. Mt. Olivet cemetery, Frederick
Addie O.	Md to Emery W. Saylor, Frederick Co.
Alice	Md to William Culler, Frederick.
Amos F.	Born 07/18/1930, died 8 days. S/o R. Franklin and Nellie R. Brandenburg. Middletown.
Ann Maria	Md Fred. Co. 03/14/1835 Henry Ridenour.
Ann Mary	Md Fred. Co. 03/19/1839 William Smith.
Anna B.	Born 03/22/1871, died 12/12/1951. Married to Smith.
Anna Catherine	Died Fred. Co. 03/07/1882, d/o John Wesley and Ann Margaret Berry Brandenburg. John Wesley md 03/22/1826 Ann Margaret Berry.
Anna Margaret	Born 06/02/1816 Fred. Co., d/o Jacob and Salome Brandenburg.
Anna Maria	Chr. 08/13/1820 Fred. Co., the d/o Jacob and Catherine Brandenburg.
Beulah Irene	Born 12/02/1912, daughter of W. B. and Lida M. Brandenburg. See entry under father's name below.
Bernard W.	Died 05/26/1884 at 9 months, 26 days. Son of George H. and E. A. Brandenburg. Kemptown.

Bertha	Born c.1872, died 10/-/1964. Md to Edward Watkins.
Catherine	Md Fred. Co. 02/01/1849 John L. Fisher.
Charles F.	Born 1885, wife Marie, born 1885. Son John P., staff sergeant, born 1917, died 1942. All buried Wolfsville Lutheran.
Charles J.	Md Mont. Co. 11/07/1892 Mary V. Weaver.
Charles P.	Born c.1878. Md Fred Co. 02/24/1899 Emma Mary Rohrback, born 05/06/1870, daughter of Daniel A. Rohrback (1845).
David	Md Fred. Co. to Mary Catherine Horine, born 02/01/1843. Lived in Tennessee.
Dorothy Elizabeth	Born 03/04/1911, md in Fred. Co. to Herbert Griesert.
Earl	Md to Maude E. VanSant, born c.1905, died 03/12/1993, daughter of Abel and Claudia VanSant of Randallstown.
Edwin C.	Lawyer in D. C., d/1935; md June, 1891 Emma Goodacre, who died 12/27/1950. Two daughters: Dorothy Bou and Ruth McCarty.
Elizabeth	Md Fred. Co. Dewalt J. Willard (1739-1808).
Elizabeth	Md Fred. Co. 11/24/1853 to Lawson Poffenberger.
Elizabeth	Md Fred. Co. 02/18/1824 Michael Motter.
Emily A.	Born 10/19/1842, died 08/23/1901. Buried at Burkittsville, Frederick County.
Emma Louise	Born 08/28/1909, md Fred. Co. to Claude Lee Buckler.
Florence	Md Carroll Co. 02/22/1911 J. Mahlon Grimm.
Francis W.	Died 1978. Md Dorothy M. Nachtman, her second marriage; she died 06/07/1996. A son, Robert W. Brandenburg, who md Lee Ann and had a son, Robert W., Jr. who had children: Michael, Robert, Joseph and Megan.
Frederick	Md Fred. Co. 02/22/1782 or 05/31/1782 to Elizabeth Sibert.
George F.	Md 12/26/1905 to Norma Brandenburg.

George Washington	Md Fred. Co. 06/03/1950 Betty Jane Cartee, born 05/17/1931
Hannah	Md Fred. Co. 03/28/1834 George Colliflower.
Hattie Ethylene	Born 01/26/1920 Fred Co. Md there Stanley Crummitt, born 10/13/1917
Helen Virginia	Born 06/08/1912, md Fred. Co. to Lawrence Townsend.
Henry	Md Fred Co. 04/15/1804 Elizabeth Gebhard.
Henry	Md Fred. Co. 08/23/1831 Charlotte Langwell.
Henry	Md Fred Co. 07/10/1793 Elizabeth Gorner.
Jacob	Chr. Fred. Co. 08/02/1818, s/o Jacob and Catharine Brandenburg.
Jefferson R.	Fred. Co. will dated 06/20/1970, not probated. Filed liber TME6, folio 340. Names wife Ruth E. and son Eugene Patrick Brandenburg.
John	Md Fred. Co. 04/12/1794 Phebe Gorner, or Garner.
John W.	Md Fred. Co. 05/12/1856 Mary M. Allerman.
John Wesley	Md 03/22/1826 to Ann Margaret Berry. Fred. County
Jonas	Md Fred. Co. 12/21/1863 Catharine Flook.
Julia Margarite	Born 1913, married James Burris. Fred Co.
Lillian	Born 1876, died 1956. Kemptown Methodist.
Lottie E.	Md Mont. Co. 12/26/1887 John W. Brown.
Mahala	Md Fred. Co. 10/20/1859 Jonas Shoemaker.
Malinda Steheley	Md Fred. Co. Elias Schlosser. Daughter of Ann Brandenburg.
Margaret Lucille	Md Fred. Co. to Samuel Lajoie.
Maria	Md Fred. Co. 12/16/1774 Samuel Bossert.
Maria	Md Fred. Co.. 05/28/1816 Philip Kramer.
Mary Ann	Born c.18 02/02/1846 David H. Knox.
Martin Calvin	Md Fred. Co. 02/18/1861 Lydia Guyton.
Mary	Md Fred. Co 24, died 09/09/1912. Middletown Reformed Church.
Mary C.	Md Fred. Co. 02/13/1860 to Abraham Wakenight.
Mary Ellen	Md Fred. Co. 05/05/1889 Emory Smith.

Mary M.	Born c.1830, died 05/08/1904 aged 74. Buried Middletown Reformed cemetery.
Mary Matilda	Md Carroll Co. 03/06/1862 George Place.
Mathias	Born c.1837, died 04/22/1897. Buried Ellerton with wife. Md 09/26/1861 Lauretta A. Blessing, born c.1836, and died 03/15/1914.
Millard W.	Born 02/01/1875, died 11/01/1938. Buried at Myersville Lutheran Church.
Milton Henry	Md Fred. Co. to Julia Emily Kemp Michael, her second marriage.
Murrill	Md to Miriam A. Zimmerman; a son, William Dean Brandenburg, born 1947
Ray M.	Died 10/14/1922, aged 0-1-12. S/o J. Roger and B. M. Brandenburg.
Ray McKinley	Born 03/08/1901, died 10/09/1908. Myersville Lutheran Church.
Ruby Frances	Born 1915 Fred Co. Md to Howard Theis.
Samuel	Md Fred. Co. 09/23/1835 Malinda Feaster.
Samuel	Md Fred. Co. 05/05/1860 Eve Ann O'Conner.
Samuel Lee	Born 07/18/1830, son of John and Anne Brandenburg. Middletown.
Sarah	Born c.1854, died 10/01/1899, aged 45-3-14. Wife of T. H. Brandenburg.
Sarah	Born 09/28/1820, died 09/19/1900. Daughter of Jacob and Priscilla Brandenburg. Buried at Mt. Carmel Church. Jacob md Fred. Co. 12/29/1812 to Priscilla Robinson.
Sarah E.	Born 08/21/1885, died 08/11/1926. Buried at Mt. Olivet, Frederick.
Sarah Jane	Md 08/11/1957 at Myersville, Carroll Gordon Zimmerman, born 03/29/1934, the s/o Edgar Allen Zimmerman (1909) and Annie Louise Cramer (1909)
Sarah L.	Born 04/30/1860, died 07/27/1860. Buried at Kemptown Methodist.
Susan Ann	Md Anne Arundel Co. 01/26/1841 Remulus Snyder.

Virginia (Smith)	Born 08/19/1902, died 02/17/1957. Buried at Mt. Olivet, Frederick.
William	Born c.1828 Howard Co., Md.; md c.1850 to Sarah Elizabeth Mullinix, born 01/30/1836 in Mont. Co., died 10/09/1895, daughter of Asbury Mullinix & Elizabeth Fleming.
William	Md Fred. Co. 06/15/1795 Christena Martin.
William	Md Fred. Co. 09/13/1806 Christiana Long.
William B.	July 6, 1923. Filed suit in Mont. Co. to divorce Lida Brandenburg.
Willie E.	Born 06/03/1897, died 02/15/1910. The son of C. J. and M. V. Brandenburg. Mt. Carmel

BIBLIOGRAPHY

American Genealogical Research Institute. *Walker Family History,* Washington, D. C. 1972.

American Historical Society. *History of Virginia, 1924*

Asplund. *Register of Baptist Churches*

Barnes. *Maryland Marriages, 1634-1777*

_____. *Maryland Marriages, 1778-1800*

_____. *Marriages and Deaths From the Maryland Gazette*

Block, Maxine, Editor. *Current Biography, Who's News and Why,* New York: H. W. Wilson Company, 1940

Bockstruck, Lloyd DeWitt. *Virginia's Colonial Soldiers*

Bowie. *Across The Years in Prince George's County*

Bowman, Tressie Nash. *Montgomery County Marriages, 1796-1850*

Brown. *Index of Marriage Licenses, Prince George's County, Maryland*

_____. *Index of Church Records, Maryland*

Brown, Ann Paxton. Personal collection of genealogical notes and abstracts; major families of Montgomery County, Maryland.

Brumbaugh. *Maryland Records.* 1915 and 1928 issues; Washington County Marriages.

_____. *Maryland Records, Colonial, Revolutionary, County and Church.*

_____. *Census of Maryland, 1776*

Burgert, Annette Kunselman. *Eighteenth Century Emigrants from German-Speaking Lands to North America.* Volume 1, The Northern Kraichgau. The Pennsylvania German Society. 1983

Burke. *Burke's Peerage and Baronetage.*

_____. *The General Armory*

Bussard, Ruthella. *The Genealogy of Peter Bossert-Bussard, 1761-1802.* Frederick, Maryland. Jeanne Bussard Workshop. 1970-1974.

Buxton, Allie May. *Family of Harry and Rosa Hurley.* Manuscript; Montgomery County Historical Society, Rockville, Maryland.

Carr, Lois Green; Menard, Russell R.; Peddicord, Louis. *Maryland at the Beginning.*

Cavey, Kathleen Tull-Burton. *Tombstones and Beyond, Prospect U. M. Church Cemetery and Marvin Chapel Church Cemetery.* Frederick County Historical Society.

Chapman. *Portrait and Biographical Record of the Sixth Congressional District, Maryland.* Chapman Publishing Company, New York. 1898

Church of Jesus Christ of Latter Day Saints. *Family group sheets, computerized ancestral files, International Genealogical Index, and other pertinent records.* Family History Center, Silver Spring, Maryland.

Clark, Edythe Maxey. *William Pumphrey of Prince George's County, Maryland, and his Descendants.* Anundsen Publishing Company. 1992.

Coldham, Peter Wilson. *The Bristol Register of Servants Sent to Foreign Plantations 1654-1686,* Genealogical Publishing Company, Baltimore. 1988

_____. *The Complete Book of Emigrants, 1607-1660,* Genealogical Publishing Co., Baltimore, 1987

Core, Earl L. *The Monongalia Story,* West Virginia: McClain Printing Company, 1974-1984

Crozier. *The General Armory*

Day, Jackson H. *The Story of the Maryland Walker Family, Including the Descendants of George Bryan Walker and Elizabeth Walker Beall.* 1957, privately printed manuscript.

Dern, John P. and Waidner, M. Marjorie. *Rauenzahner to Routson, A Family on the Move.* Picton Press, Camden, Maine. 1993

Doliante, Sharon J. *Maryland and Virginia Colonials: Genealogies of Some Colonial Families.* Genealogical Publishing Co. Baltimore, Md. 1991

Ferrill, Matthew & Gilchrist, Robert. *Maryland Probate Records 1635-1777.* Volume 9.

Filby. *Passenger and Immigration Lists Index.*

Fleming, Bertha Ann. *The Brandenburg Family in America.* Not published; private compilation deposited with the Frederick County, Maryland, Historical Society.

Fry, Joshua & Jefferson, Peter. *Map of Virginia, North Carolina, Pennsylvania, Maryland, New Jersey 1751.* Montgomery County, Md Library, Atlas Archives.

Gaithersburg, Maryland, City. *Gaithersburg, The Heart of Montgomery County.* Privately printed. 1978

Gartner Funeral Home, Gaithersburg, Maryland. *Alphabetical computer print-out of funerals and dates.*

Goldsborough. *Maryland Line in the Confederacy.*

Hamlin, Charles Hughes. *Virginia Ancestors and Adventurers.* 1975.

Hardisty. *Historical and Geographical Encyclopedia, 1884.*

Hardisty. H. H. *Presidents, Soldiers, Statesmen.*

Hardy, Stella Pickett. *Colonial Families of the Southern States of America.* Genealogical Publishing Co., Baltimore, 1981

Hinke and Reinecke. *Evangelical Reformed Church, Frederick, Maryland*

Hinman-Sotcher. *Genealogies of Pennsylvania Families.* Pennsylvania Genealogical Magazine, Volume II

Holdcraft, Jacob Mehrling. *Names in Stone; 75,000 Cemetery Inscriptions From Frederick County, Maryland.* Ann Arbor, Michigan. 1966.

Hopkins, G. M. *Atlas of Montgomery County, Maryland.*

Hurley, William N., Jr. *Hurley Families in America, Volumes 1 and 2,* Bowie, Md., Heritage Books, Inc. 1995

_____. *The Ancestry of William Neal Hurley, III,* Chelsea, Michigan: BookCrafters, 1985

Jacobs, Elizabeth Jeanne King. *Personal papers and records.*

Jones, Henry Z., Jr. *More Palatine Families, Some Immigrants to the Middle Colonies 1717-1776 and their European Origins.* Universal City, California. 1991

Jourdan, Elise Greenup. *The Land Records of Prince George's County, Maryland, 1710-1717*

Lebherz, Margaret Biser Green. *Biser Family Journals, Volumes 1, 2 and 3.* Privately printed. 1991. Frederick County Library Collection.

Liebegott. *The Liebegott Collection (247 volumes).* Martinsburg public library, Martinsburg, Blair County, Pennyslvania

London House and Maxwell. *Prominent Families in America wih British Ancestry.*

Lord, Elizabeth M. *Burtonsville, Maryland Heritage, Genealogically Speaking*

MacLysaght, Edward. *Irish Families, Their Names, Arms and Origins*

Malloy, Mary Gordon; Sween, Jane C.; Manuel, Janet D. *Abstract of Wills, Montgomery County, Maryland 1776-1825*

Malloy, Mary Gordon; Jacobs, Marian W. *Genealogical Abstracts, Montgomery County Sentinel, 1855-1899*

Manuel, Janet Thompson. *Montgomery County, Maryland Marriage Licenses, 1798-1898*

Maryland State. *Archives of Maryland*, all volumes.

Maryland Hall of Records. *Wills, estates, inventories, births, deaths, marriages, deeds and other reference works relative to counties of Maryland.*

_____. *Maryland Calendar of Wills.* Eight volumes.

_____. *Maryland Historical Society Magazine.*

_____. *Vestry Book of St. John's Episcopal Parish Church, 1689-1810.* Original.

Montgomery County Court Records. *Wills, inventories of estate, deeds.* Rockville, Maryland.

Montgomery County Historical Society, Rockville, Maryland. *Folder files; census, church, correspondence, newspaper, manuscripts, library, and family records.*

_____. *Queen Anne Parish Records, 1686-1777*

_____. *King George Parish Records 1689 - 1801*

_____. *King George Parish Records 1797-1878*

_____. *St. Paul's at Baden, Parish Records*

_____. *Frederick County Maryland Marriage Licenses*

_____. *Montgomery County Marriages*

_____. *1850 Census, Montgomery County, Maryland*

_____. *1850 Census, Prince George's County, Maryland*

_____. *Pioneers of Old Monocacy*

Mormon Church, Genealogical Library. Archival family group sheets and other records.

_____. *International Genealogical Index.* North Carolina, Tennessee, Maryland, Pennsylvania, Ohio, Kentucky, Alabama, Virginia and other states.

Morrow and Morrow. *Marriages of Washington County, Maryland, An Index, 1799-1866.* DAR library, Washington, D. C.

Myers, Margaret Elizabeth. *Marriage Licenses of Frederick County, Maryland 1778-1810.* Family Line Publications. 1986

_____. *Marriage Licenses of Frederick County, Maryland 1811-1840.* Family Line Publications. 1987

_____. *Marriage Licenses of Frederick County, Maryland 1841-1865.* Family Line Publications. 1988

_____. *George Zimmerman and Descendants of Frederick County, Maryland 1714-1987.* Family Line Publications. 1987.

National Genealogical Society Quarterly. Volume 72, Number 3

Napoli, J. Belle. *Hobbs and Related Families.* 1982, unpublished, Library of Montgomery County Historical Society.

Newman, Harry Wright. *Mareen Duvall of Middle Plantation.* Privately published 1952. Washington, D. C.

Omans, Donald James and Nancy West. *Montgomery County Marriages 1798-1875.* Maryland.

Pennsylvania, author unknown. *History of Bedford, Somerset and Fulton Counties, Pennsylvania.* 1884

_____. *History of Huntington and Blair Counties, Pennsylvania.* 1883

Pennsylvania. Miscellaneous court records, local courthouses; wills, estates, inventories, deeds, estates, etc.

Pioneer Historical Society and Library, Bedford, Pennsylvania. Collections of genealogical importance; obituaries, newspapers, family folders, cemetery records, publications, etc.

Prince George's County, Md Historical Society. *Index to the Probate Records of Prince George's County, Maryland, 1696-1900*

_____. *Prince George's County Land Records, Volume A, 1696-1702.* Bowie, Maryland, 1976

_____. *1850 Census, Prince George's County, Maryland.* Bowie, Maryland, 1978

_____. *1828 Tax List Prince George's County, Maryland.* Bowie, Maryland, 1985.

Reinton, Louise Joyner. *Prince George's County, Md. Piscataway or St. John's Parish (now called King George's Parish. Index to Register, 1689-1878.*

Remsberg, Reverend W. L. *Genealogy of the Remsberg Family in America.* The Valley Register, Middletown, Md. 1912

Ridgely. *Historic Graves of Maryland and the District of Columbia*

Rohrbaugh, Lewis Bunker. *Rohrbach Genealogy.* Dando-Schaff Printing & Pub. Co. Philadelphia. 1970

Russell, Donna Valley. *Western Maryland Genealogy.* Volumes 1 thru 12. Catoctin Press, Middletown, Md. 1985-1996

Sargent. *Stones and Bones, Cemetery Records of Prince George's County, Maryland.*

Scharff. *History of Western Maryland*

Schildknecht, Calvin E. *Monocacy and Catoctin, Volumes 1 thru 111.* Gettysburg, Pa. 1994

Simmendinger, Ulrich. *The Simmendinger Register.* St. Johnsville, New York: Reprinted by the Enterprise and News, 1934.

Skinner, V. L., Jr. *Abstracts of the Prerogative Court of Maryland, 1726-1729*

Skordas, Gust. *Early Settlers of Maryland*
_____. (Perhaps). *Servants to Foreign Plantations*

St. Clair. *St. Clair's Bedford: The History and Genealogy of Bedford County, Pennsylvania.* Several volumes, Pioneer Library, Bedford, Pa.

Strassburger, Ralph Beaver, LL.D. *Pennsylvania German Pioneers.* Genealogical Publishing Co., Inc. Baltimore, second printing in two volumes. 1980

Tepper, Michael. *Emigrants to the Middle Colonies.*
_____. *Passengers to America.* Genealogical Publishing Company, Baltimore, 1979

Tombstone Records. *Bethesda United Methodist Church, Browningsville, Maryland. Forest Oak Cemetery, Gaithersburg, Maryland. Goshen United Methodist Church (now Goshen Mennonite Church), Laytonsville, Maryland. St. Paul's Methodist Church, Laytonsville, Maryland.*

Unknown author. *History of Tennessee*, with sketches of Gibson, Orion, Weakley, Dyer and Lake Counties. Nashville, Tenn. 1887

_____. *Portrait & Biographical Record, 6th Congressional District of Maryland, 1898.* Montgomery County Historical Society

_____. *Historie Catholicae Iberniae Compendium*

_____. *History and Biographical Record of Washington County, Maryland.* Hagerstown public library.

_____. *Groff Book, a Family Genealogy.* Washington County, Maryland, Historical Society

_____. *Biographical Cyclopedia of Representative Men of Maryland and District of Columbia.* 1879.

VanHorn, R. Lee. *Out of the Past.*

Virginia State Library and Archives, Richmond. Wills, estates, inventories, births, deaths, marriages, deeds and other reference works relative to counties of Virginia.

Wampler, Roy H. *The Derr Family 1750-1986.* Gateway Press, Inc. Baltimore, Md. 1987

Washington County, Maryland. Folder files of the County Historical Society; correspondence and family records; courthouse records of wills, estates, deeds, births, deaths and marriages.

Washington County, Maryland Library. *Church Records, Zion Reformed Church at Hagerstown.*

Welsh, Luther W., A.M., M.D. *Ancestral Colonial Families, Genealogy of The Welsh and Hyatt Families of Maryland and Their Kin.* Lambert Moon Printing Co., Independence, Missouri. 1928.

Williams, T. J. C. *History of Frederick County, Maryland.* Two volumes. L. R. Titsworth & Co. 1910.

_____. *History of Washington County, Maryland*

Williams, Ruth Smith; Griffin, Margarette Glenn. *Bible Records of Early Edgecombe, North Carolina*

Wimberly, Bessie Jewel Mayes. *The William Kindley Family Genealogy, His Nine Sons and Their Descendants.* Washington, D. C. Privately printed. Undated.

Wright, F. Edward. *Maryland Militia, War of 1812.*

INDEX

All names appearing in the text have been indexed, with reference to each page on which they appear. Most names are accompanied by a date, generally indicating date of birth, in order to differentiate between individuals having the same given name. In some cases where birth dates are not available, dates of marriage or death will appear, such as m/1825 or d/1876. In the case of common names such as John or Mary, where no date is specified, the references are without question to more than one individual.

Baker, J. L., 101
Baker, John T. 1851, 149
Baker, Mary J. 1869, 146
Baker, Nancy, 97
Baker, Rudelle Brandenburg 1914, 149
Baker, Susan L. 1954, 149
Baker, Thomas, 102
Baker, William Andrew 1880, 149
Barker, Nancy Ann, 93
Barkman, David, Jr. 1830, 32
Barnes, Anna Louise 1920, 159
Barnes, Dorothy Pauline 1917, 159
Barnes, Eleanor Irene Virginia 1934, 161
Barnes, Herbert Day 1891, 159
Barnes, James Oliver 1860, 159
Barnes, James Raymond Hamilton 1927, 161
Barnes, Jamie Luanne, 161
Barnes, Marion Evangeline 1917, 161, 172
Barnes, Matilda, 93
Barnes, Mazie Emma 1926, 161
Barnes, Patricia Lee 1945, 160
Barnes, Phyllis 1928, 174
Barnes, Raymond Oliver 1893, 161
Barnes, Vivian Bernice 1923, 160
Barr, William Arnold, 77
Bartgis, Clara, 105
Barton, Ida, 144
Basford, Rachel, 111
Bass, No given name, 201
Beach, No given name, 11
Beachley, Edith M., 105
Beachley, John D., 105
Beall, Barry, 167
Beall, Betty Marie 1926, 166

Beall, David Otho, 92
Beall, Laura Washington 1859, 156
Beall, Mark Willis 1950, 167
Beall, Melanie Ann 1953, 167
Beall, Nettie F. 1872, 130
Beall, Wendy Jeanine 1959, 167
Beall, Willis Webster 1927, 166
Beard, George C., 94
Beard, Laura Jane 1815, 94
Beasley, Lucetta, 91
Beasman, Caroline, 184
Beavers, William 1797, 89
Beck, Beth Luella 1969, 173
Beck, Charles Franklin, II 1929, 172
Beck, Charles Franklin, III 1964, 172
Bell, Alice, 26
Bell, Cory Michael 1981, 131
Bell, Diane, 26
Bell, Donald Wilford 1934, 131
Bell, Fred, 26
Bell, Gary Wayne 1960, 131
Bell, John H., 114
Bell, Leslie Ann 1988, 131
Bell, Michael Donald 1956, 131
Bell, Pattie Lynn 1962, 131
Bell, Phenton, 94
Bell, Stacy Lorraine 1983, 131
Bellmyer, Abba, 59
Bennett, Belinda Berniece 1971, 160
Bennett, Clifton Wayne 1972, 161
Bennett, Linda Amelia 1913, 121
Bennett, Margaret Jane 1924, 27
Bennett, Ormus Durrett 1946, 160
Benning, Josephine, 131
Berger, Joe, 26
Berger, Joe, Jr., 26

Berger, Rosalee, 26
Berry, Ann Margaret, 206, 208
Best, Edna, 77
Beyer, Catherine, 6
Biniger, Carrie 1886, 14
Binkley, Reuben 1816, 97
Biser, Charles C., 78
Biser, Edward S., 78
Biser, Emma Alice 1862, 78
Biser, Ezra 1820, 78
Biser, Frederick, 67
Biser, Frederick 1763, 78
Biser, George Washington 1838,
   78
Biser, Harvey G., 78
Biser, John Jacob 1793, 78
Biser, Joshua Frederick 1841, 78
Biser, Lulu M., 78
Biser, Mary 1801, 67
Biser, No given name, 35
Biser, Thaddeus M., 72
Biser, Wellington Frederick, 78
Bishop, Ray Edward 1949, 118
Bishop, Seth Edward, 118
Black, Michael Doran 1971, 83
Black, Thomas C. 1930, 83
Blackwell, Joseph, 90
Blanche, David Forbes, 128
Blanche, Gary David 1968, 128
Blanche, Glen Bradley 1971, 128
Blanche, Greg Thomas 1965,
   128
Blanche, Nan, 128
Blanche, Thomas, 128
Blank, Linda Jean 1948, 39
Blank, Ralph Leon, 39
Blessing, Lauretta A. 1836, 209
Blewett, Alan G. 1931, 155
Blewett, Carla Elaine 1960, 155
Blewett, Ronald Rush 1961, 155
Blickenstaff, Charles, 33
Bliss, Allen 1932, 125

Bliss, Dawn 1958, 125
Bolger, James L. 1903, 118
Bolton, Elizabeth, 128
Bolton, Frances Elizabeth, 127
Boone, Charles, 35, 133
Boone, Jean, 35, 133
Boone, Myrtle, 27
Boone, Vicki Marie 1953, 35,
   133
Bossert, Samuel, 208
Boswell, Walter George, 77
Bou, No given name, 207
Bowlus, Clarence Melvin 1876,
   13
Bowlus, Lula 1880, 13
Bowlus, Pearl, 13
Bowman, Deborah 1819, 93
Bowman, Sarah Elizabeth 1906,
   146
Bowman, Thomas 1822, 90
Boyer, Emma Cassandra 1868,
   115, 119
Boyer, John, 112
Boyer, Larry, 82
Boyer, Lois, 82
Boyer, Sarah Rebecca 1874, 167
Boyle, Kenneth Howell 1934,
   153
Brady, Florence, 76
Brady, John, 76
Bragunier, Ida, 70
Branaman, Will, 108
Brandenburg, Aaron 1761, 6, 49,
   51, 53, 57, 58, 60, 61
Brandenburg, Aaron 1800, 50
Brandenburg, Aaron 1814, 51
Brandenburg, Aaron 1815, 53,
   54, 58
Brandenburg, Aaron Douglas
   1859, 56
Brandenburg, Abraham, 65

Brandenburg, Absalom Henson 1799, 93
Brandenburg, Absolom, 206
Brandenburg, Absolom 1786, 97
Brandenburg, Achsah 1852, 203
Brandenburg, Ada E. 1874, 84
Brandenburg, Adam Grant 1865, 52
Brandenburg, Addie D. 1870, 113
Brandenburg, Addie O., 206
Brandenburg, Agnes 1868, 177
Brandenburg, Albert 1839, 62
Brandenburg, Albert 1866, 189
Brandenburg, Albert Harp 1905, 72
Brandenburg, Alexander Henry, 2, 4, 5, 87, 101
Brandenburg, Alice, 206
Brandenburg, Alice A. 1907, 183
Brandenburg, Alice C. 1899, 23
Brandenburg, Alice Catherine 1864, 22
Brandenburg, Alice Salome 1845, 188
Brandenburg, Allen 1829, 74
Brandenburg, Althea Anna 1869, 60
Brandenburg, Alton P. 1904, 141
Brandenburg, Alura 1858, 136
Brandenburg, Alvey Raymond 1863, 31, 43
Brandenburg, Alvin, 141
Brandenburg, Amanda 1911, 189
Brandenburg, Amanda C. 1857, 206
Brandenburg, Amanda Louise 1892, 193
Brandenburg, Amelia, 198
Brandenburg, Amelia 1894, 198
Brandenburg, Amelia A. 1846, 95

Brandenburg, Amonias 1848, 52
Brandenburg, Amos 1902, 188
Brandenburg, Amos F. 1930, 206
Brandenburg, Amos Lyle 1899, 55
Brandenburg, Amos W. 1845, 188
Brandenburg, Amos Warner 1873, 55
Brandenburg, Amy Altana 1897, 55
Brandenburg, Amy Luelda 1879, 56
Brandenburg, Amy M. 1898, 20
Brandenburg, Amy Viola 1897, 70
Brandenburg, Andrew J. 1866, 139
Brandenburg, Andrew J. 1890, 185
Brandenburg, Andrew R. 1835, 52
Brandenburg, Angela Ann 1983, 130
Brandenburg, Anita Kay 1943, 191
Brandenburg, Ann, 5, 208
Brandenburg, Ann 1766, 49
Brandenburg, Ann Elizabeth 1833, 74
Brandenburg, Ann Maria, 206
Brandenburg, Ann Maria 1797, 10
Brandenburg, Ann Mary, 206
Brandenburg, Ann Priscilla 1831, 112, 151, 152, 156, 157, 159, 162, 171, 174
Brandenburg, Ann Rebecca 1823, 12
Brandenburg, Anna, 2
Brandenburg, Anna 1787, 51
Brandenburg, Anna 1860, 57

Brandenburg, Anna B. 1871, 206
Brandenburg, Anna Catherine, 206
Brandenburg, Anna E. 1901, 113
Brandenburg, Anna Jane 1897, 22
Brandenburg, Anna M. 1869, 186
Brandenburg, Anna Margaret 1816, 206
Brandenburg, Anna Maria 1820, 206
Brandenburg, Anna Myrtle 1878, 148
Brandenburg, Anna Rebecca 1841, 84
Brandenburg, Anne, 209
Brandenburg, Annie 1847, 56
Brandenburg, Annie 1888, 205
Brandenburg, Annie B. 1872, 20
Brandenburg, Annie E. 1861, 15
Brandenburg, Annie E. 1892, 33, 73
Brandenburg, Annie G. 1879, 137, 141
Brandenburg, Annie Lauretta 1914, 137, 141
Brandenburg, Annie P. 1900, 189
Brandenburg, Annie R. 1898, 84
Brandenburg, Annie Virginia 1884, 34
Brandenburg, Anthony, 51
Brandenburg, Archie 1893, 16
Brandenburg, Archie Lowell 1901, 17
Brandenburg, Archie Merhle 1902, 189
Brandenburg, Arline E. 1918, 24
Brandenburg, Arminta A. 1881, 182
Brandenburg, Arnold 1916, 201

Brandenburg, Arthur 1919, 178
Brandenburg, Arthur A. 1886, 178
Brandenburg, Arthur Carl 1940, 45
Brandenburg, Arthur F. 1884, 203
Brandenburg, Arthur R. 1933, 194
Brandenburg, Arthur W. 1910, 194
Brandenburg, Atlee Francis 1896, 37
Brandenburg, Atlee Leucien 1892, 43
Brandenburg, Audrey 1920, 18
Brandenburg, Austin M. 1898, 43
Brandenburg, Austin T. 1918, 72
Brandenburg, B. M., 209
Brandenburg, Barbara, 2, 101
Brandenburg, Barbara Ann 1934, 40
Brandenburg, Barbara Lynn 1958, 165, 173
Brandenburg, Beatrice, 201
Brandenburg, Benjamin M. 1844, 53
Brandenburg, Bernard W. 1884, 206
Brandenburg, Berniece E. 1881, 186
Brandenburg, Bertha 1872, 207
Brandenburg, Bertha Ruth, 46
Brandenburg, Bertie 1884, 178
Brandenburg, Bessie 1889, 177
Brandenburg, Bessie M., 141
Brandenburg, Bessie Marie 1896, 70
Brandenburg, Bessie V. 1880, 16
Brandenburg, Bethany Yvette 1984, 130

Brandenburg, Betty, 26
Brandenburg, Betty Claire 1925, 164
Brandenburg, Betty Elaine 1925, 164
Brandenburg, Betty Estelle 1929, 138
Brandenburg, Betty Grace 1922, 44
Brandenburg, Betty Jean 1940, 83
Brandenburg, Beulah 1892, 197
Brandenburg, Beulah Irene 1912, 206
Brandenburg, Beulah J. 1909, 33
Brandenburg, Blanche E. 1897, 139
Brandenburg, Bonnie Lee 1942, 37
Brandenburg, Bradley Carlton 1920, 128
Brandenburg, Bradley Claytus 1895, 128
Brandenburg, Bradley F. 1888, 21
Brandenburg, Bradley Jefferson 1863, 116, 127, 133
Brandenburg, Bradley Monroe 1916, 127
Brandenburg, Bradley Thomas 1937, 133
Brandenburg, Brenda Lee 1962, 190
Brandenburg, Brian Taft 1974, 195
Brandenburg, Bruce W. 1914, 33
Brandenburg, C. Edward 1917, 34
Brandenburg, C. J., 210
Brandenburg, C. Upton Caldwell 1922, 37
Brandenburg, Calmeda 1879, 33

Brandenburg, Calvin G. 1902, 179
Brandenburg, Calvin R. 1863, 70
Brandenburg, Capitola E. 1862, 113
Brandenburg, Carl L. 1906, 197
Brandenburg, Carl S. 1898, 183
Brandenburg, Carleton William 1872, 18
Brandenburg, Carol, 201
Brandenburg, Carol A., 194
Brandenburg, Carol Ann 1945, 37
Brandenburg, Caroline 1836, 98
Brandenburg, Caroline 1840, 62
Brandenburg, Caroline 1872, 52
Brandenburg, Carolyn Yvonne 1929, 44
Brandenburg, Carrie 1884, 197
Brandenburg, Carrie E. 1880, 16
Brandenburg, Carrie Edna 1898, 194
Brandenburg, Carrie Lucinda 1883, 72
Brandenburg, Carrie Naomi 1962, 40
Brandenburg, Carroll T. 1905, 113
Brandenburg, Catharine, 208
Brandenburg, Catharine 1813, 92
Brandenburg, Catharine 1827, 74
Brandenburg, Catherine, 10, 206
Brandenburg, Catherine 1765, 6
Brandenburg, Catherine 1785, 97
Brandenburg, Catherine 1795, 65, 78
Brandenburg, Catherine 1807, 89
Brandenburg, Catherine 1813, 90
Brandenburg, Catherine 1841, 62
Brandenburg, Catherine A. 1834, 98

Brandenburg, Catherine m/1849, 207

Brandenburg, Charles, 190

Brandenburg, Charles 1868, 57

Brandenburg, Charles 1873, 196

Brandenburg, Charles 1889, 21

Brandenburg, Charles A., 194

Brandenburg, Charles A. 1902, 23

Brandenburg, Charles A. 1907, 24

Brandenburg, Charles Austin 1932, 194

Brandenburg, Charles Emerson 1916, 18

Brandenburg, Charles Emory 1912, 26

Brandenburg, Charles F., 43

Brandenburg, Charles F. 1885, 189, 207

Brandenburg, Charles Franklin 1946, 37

Brandenburg, Charles Frederick 1892, 26

Brandenburg, Charles H., 81

Brandenburg, Charles J. m/1892, 207

Brandenburg, Charles L. 1899, 21

Brandenburg, Charles Malocton 1858, 21, 25

Brandenburg, Charles P. 1874, 188

Brandenburg, Charles P. 1878, 207

Brandenburg, Charles P. 1889, 43

Brandenburg, Charles P., Jr. 1912, 188

Brandenburg, Charles S. 1883, 21

Brandenburg, Charles Tyson 1900, 37

Brandenburg, Charles W. 1865, 196

Brandenburg, Charlotte 1837, 114

Brandenburg, Charlotte E. 1864, 139

Brandenburg, Charlotte Lavinia 1851, 115, 120

Brandenburg, Charlotte Virginia 1929, 165

Brandenburg, Chester Robert 1870, 32, 46

Brandenburg, Christine, 194

Brandenburg, Clara E. 1884, 33

Brandenburg, Clarence 1883, 16

Brandenburg, Clarence C. 1897, 84

Brandenburg, Clarence C. d/1923, 23

Brandenburg, Clarence Frederick 1925, 27

Brandenburg, Clarence Main 1876, 71

Brandenburg, Clarence Marshall 1885, 26

Brandenburg, Clarence Millard 1906, 26

Brandenburg, Claude Fillmore 1903, 140

Brandenburg, Clay K. 1893, 69

Brandenburg, Clayton E. 1883, 21

Brandenburg, Clemmie M. 1870, 74

Brandenburg, Cleveland LeRoy 1882, 149

Brandenburg, Clifford B. 1905, 179

Brandenburg, Clifford Earl 1906, 17

Brandenburg, Clinton C. 1851, 56

Brandenburg, Clyde Konine 1871, 60

Brandenburg, Clyde Sanderson 1897, 17

Brandenburg, Columbia May 1912, 26

Brandenburg, Conrad, 101

Brandenburg, Constance A. 1937, 83

Brandenburg, Constance Marie 1924, 128

Brandenburg, Cora E. 1872, 113

Brandenburg, Cora P. 1901, 183

Brandenburg, Cora W. 1860, 196

Brandenburg, Cordelia A. 1859, 30

Brandenburg, Cornelia Ann 1832, 80

Brandenburg, Cornelius, 18

Brandenburg, Cornelius E. 1824, 15, 27

Brandenburg, Cornelius Edward 1852, 21

Brandenburg, Cornelius Upton 1850, 30, 45

Brandenburg, Cyrus P., 30

Brandenburg, Cyrus P. 1885, 33

Brandenburg, Daniel, 66

Brandenburg, Daniel 1805, 83

Brandenburg, Daniel 1823, 79, 80, 81

Brandenburg, Daniel 1841, 62

Brandenburg, Daniel 1843, 62

Brandenburg, Daniel 1890, 182

Brandenburg, David, 192, 207

Brandenburg, David 1772, 91

Brandenburg, David 1795, 65, 73, 75

Brandenburg, David 1804, 91

Brandenburg, David 1812, 94

Brandenburg, David 1818, 95

Brandenburg, David 1841, 98

Brandenburg, David Lloyd 1960, 130

Brandenburg, David S. 1872, 186

Brandenburg, David, Jr. 1841, 74

Brandenburg, Dawn Lee 1954, 44

Brandenburg, Dawn Shirley 1942, 128

Brandenburg, Debora Jean 1959, 130

Brandenburg, Debra Lynn 1960, 195

Brandenburg, Delila 1813, 53

Brandenburg, Delilah 1811, 90

Brandenburg, Della M. 1893, 139

Brandenburg, Diana, 202

Brandenburg, Donald 1907, 188

Brandenburg, Dorothy, 36, 138, 207

Brandenburg, Dorothy A. 1868, 52

Brandenburg, Dorothy Elizabeth 1911, 207

Brandenburg, Dorsey 1900, 186

Brandenburg, Dorsey W. 1859, 185

Brandenburg, Dortha Lavon 1910, 56

Brandenburg, E. A., 206

Brandenburg, E. Mary 1892, 186

Brandenburg, Earl, 207

Brandenburg, Earl 1891, 61

Brandenburg, Earl D. 1893, 118

Brandenburg, Earl H., 34

Brandenburg, Edgar Allen 1896, 20

Brandenburg, Edgar L. 1900, 71

Brandenburg, Edith E. 1910, 183

Brandenburg, Edith M. 1905, 139

Brandenburg, Edna M. 1890, 178

Brandenburg, Edna Naomi 1896, 69

Brandenburg, Edna P. d/1981, 138

Brandenburg, Edward F. 1916, 177

Brandenburg, Edward Franklin 1870, 70

Brandenburg, Edwin C., 207

Brandenburg, Edythe Charlotte 1925, 38

Brandenburg, Effie Alberta M. 1872, 74

Brandenburg, Effie C. 1887, 181

Brandenburg, Effie Clearfield 1877, 148

Brandenburg, Effie May 1877, 15

Brandenburg, Eleanor, 26

Brandenburg, Eleanor Virginia 1920, 191

Brandenburg, Eli, 29, 71

Brandenburg, Eli 1830, 67

Brandenburg, Elias, 51

Brandenburg, Elias 1837, 182

Brandenburg, Eliphalet 1818, 51

Brandenburg, Eliza 1816, 92

Brandenburg, Eliza A. 1823, 57

Brandenburg, Eliza A. 1825, 74, 75

Brandenburg, Eliza J. 1847, 53

Brandenburg, Elizabeth, 118, 207

Brandenburg, Elizabeth 1764, 6

Brandenburg, Elizabeth 1769, 90

Brandenburg, Elizabeth 1796, 88, 91

Brandenburg, Elizabeth 1800, 50, 58

Brandenburg, Elizabeth 1810, 51

Brandenburg, Elizabeth 1816, 90, 97

Brandenburg, Elizabeth 1818, 94

Brandenburg, Elizabeth 1821, 12

Brandenburg, Elizabeth 1822, 67

Brandenburg, Elizabeth 1826, 90

Brandenburg, Elizabeth 1828, 112

Brandenburg, Elizabeth 1829, 54

Brandenburg, Elizabeth 1833, 184

Brandenburg, Elizabeth 1875, 186

Brandenburg, Elizabeth Ann 1820, 95

Brandenburg, Elizabeth Belle, 52

Brandenburg, Elizabeth C. 1925, 119

Brandenburg, Elizabeth m/1824, 207

Brandenburg, Elizabeth m/1853, 207

Brandenburg, Ella 1852, 81

Brandenburg, Ella 1865, 57

Brandenburg, Ella May 1861, 113

Brandenburg, Ella May 1874, 113

Brandenburg, Ellea M. 1861, 183

Brandenburg, Ellen Frances 1852, 81

Brandenburg, Elmer Caleb 1865, 31, 45

Brandenburg, Elmer Granville 1880, 72

Brandenburg, Elsie U. 1895, 186

Brandenburg, Elsie V. 1878, 30

Brandenburg, Elsie V. 1891, 138

Brandenburg, Emanuel 1833, 112

Brandenburg, Emily 1827, 112, 135

Brandenburg, Emily 1894, 198
Brandenburg, Emily A. 1842, 207
Brandenburg, Emma 1862, 56
Brandenburg, Emma 1884, 69
Brandenburg, Emma C. 1864, 15
Brandenburg, Emma F. 1866, 74
Brandenburg, Emma Grace, 138
Brandenburg, Emma Louise 1909, 207
Brandenburg, Emma M. 1873, 196
Brandenburg, Emmet G. 1892, 34
Brandenburg, Emory Maurice 1904, 83
Brandenburg, Enoch P. 1782, 6
Brandenburg, Erma 1920, 24
Brandenburg, Erma Frances 1892, 82
Brandenburg, Ernest L. 1919, 34
Brandenburg, Ernest R. 1879, 182
Brandenburg, Ernie Lee 1951, 38
Brandenburg, Ernie Lee, Jr. 1971, 38
Brandenburg, Esta R. 1878, 33
Brandenburg, Estelle 1889, 33
Brandenburg, Estie C. 1868, 74
Brandenburg, Ethel 1896, 198
Brandenburg, Ethel B. 1915, 24
Brandenburg, Etta 1908, 189
Brandenburg, Etta M. 1877, 182
Brandenburg, Eugene Hauver 1925, 44
Brandenburg, Eugene Patrick, 208
Brandenburg, Eunice Estella 1872, 146
Brandenburg, Eva 1864, 56
Brandenburg, Eva 1884, 182

Brandenburg, Eva Blanche 1909, 24
Brandenburg, Eva C. 1905, 47
Brandenburg, Eva I. 1904, 194
Brandenburg, Eve 1763, 6
Brandenburg, Eveline, 51
Brandenburg, Evelyn Crothers 1907, 35, 132
Brandenburg, Evelyn Louise, 141
Brandenburg, Everett 1907, 178
Brandenburg, Ezra 1826, 111
Brandenburg, Ezra Stewart 1868, 117
Brandenburg, Fairy 1903, 131
Brandenburg, Faye Elizabeth 1950, 39
Brandenburg, Finis Edgar 1917, 56
Brandenburg, Flora Edith 1890, 192
Brandenburg, Florence, 28
Brandenburg, Florence 1886, 182
Brandenburg, Florence C. 1872, 141
Brandenburg, Florence E. 1864, 197
Brandenburg, Florence m/1911, 207
Brandenburg, Floyd Clayton 1934, 129
Brandenburg, Floyd Hulbert 1880, 61
Brandenburg, Forrest Dean 1933, 17
Brandenburg, Frances, 118
Brandenburg, Frances Cecelia 1865, 17
Brandenburg, Frances Ollie, 26
Brandenburg, Francis Marion 1844, 54
Brandenburg, Francis Merrill 1899, 55

Brandenburg, Francis W. d/1978, 207

Brandenburg, Frank, 18

Brandenburg, Frank 1854, 57

Brandenburg, Frank C. 1889, 43

Brandenburg, Frank E. 1910, 16

Brandenburg, Frank J. 1911, 181

Brandenburg, Franklin J. 1875, 181

Brandenburg, Franklin Rudell 1940, 165

Brandenburg, Freda M. 1909, 205

Brandenburg, Freddie, 26

Brandenburg, Frederick 1788, 65, 66

Brandenburg, Frederick m/1782, 207

Brandenburg, Gabriel Swan 1850, 95

Brandenburg, Gale W. 1919, 33

Brandenburg, Galen Barkley 1949, 44

Brandenburg, Garrison McLain 1845, 114, 145

Brandenburg, Gary Wayne 1948, 195

Brandenburg, George 1806, 197

Brandenburg, George 1816, 199

Brandenburg, George 1854, 56

Brandenburg, George 1918, 34

Brandenburg, George Clinton 1878, 56

Brandenburg, George E. 1877, 186

Brandenburg, George E. L. H. 1842, 114

Brandenburg, George F. 1883, 203

Brandenburg, George F. m/1905, 207

Brandenburg, George Floyd 1893, 127

Brandenburg, George H., 206

Brandenburg, George Henson 1802, 93

Brandenburg, George Keifer 1883, 34

Brandenburg, George Martin 1825, 15

Brandenburg, George Nevin 1925, 192

Brandenburg, George W. 1856, 202

Brandenburg, George W. 1873, 15

Brandenburg, George Washington 1819, 92

Brandenburg, George Washington 1842, 61

Brandenburg, George Washington 1875, 23

Brandenburg, George Washington m/1950, 208

Brandenburg, George Washington, Jr., 24

Brandenburg, George William 1871, 20

Brandenburg, George Wilson 1861, 69

Brandenburg, Georgia Mae 1938, 201

Brandenburg, Gertrude 1890, 197

Brandenburg, Gertrude 1899, 178

Brandenburg, Gladys P. 1912, 206

Brandenburg, Glencora Elizabeth 1868, 23

Brandenburg, Glenn Hoffmeier 1897, 82

Brandenburg, Gloria Edwina, 26

Brandenburg, Gloria Irene 1930, 40
Brandenburg, Gloria Lee, 187
Brandenburg, Goldie, 146
Brandenburg, Gorman C. 1893, 22
Brandenburg, Grace E., 194
Brandenburg, Grace Edith 1883, 61
Brandenburg, Grace Ellen, 25
Brandenburg, Grace Estelle 1898, 44
Brandenburg, Grace G. 1922, 45
Brandenburg, Grace Rebecca 1899, 82
Brandenburg, Grayson E. 1877, 21
Brandenburg, Green A. 1830, 98
Brandenburg, Green C. 1808, 94
Brandenburg, Guy 1884, 68
Brandenburg, Hannah 1789, 10
Brandenburg, Hannah B. 1879, 188
Brandenburg, Hannah m/1834, 208
Brandenburg, Hanson Ezra 1895, 118
Brandenburg, Harley, 17
Brandenburg, Harold Alvin 1928, 44
Brandenburg, Harold Alvin, Jr. 1957, 44
Brandenburg, Harold Penfield 1902, 55
Brandenburg, Harold Thomas, 202
Brandenburg, Harold Thomas, Jr., 202
Brandenburg, Harold W., 194
Brandenburg, Harriet Lois 1850, 61
Brandenburg, Harriett 1828, 67

Brandenburg, Harriett 1918, 34
Brandenburg, Harry 1894, 69
Brandenburg, Harry E., 34
Brandenburg, Harry L. 1876, 188
Brandenburg, Harry Roscoe 1896, 22
Brandenburg, Hattie Ethylene 1920, 208
Brandenburg, Hazel 1911, 178
Brandenburg, Hazel B., 202
Brandenburg, Hazel C. 1900, 194
Brandenburg, Hazel O. 1910, 69
Brandenburg, Heinrich, 3
Brandenburg, Helen 1903, 69
Brandenburg, Helen 1918, 178
Brandenburg, Helen Adele 1908, 72
Brandenburg, Helen C. 1897, 21
Brandenburg, Helen M. 1898, 113
Brandenburg, Helen V. 1907, 16
Brandenburg, Helen Virginia 1912, 208
Brandenburg, Henning R. 1897, 189
Brandenburg, Henry, 5
Brandenburg, Henry 1765, 88
Brandenburg, Henry 1792, 65, 67
Brandenburg, Henry 1795, 10, 28, 29
Brandenburg, Henry 1823, 52
Brandenburg, Henry 1827, 97
Brandenburg, Henry Adolph 1785, 49, 53
Brandenburg, Henry E. 1832, 62
Brandenburg, Henry E. 1845, 52
Brandenburg, Henry Emerson 1798, 88
Brandenburg, Henry Levi 1853, 30, 32
Brandenburg, Henry m/1793, 208

Brandenburg, Henry m/1804, 208

Brandenburg, Henry m/1831, 208

Brandenburg, Henry T. 1782, 6

Brandenburg, Hepzibah 1835, 114

Brandenburg, Herman E. 1912, 33

Brandenburg, Hester 1788, 98

Brandenburg, Hester 1798, 91

Brandenburg, Hester 1800, 88

Brandenburg, Hester 1808, 94

Brandenburg, Hester 1819, 90

Brandenburg, Hester 1820, 97

Brandenburg, Hilda C. d/1914, 24

Brandenburg, Hilda E. 1909, 139

Brandenburg, Homer Guy 1884, 68

Brandenburg, Hoye Elwood 1917, 191

Brandenburg, Hubert A. 1925, 70

Brandenburg, Ida M. 1878, 179

Brandenburg, Ira 1888, 33

Brandenburg, Ira Clayton 1890, 82

Brandenburg, Ira Franklin 1933, 40

Brandenburg, Irene 1872, 57

Brandenburg, Irving T. 1922, 37

Brandenburg, Isaac 1797, 65, 79, 80

Brandenburg, Isabel 1922, 191

Brandenburg, Isabella 1904, 198

Brandenburg, Israel 1811, 50

Brandenburg, Ivy M. 1896, 194

Brandenburg, J. Andrew 1889, 185

Brandenburg, J. B. 1875, 179

Brandenburg, J. Roger, 209

Brandenburg, Jacob, 1, 2, 10, 102, 103, 206, 208, 209

Brandenburg, Jacob 1783, 65, 66

Brandenburg, Jacob 1792, 50, 57

Brandenburg, Jacob 1818, 208

Brandenburg, Jacob 1832, 185

Brandenburg, Jacob d/1838, 101, 102, 106, 111

Brandenburg, Jacob E. 1873, 186

Brandenburg, Jacob Earl 1896, 17

Brandenburg, Jacob Samuel 1863, 16

Brandenburg, James 1827, 92

Brandenburg, James 1834, 62

Brandenburg, James 1861, 198

Brandenburg, James A. d/1906, 22

Brandenburg, James Adam 1830, 16

Brandenburg, James Buchanan 1856, 21

Brandenburg, James C. 1808, 90

Brandenburg, James C. 1832, 52

Brandenburg, James C. 1868, 70

Brandenburg, James Calvin 1815, 89

Brandenburg, James E. 1864/66, 183

Brandenburg, James M. 1859, 56

Brandenburg, James Michael 1966, 165, 173

Brandenburg, James Oscar 1933, 165, 173

Brandenburg, James R. 1900, 183, 198

Brandenburg, James W. 1887, 178

Brandenburg, James William, III, 202

Brandenburg, James William, Jr. d/1960, 202

Brandenburg, Jane 1805, 94
Brandenburg, Jeanette 1915, 205
Brandenburg, Jefferson 1915, 36
Brandenburg, Jefferson R., 208
Brandenburg, Jeffrey Keith 1966, 166
Brandenburg, Jeffrey Lynn 1963, 44
Brandenburg, Jennie, 33
Brandenburg, Jennie 1890, 69
Brandenburg, Jennie May 1889, 69
Brandenburg, Jeremiah Elsworth 1925, 138
Brandenburg, Jesse, 102, 138
Brandenburg, Jesse B. 1824, 111, 114, 127
Brandenburg, Jesse D. 1878, 186
Brandenburg, Jesse L. 1857, 197
Brandenburg, Jesse R. 1879, 182
Brandenburg, Jesse S. 1898, 119
Brandenburg, Jesse T. 1861, 186
Brandenburg, Jesse W. 1838, 184
Brandenburg, Jessie Fay 1892, 127, 133
Brandenburg, JoAnne, 192
Brandenburg, Joel 1830, 79
Brandenburg, Johan Andonges, 3
Brandenburg, Johann Andonges 1711, 2
Brandenburg, John, 29, 102, 209
Brandenburg, John 1760, 5
Brandenburg, John 1779, 95
Brandenburg, John 1799, 10
Brandenburg, John 1802, 93, 96
Brandenburg, John 1804, 50, 60
Brandenburg, John 1830, 92
Brandenburg, John 1841, 54
Brandenburg, John 1844, 98
Brandenburg, John 1845, 62
Brandenburg, John 1885, 178

Brandenburg, John Adam 1830, 16
Brandenburg, John Conrad, 2
Brandenburg, John David 1827, 188, 190
Brandenburg, John F. 1891, 24
Brandenburg, John F. 1892, 22
Brandenburg, John Henson 1801, 93
Brandenburg, John M. 1837, 52
Brandenburg, John M. 1885, 186
Brandenburg, John m/1794, 208
Brandenburg, John Martin, 2, 4
Brandenburg, John Nathaniel 1822, 12, 19, 25
Brandenburg, John P. 1917, 207
Brandenburg, John R. 1873, 20
Brandenburg, John R. 1917, 178
Brandenburg, John Swan 1812, 95
Brandenburg, John T., 18
Brandenburg, John Thomas 1878, 184
Brandenburg, John W. m/1856, 208
Brandenburg, John Wesley 1872, 189
Brandenburg, John Wesley m/1826, 206, 208
Brandenburg, John William 1840, 60
Brandenburg, John William 1901, 20
Brandenburg, John William Edward 1849, 19
Brandenburg, John Wilson 1849, 52
Brandenburg, Jonas m/1863, 208
Brandenburg, Jonathan 1775, 93
Brandenburg, Jonathan 1797, 89
Brandenburg, Jonathan 1821, 92
Brandenburg, Joseph, 207

Brandenburg, Lawrence 1915, 177

Brandenburg, Leah Ann 1831, 74

Brandenburg, Leah L. 1887, 182

Brandenburg, Leah Marlene 1983, 130

Brandenburg, Leah R., 194

Brandenburg, Lee Ann, 207

Brandenburg, Lee Edward 1941, 36

Brandenburg, Lee Jeffrey 1972, 73

Brandenburg, Lela M. 1885, 205

Brandenburg, Lemuel 1801, 102, 111, 114, 135, 136, 143, 145, 151

Brandenburg, Lemuel 1838, 114

Brandenburg, Lemuel F. 1871, 183

Brandenburg, Lemuel Reece 1870, 146

Brandenburg, Leo 1899, 198

Brandenburg, Leo 1908, 23

Brandenburg, Leroy, 119

Brandenburg, Leroy 1903, 178

Brandenburg, Leroy 1906, 196

Brandenburg, Leslie Clarence 1894, 22

Brandenburg, Leslie F. 1886, 16

Brandenburg, Leta Mae 1899, 55

Brandenburg, Levi 1863, 177

Brandenburg, Levi 1880, 33

Brandenburg, Levi H. 1859, 183

Brandenburg, Lewis Henry 1878, 71

Brandenburg, Lida, 210

Brandenburg, Lida M., 206

Brandenburg, Lillian 1876, 208

Brandenburg, Lillian 1909, 178

Brandenburg, Lillian E. 1916, 181

Brandenburg, Lillian G. 1913, 24

Brandenburg, Lillie 1877, 148

Brandenburg, Linda 1949, 73

Brandenburg, Linda L., 194

Brandenburg, Lizzie, 97

Brandenburg, Lizzie Sue 1865, 81

Brandenburg, Lloyd Claytus, 129

Brandenburg, Lloyd R. 1895, 34

Brandenburg, Lois Marie 1926, 17

Brandenburg, Lola 1898, 203

Brandenburg, Lola Ethel 1894, 55

Brandenburg, Lola May 1895, 140

Brandenburg, Lori Ann 1960, 40

Brandenburg, Lorraine, 140

Brandenburg, Lorraine Mae, 190

Brandenburg, Lottie E. m/1887, 208

Brandenburg, Louis N. 1880, 127

Brandenburg, Louisa 1857, 32

Brandenburg, Louise S. 1911, 205

Brandenburg, Louisiana 1816, 95

Brandenburg, Louisiana 1819, 97

Brandenburg, Lovetta 1889, 36

Brandenburg, Lucile Eleanor 1900, 55

Brandenburg, Lucinda 1830, 54

Brandenburg, Lucinda 1832, 112

Brandenburg, Lucinda 1843, 75

Brandenburg, Lucinda C. 1840, 23

Brandenburg, Lucinda C. 1843, 18

Brandenburg, Lucy 1855, 119

Brandenburg, Lucy Jane 1847, 98

Brandenburg, Luelda 1866, 56

Brandenburg, Lula G. 1894, 185

Brandenburg, Lula G. 1917, 185
Brandenburg, Lula M. 1872, 181
Brandenburg, Lura Lucille 1914, 56
Brandenburg, Lydia Ann 1825, 79
Brandenburg, Lydia Ellen 1853, 56
Brandenburg, Lydia J. 1850, 182
Brandenburg, Lysle 1913, 183
Brandenburg, M. V., 210
Brandenburg, Mabel Elson 1887, 61
Brandenburg, Mack, 201
Brandenburg, Maggie 1865, 198
Brandenburg, Mahala 1804, 102, 106
Brandenburg, Mahala 1834, 73
Brandenburg, Mahala 1836, 74
Brandenburg, Mahala m/1859, 208
Brandenburg, Maisie A. 1904, 183
Brandenburg, Malcolm L., 128
Brandenburg, Malinda 1820, 67
Brandenburg, Malinda C. 1822, 29
Brandenburg, Malinda Steheley, 208
Brandenburg, Mamie A. 1895, 43
Brandenburg, Manzella Ellen 1847, 19
Brandenburg, Marcellus E. 1879, 21
Brandenburg, Margaret 1822, 90
Brandenburg, Margaret 1835, 196
Brandenburg, Margaret 1849, 186
Brandenburg, Margaret E. 1884, 188

Brandenburg, Margaret Lucille, 208
Brandenburg, Margaret M. 1839, 52
Brandenburg, Margarita J. 1917, 25
Brandenburg, Margretta Susanna Rebecca 1906, 71
Brandenburg, Maria, 5
Brandenburg, Maria 1823, 73
Brandenburg, Maria Ann 1820, 11
Brandenburg, Maria m/1774, 208
Brandenburg, Maria m/1846, 208
Brandenburg, Mariah 1817, 92
Brandenburg, Marianna Jane 1916, 24, 193
Brandenburg, Marie 1885, 207
Brandenburg, Marion Granville 1857, 69, 71
Brandenburg, Marion Ruby 1897, 55
Brandenburg, Marjorie 1904, 188
Brandenburg, Marjorie A. 1919, 137
Brandenburg, Marjorie Eva 1901, 17
Brandenburg, Mark Alan 1963, 130
Brandenburg, Marshall E. 1927, 39
Brandenburg, Martha 1800, 91
Brandenburg, Martha Adelaide 1943, 40
Brandenburg, Martha Ann 1855, 56
Brandenburg, Martha C. 1840, 53
Brandenburg, Martha Elizabeth 1872, 183
Brandenburg, Martha Ellen 1850, 98

Brandenburg, Martha Jane 1817, 89

Brandenburg, Martha Jane 1846, 61

Brandenburg, Martha L. 1838, 185

Brandenburg, Martha Sophia 1888, 35, 133

Brandenburg, Martin Calvin m/1861, 208

Brandenburg, Martin L. 1881, 84

Brandenburg, Martin Rufus 1856, 30, 34

Brandenburg, Mary, 51, 102, 104

Brandenburg, Mary 1787, 50

Brandenburg, Mary 1792, 88

Brandenburg, Mary 1802, 50

Brandenburg, Mary 1808, 51

Brandenburg, Mary 1820, 97

Brandenburg, Mary 1858, 57

Brandenburg, Mary 1871, 188

Brandenburg, Mary A., 67

Brandenburg, Mary A. 1874, 21

Brandenburg, Mary A. 1889, 141

Brandenburg, Mary Alice 1918, 26

Brandenburg, Mary Ann 1782, 6

Brandenburg, Mary Ann 1824, 208

Brandenburg, Mary Ann 1828, 79

Brandenburg, Mary Ann 1831, 61

Brandenburg, Mary Ann 1843, 54

Brandenburg, Mary Ann d/1837, 54

Brandenburg, Mary Barbara d/1852, 21

Brandenburg, Mary C. 1888, 203

Brandenburg, Mary C. m/1860, 208

Brandenburg, Mary Catherine 1875, 20

Brandenburg, Mary Catherine 1886, 35

Brandenburg, Mary E., 31

Brandenburg, Mary E. 1826, 29

Brandenburg, Mary E. 1867, 15

Brandenburg, Mary E. 1870, 189

Brandenburg, Mary E. 1897, 177

Brandenburg, Mary E. 1898, 23

Brandenburg, Mary Eliza 1811, 95

Brandenburg, Mary Elizabeth 1853, 21

Brandenburg, Mary Ellen 1848, 75

Brandenburg, Mary Ellen 1852, 52

Brandenburg, Mary Ellen m/1889, 208

Brandenburg, Mary Emma 1923, 38

Brandenburg, Mary G. 1897, 177

Brandenburg, Mary Helen 1926, 164

Brandenburg, Mary J. 1889, 196

Brandenburg, Mary Jane 1846, 181

Brandenburg, Mary L. 1871, 23

Brandenburg, Mary M. 1830, 209

Brandenburg, Mary M. 1867, 186

Brandenburg, Mary M. C. 1884, 182

Brandenburg, Mary m/1801, 10

Brandenburg, Mary m/1816, 208

Brandenburg, Mary Magdalena Clementine America 1848, 21

Brandenburg, Mary Manzella 1849, 114

Brandenburg, Mary Margaret, 190

Brandenburg, Mary Matilda m/1862, 209

Brandenburg, Mary Naomi, 141

Brandenburg, Mary Roberta 1865, 116

Brandenburg, Mathew J. 1842, 53

Brandenburg, Mathias, 1, 2, 103

Brandenburg, Mathias 1744, 4, 5, 87, 88

Brandenburg, Mathias 1763, 6, 65, 66, 67, 73, 78, 79, 83

Brandenburg, Mathias 1837, 209

Brandenburg, Matilda 1840, 114

Brandenburg, Matilda May 1869, 146

Brandenburg, Maude 1898, 198

Brandenburg, Maude 1906, 189

Brandenburg, Maude G. 1889, 20

Brandenburg, Maude Myrtle 1875, 60

Brandenburg, Maulty D. 1881, 149

Brandenburg, Maurice Clayton 1859, 81

Brandenburg, Max A. 1920, 206

Brandenburg, Maxine V., 187

Brandenburg, Maysie Nadine 1897, 130

Brandenburg, Megan, 207

Brandenburg, Merhl H. 1910, 33

Brandenburg, Merhl Hyatt 1910, 133

Brandenburg, Michael, 207

Brandenburg, Michael 1956, 37

Brandenburg, Michael Edward 1962, 40

Brandenburg, Michelle Elizabeth 1989, 130

Brandenburg, Mildred 1901, 188

Brandenburg, Mildred D. 1899, 196

Brandenburg, Mildred E. 1907, 47

Brandenburg, Mildred I. 1911, 24

Brandenburg, Millard W. 1875, 84, 209

Brandenburg, Millson F., 201

Brandenburg, Milton Henry, 209

Brandenburg, Minerva, 51

Brandenburg, Molly, 52

Brandenburg, Morgan 1837, 54

Brandenburg, Moses 1822, 52

Brandenburg, Moses 1834, 54

Brandenburg, Murrill, 209

Brandenburg, Murrill P. 1915, 178

Brandenburg, Musetta Berniece 1925, 18

Brandenburg, Myrtle Oneida, 26

Brandenburg, Myrtle Oneida 1901, 27

Brandenburg, Nancy 1799, 90

Brandenburg, Nancy 1803, 88

Brandenburg, Nancy 1811, 96

Brandenburg, Nancy 1818, 54

Brandenburg, Nancy Amanda 1810, 94

Brandenburg, Nancy Anne 1797, 50

Brandenburg, Nancy J. 1890, 178

Brandenburg, Nancy Joan 1936, 45

Brandenburg, Nancy Kay, 139

Brandenburg, Nancy Lee 1962, 165, 173

Brandenburg, Nellie M. 1882, 30, 42

Brandenburg, Nellie R., 206

Brandenburg, Nellie Rhoda, 187

Brandenburg, Robert F. 1905, 24
Brandenburg, Robert Franklin, 187
Brandenburg, Robert J. 1912, 181
Brandenburg, Robert J. 1918, 177
Brandenburg, Robert Jesse 1879, 182
Brandenburg, Robert Leroy 1927, 165
Brandenburg, Robert Matthew 1976, 130
Brandenburg, Robert W., 207
Brandenburg, Robert W., Jr., 207
Brandenburg, Rodger J. 1901, 21
Brandenburg, Rodney, 141
Brandenburg, Roland 1922, 70
Brandenburg, Roma Lee 1939, 128
Brandenburg, Ronald L. 1942, 72
Brandenburg, Rosalie 1936, 165
Brandenburg, Rosanna Catherine Magdalena 1838, 18
Brandenburg, Roscoe Hamilton 1901, 47
Brandenburg, Ross 1888, 45
Brandenburg, Roy G. 1890, 205
Brandenburg, Roy O. W. 1898, 138
Brandenburg, Roy R., 33
Brandenburg, Roy Vern 1890, 16
Brandenburg, Ruby Frances 1915, 209
Brandenburg, Rudell Leroy 1905, 164
Brandenburg, Rudolph 1924, 195
Brandenburg, Rudolph L. 1907, 205
Brandenburg, Rufus 1898, 203
Brandenburg, Rufus 1916, 203

Brandenburg, Rufus Edgar 1893, 36
Brandenburg, Rufus Edgar 1914, 36
Brandenburg, Rufus Mahlon d/1917, 17
Brandenburg, Russell F. 1891, 44
Brandenburg, Russell R. 1905, 23
Brandenburg, Russell T., 45
Brandenburg, Ruth, 207
Brandenburg, Ruth 1790, 98
Brandenburg, Ruth Ann 1814, 94
Brandenburg, Ruth E., 208
Brandenburg, Ruth Gwenn 1894, 17
Brandenburg, Ruth M. 1896, 47
Brandenburg, Ruth Valerie 1926, 129
Brandenburg, Ryan Mark 1987, 130
Brandenburg, S. 1886, 205
Brandenburg, Sabina, 51
Brandenburg, Sadie Ellen 1883, 42
Brandenburg, Sallie V., 43
Brandenburg, Sally, 98
Brandenburg, Sally 1800, 90
Brandenburg, Salome, 206
Brandenburg, Samuel 1735, 49
Brandenburg, Samuel 1756, 5, 9, 10, 28
Brandenburg, Samuel 1774, 92
Brandenburg, Samuel 1783, 6
Brandenburg, Samuel 1784, 49, 51
Brandenburg, Samuel 1786, 98
Brandenburg, Samuel 1820, 51
Brandenburg, Samuel 1823, 57
Brandenburg, Samuel 1824, 29, 32, 34, 41, 43, 45, 46
Brandenburg, Samuel 1827, 92

Brandenburg, Samuel Clayton 1866, 22, 24
Brandenburg, Samuel Dooley 1800, 90
Brandenburg, Samuel E. 1847, 52
Brandenburg, Samuel Edward 1868, 113
Brandenburg, Samuel Gideon 1891, 36
Brandenburg, Samuel K. 1890, 43
Brandenburg, Samuel Keefer 1881, 33
Brandenburg, Samuel Lee 1830, 209
Brandenburg, Samuel m/1835, 209
Brandenburg, Samuel m/1860, 209
Brandenburg, Samuel Ray 1901, 44
Brandenburg, Samuel Ray, Jr. 1923, 44
Brandenburg, Samuel Rice 1910, 47
Brandenburg, Samuel Rue 1910, 47
Brandenburg, Samuel Tracy 1858, 30, 41
Brandenburg, Samuel, Jr. 1793, 9, 10, 19, 27
Brandenburg, Sandra Jane 1944, 195
Brandenburg, Sanford 1811, 92
Brandenburg, Sarah 1781, 96
Brandenburg, Sarah 1808, 50
Brandenburg, Sarah 1809, 89, 92
Brandenburg, Sarah 1812, 51
Brandenburg, Sarah 1820, 209
Brandenburg, Sarah 1823, 54
Brandenburg, Sarah 1854, 209

Brandenburg, Sarah 1886, 21
Brandenburg, Sarah Ann 1823, 97
Brandenburg, Sarah Ann 1836, 80
Brandenburg, Sarah Ann Rebecca 1862, 22
Brandenburg, Sarah C. 1861, 113
Brandenburg, Sarah D. 1886, 203
Brandenburg, Sarah E., 33
Brandenburg, Sarah E. 1821, 197
Brandenburg, Sarah E. 1843, 198
Brandenburg, Sarah E. 1860, 136
Brandenburg, Sarah E. 1885, 209
Brandenburg, Sarah Henrietta 1770, 88
Brandenburg, Sarah Jane 1937, 192
Brandenburg, Sarah Jane m/1957, 209
Brandenburg, Sarah L. 1860, 209
Brandenburg, Sarah Louisa 1843, 114, 143
Brandenburg, Sarah M. 1890, 22
Brandenburg, Sarah R. 1917, 206
Brandenburg, Saris G. 1886, 205
Brandenburg, Seany Elizabeth 1845, 95
Brandenburg, Sellman J. 1898, 119
Brandenburg, Sharon Kay 1957, 130
Brandenburg, Sharon Lee 1956, 40
Brandenburg, Sherri Ann 1963, 165
Brandenburg, Shirley, 118
Brandenburg, Shirley Ann 1934, 165
Brandenburg, Silas 1825, 57

Brandenburg, Solomon, 49
Brandenburg, Solomon 1700, 2, 4, 5, 87, 101
Brandenburg, Solomon 1777, 94
Brandenburg, Solomon 1803, 91
Brandenburg, Solomon Preston 1794, 88
Brandenburg, Stephen 1861, 198
Brandenburg, Stephen Thomas 1968, 83
Brandenburg, Steven Taft 1973, 195
Brandenburg, Steven Thomas 1943, 44
Brandenburg, Stewart Johnson 1865, 113
Brandenburg, Sue Fair 1945, 191
Brandenburg, Susan, 52
Brandenburg, Susan 1811, 89
Brandenburg, Susan 1821, 54
Brandenburg, Susan 1823, 92
Brandenburg, Susan A. 1874, 183
Brandenburg, Susan Ann m/1841, 209
Brandenburg, Susan L. 1894, 140
Brandenburg, Susannah 1790, 10
Brandenburg, Susannah 1795, 50, 57
Brandenburg, Susannah 1816, 51
Brandenburg, Susannah 1847, 98
Brandenburg, Susie L. 1860, 137
Brandenburg, Sybell R. 1873, 120
Brandenburg, T. H., 209
Brandenburg, Teri 1954, 195
Brandenburg, Thelma 1909, 181
Brandenburg, Theodore McAuley 1855, 68
Brandenburg, Thomas 1842, 84

Brandenburg, Thomas Emory 1941, 83
Brandenburg, Thomas Hamilton 1860, 22
Brandenburg, Thomas Simmon 1839, 60
Brandenburg, Thomas Solomon Independence 1822, 95
Brandenburg, Tilghman J. 1910, 139
Brandenburg, Timothy Wayne 1959, 40
Brandenburg, Tyson Willard 1956, 40
Brandenburg, Veronica M. 1955, 37
Brandenburg, Victor 1906, 198
Brandenburg, Vinnie Frederica 1904, 71
Brandenburg, Viola Virginia 1905, 71
Brandenburg, Virgie H. 1892, 16
Brandenburg, Virginia Ann 1925, 69
Brandenburg, Virginia L., 194
Brandenburg, Virginia T. 1869, 185
Brandenburg, Vivian May 1912, 72
Brandenburg, W. B., 206
Brandenburg, W. Clinton, 184
Brandenburg, Walter Edgar 1871, 55
Brandenburg, Walter Edgar 1918, 55
Brandenburg, Walter G. 1872, 196
Brandenburg, Walter L. 1896, 113
Brandenburg, Walter V. 1910, 183
Brandenburg, Wanda L., 194

Brandenburg, Wayne L., 187
Brandenburg, Wilbur 1897, 113
Brandenburg, Wilbur H., 43
Brandenburg, Wilhelm Heinrich 1722, 4, 5, 6, 9, 49, 65, 87
Brandenburg, Wilhemina Anna 1859, 116
Brandenburg, William, 1, 102, 103
Brandenburg, William 1758, 5, 6
Brandenburg, William 1785, 6
Brandenburg, William 1790, 50, 53, 54
Brandenburg, William 1822, 57
Brandenburg, William 1828, 210
Brandenburg, William 1862, 57
Brandenburg, William 1886, 197
Brandenburg, William 1897, 186
Brandenburg, William A. 1917, 203
Brandenburg, William A. d/1963, 141
Brandenburg, William Aaron 1869, 55
Brandenburg, William Aaron 1910, 55
Brandenburg, William Arnold 1917, 137
Brandenburg, William Asbury 1887, 137
Brandenburg, William Aubrey 1917, 37
Brandenburg, William Aubrey, Jr. 1948, 37
Brandenburg, William B., 210
Brandenburg, William Bromwell 1869, 140
Brandenburg, William Dean 1947, 209
Brandenburg, William Dewey 1899, 140

Brandenburg, William E. 1900, 113
Brandenburg, William Elmer 1904, 41
Brandenburg, William H. 1758, 49
Brandenburg, William H. 1862, 112
Brandenburg, William H. 1909, 21
Brandenburg, William Hanson 1863, 189, 190
Brandenburg, William Henry, 2
Brandenburg, William Howard Taft 1908, 194
Brandenburg, William L. 1872, 182
Brandenburg, William L. 1906, 16
Brandenburg, William Lee 1826, 66
Brandenburg, William M. 1877, 181
Brandenburg, William m/1795, 210
Brandenburg, William m/1806, 210
Brandenburg, William R. 1829, 112, 136
Brandenburg, William S., 51
Brandenburg, William S. 1836, 52
Brandenburg, William Washington 1873, 70
Brandenburg, Willie B. 1874, 186
Brandenburg, Willie E. 1897, 210
Brandenburg, Wilmer H. 1901, 43
Brandenburg, Windsor M. 1890, 117

243

Butt, Donald Eugene, Jr. 1955, 121

Butt, Jacob Watkins 1987, 121

Butt, Kathleen Lee 1984, 121

Butt, Mark Timothy 1958, 121

Butts, Charles Earl 1893, 70

Buxton, Basil Francis 1843, 115, 120

Buxton, Brook, 115

Buxton, Delma Viola 1893, 120

Buxton, Emma Rose 1874, 115

Buxton, Helen E. 1880, 116, 120

Buxton, Upton, 120

Byerly, Rebecca, 10

—C—

Calhoon, George, 95

Campbell, Edward, 137

Cantrell, Marsha Lynn 1946, 134

Cantrell, Verdin Smith, 134

Carmichael, Henry, 56

Carmin, Sarah Jane 1848, 52

Cartee, Betty Jane 1931, 208

Cartee, Mary Ellen, 190

Carter, Adaline 1842, 60

Cary, Allen, 156

Castle, Effie, 19

Castle, George, 19

Castle, Joseph E., 19

Castle, Mary, 19

Castle, Rebecca, 19

Cawthorn, Charles, 136

Chain, Sarah L. 1918, 149

Chance, 101, 102, 106, 111

Chance Resurveyed, 101

Chandler, Claude Swenson, 154

Charley, Lydia 1803, 94

Chase, Julia Ann 1941, 158

Chase, Philip Scott 1953, 158

Chase, Theodore W., III 1940, 158

Chase, Theodore W., Jr. 1914, 158

Chertoff, Gordon Alan, 161

Chick, Marie Allen 1921, 170

Chittester, Hannah, 51

Christianson, Ralph, 56

Clagett, Nathan, 145

Clark, Della May 1890, 17

Clay, Barry, 147

Clay, Bonnie Lou, 147

Clay, Carol, 144

Clay, Jackson, 144

Clay, Linda, 144

Clay, Mabel, 144

Clay, Mary Margaret, 116

Clay, Paul B., 147

Clay, Paul Dale, 147

Clay, Sterling, 144

Clay, Thelma, 144

Clay, Thomas Glen, 147

Clem, Blaine Edward, 25

Clickner, Dale Thomas 1930, 125

Clickner, Dale Thomas, Jr. 1960, 125

Clickner, James Andrew 1961, 125

Cline, Charles, 22

Cline, Charles L., 22

Cline, Elmer, 22

Cline, Harry, 22

Cline, John, 22

Cline, Michael Lee 1951, 123

Cline, Robin Lynne 1954, 124

Cline, Walter Lee 1898, 123

Cline, Walter Lee 1926, 123

Coblentz, Albert Martin 1883, 81

Coblentz, Annie Remsburg 1876, 81

Coblentz, Calvin R. 1863, 81

Coblentz, Catherine, 13

Coblentz, Elizabeth, 80

Coblentz, Henry 1807, 81
Coblentz, L. P., 14
Coblentz, Lizzie Adeline 1888, 81
Coblentz, Martin Calvin 1849, 81
Coblentz, Mary Margaret 1765, 78
Coblentz, Maurice Daniel 1885, 81
Coblentz, Philip 1812, 81
Coblentz, Victor Clayton 1878, 81
Coblentz, Walter Calvin 1880, 81
Coblentz, William Henry 1874, 81
Cochran, No given name, 107
Cole, Thomas, 53
Collier, Beverly Diane 1944, 153
Collier, Janice Gayle 1946, 153
Collier, Jayne Blair 1953, 153
Collier, Joseph Bernard 1921, 153
Colliflower, George, 208
Collins, John 1848, 61
Combs, Elizabeth Ann, 92
Compton, Rosemary, 130
Condon, Mary Catherine, 116
Congleton, Isaac 1805, 90
Conoway, Cora, 184
Conoway, Margaret 1876, 183
Conrad, William J., 98
Cook, Henry, 184
Coon, George, 139
Cooper, Melissa Jane 1849, 60
Cordi, Estella 1886, 26
Covell, Carrie Lynn 1972, 38
Covell, Jonathan Forrest 1916, 38
Covell, Jonathan Wayne 1950, 38

Covell, Lorna Jean 1946, 38
Covell, Thomas Bernard 1948, 38
Craig, Mariah, 94
Cramer, Annie Louise 1909, 209
Cramer, John, 10
Crawford, Carroll, 183
Crawford, Clara Leone 1880, 12
Crawford, Jane 1808, 93
Crawford, Margaret, 183
Crew, Terry 1957, 153
Crone, Alta Susan 1886, 14
Crone, Chancellor Livingston 1857, 14
Crone, Charles Thomas 1888, 14
Crone, Flora Rebecca 1884, 14
Crone, Frederick Lewis 1882, 14
Crook, Adaline O. 1817, 89
Crook, John 1798, 88
Crum, Shirley Ann 1935, 168
Crummitt, Stanley 1917, 208
Crumpacker, Summer, 108
Crutcher, Burr Harrison 1804, 94
Culler, William, 206
Cummings, Catherine 1780, 96
Currier, Joseph C., 58
Cutsail, Julie Ann 1965, 83
Cutsail, Lawrence, Jr. 1934, 83

—D—

Dabbadanza, Betty, 27
Dabbadanza, Vincent, 27
Dailey, Douglas Alan, 134
Darby, No given name, 146
Darby, Windsor D., 146
Dasher, Elizabeth, 142
David, Ralph, 186
Davies, Gene Richard, 154
Davies, Shirley Jean 1943, 154
Davis, Jama Cheri 1954, 192
Davis, James K., 192

Davis, James Kent 1955, 192
Davis, John, 77
Davis, Kathryn Debra 1975, 161
Davis, Laura Helen 1874, 162
Davis, R. Lee, 162
Davis, R. Leslie 1891, 162
Davis, Robert Francis 1954, 161
Davis, Ruth 1904, 172
Dawson, Harriett, 91
Day, Addison Singleton 1856, 151, 156
Day, Alan Christopher 1962, 168
Day, Alice Marie 1922, 163
Day, Altona Bovincia Clintinchia 1857, 151
Day, Anna Lucille 1902, 164
Day, Annie Griffith 1896, 157
Day, Barbara Ann 1938, 167
Day, Barbara Loretta 1939, 155
Day, Basil Boyer 1936, 168
Day, Basil Boyer, Jr. 1958, 168
Day, Brenda Jean 1948, 166
Day, Brian Keith 1968, 168
Day, Carol Ann 1968, 166
Day, Carroll Davis 1944, 166
Day, Cheryl Ann 1954, 167
Day, Cindy Lou 1957, 167
Day, Clara Lavinia 1913, 154
Day, Clarence Emory 1901, 163
Day, Claude Randolph 1906, 154
Day, Daisy May 1891, 156
Day, David Ellis 1943, 157
Day, David Franklin 1949, 156
Day, Doris Jane 1946, 170
Day, Dorothy Jean 1929, 166
Day, Douglas Edsel 1945, 157
Day, Douglas Robert 1961, 170
Day, Effie Madeline 1912, 169
Day, Emil Rodney 1921, 155
Day, Ethel Virginia 1897, 162
Day, Evelyn Jane 1933, 168
Day, Evelyn Louise 1943, 170

Day, Gary Wayne 1952, 166
Day, Gayle Marie 1953, 168
Day, Gregory Robert 1966, 157
Day, Hanford Perry 1916, 170
Day, Harold Lewis 1888, 158
Day, Harriet Emma 1863, 151, 159
Day, Harrison Edward 1888, 156
Day, Helen Mildred 1909, 168
Day, Howard Michael 1948, 157
Day, Ira Eugene 1880, 152
Day, Ivah May 1901, 174
Day, James Murray 1926, 166
Day, James Sellman 1899, 162
Day, James Start 1865, 151, 162
Day, Janet Louise 1937, 168
Day, Janice June Louise 1904, 153
Day, Jean Shirley 1951, 156
Day, Jesse Downey, Jr. 1914, 156
Day, Joan Marie 1954, 166
Day, Joelle Denise 1971, 157
Day, John Marvin 1951, 168
Day, Joseph Loren 1965, 175
Day, Judith Elaine 1953, 167
Day, Karen 1957, 156
Day, Kelsel Williams 1907, 167
Day, Kelsel Williams, Jr. 1931, 167
Day, Kenneth Berkely 1964, 166
Day, Kenneth Lee 1930, 166
Day, Kevin Scott 1955, 168
Day, Langdon Storrs 1871, 151, 174
Day, Larry Langdon 1962, 175
Day, Latimer W. 1852, 152
Day, Lattimer W. 1852, 151, 152
Day, Laura Ann 1915, 156
Day, Laura Arvilla 1867, 151, 171
Day, Laura Helen 1920, 163
Day, Leroy Edward 1927, 156

Dodson, Adam Charles 1983, 122

Dodson, Bedford Ashley 1936, 122

Dodson, Norman Bedford 1954, 122

Dorsey, Emma C., 184

Dorsey, Paige, 192

Doub, Sarah A. 1831, 76

Dowell, Christopher M., 95

Drake, Aaron 1825, 58

Drake, Edward 1782, 57

Drake, Julia Ann 1816, 58

Drake, Mary 1826, 58

Drake, Peter 1828, 58

Drake, Rebecca, 50, 54

Drake, Rebecca 1819, 58

Drake, Sarah E. 1832, 58

Draper, No given name, 42

Dreisonstok, Daniel Jacob 1986, 195

Dreisonstok, John, 195

Dreisonstok, John Dustin 1981, 195

Drewry, Beverly Jean 1950, 143

Drisch, Christy Lynn 1973, 166

Drisch, Robert Osborne 1946, 166

Driskill, Jack, 132

Driskill, Linda Ann 1953, 132

Driskill, Mary, 132

Drummond, James, 26

Dudley, Peter, 54

Dunn, Lewis Mankor 1867, 62

Dunn, Okey 1874, 62

Dutrow, Eleanora 1838, 78

Duvall, Alfrieda Mae 1940, 169

Duvall, Alice Louise 1971, 160

Duvall, Barbara, 138

Duvall, Brandon Woodrow 1913, 159

Duvall, Christopher Brandon 1969, 160

Duvall, Ethel, 128

Duvall, Herbert Sherwood 1945, 160

Duvall, Jeannette Louise 1944, 160

Duvall, Jerry Brandon 1943, 159

Duvall, No given name, 138

Dwelly, Mamie 1874, 59

Dwyer, Paul, 26

Dwyer, Ronald Paul, 26

—E—

Eagle, Sandra Lynn 1944, 160

Easterday, Anita, 139

Easterday, Hubert Conrad 1902, 71

Easterday, Jordon Alan, 139

Easterday, No given name, 43, 139

Easterday, Robert Franklin, 139

Easterday, Sandra Kay, 139

Eaves, Ruth 1917, 36

Egbert, James, 50

Ehrenberg, Ernest 1891, 171

Eisenbeis, Sally Jo 1937, 168

Eisenberg, Sally Jo 1937, 168

Ekeberg, Marquis A. 1861, 59

Emswiler, Charles William 1925, 165

Emswiler, David Leroy 1953, 173

Emswiler, Donald Lee 1954, 165

Emswiler, George Evert 1931, 173

Emswiler, Kirk Walker 1959, 173

Emswiler, Larry Wayne 1953, 165

Gaver, William, 33
Gay, Helen Howard 1875, 61
Gaylor, Mary Gertrude 1923, 70
Gebhard, Elizabeth, 208
Geisler, Amy Marie 1982, 35, 133
Geisler, Barbara, 35
Geisler, Carole Jean 1961, 35, 133
Geisler, Donna Kay 1956, 35, 133
Geisler, Edwin B., 35
Geisler, Elizabeth 1914, 35
Geisler, Emma S., 35
Geisler, Gary Lee 1952, 35, 133
Geisler, James Wesley 1896, 35, 133
Geisler, Lori Ann 1963, 35, 133
Geisler, M. Frances, 35
Geisler, Mary Lucille, 35
Geisler, William Wesley 1927, 35, 133
Gephart, Elizabeth, 6
Gerhart, Melva 1948, 126
Gibson, Letitia, 53
Gill, David Ernest 1970, 173
Gill, John Arthur 1925, 173
Glaze, Basil Russell, 129
Glaze, Cathie May 1952, 129
Glaze, John Russell 1922, 128
Glaze, Judith Marie 1947, 129
Golden, Michael Oliver 1862, 12
Goodacre, Emma, 207
Gordon, Mary Jane F. 1836, 90
Gorner, Elizabeth, 208
Gorner, Phebe, 208
Gosnell, Tyson, 184
Gough, Muriel, 17
Grable, John, 89
Grable, Solomon, 89
Graf, Hans, 3
Graf, Jagli, 3

Graham, No given name, 122, 123
Granahan, No given name, 124
Graser, Mary Catherine, 38
Gravett, Sarah, 92
Green, Effie Mary 1870, 70
Green, John W. 1846, 70
Green, Rosia Mary 1942, 170
Green, Thomas C., 97
Gregory, Fred Watkins 1949, 73
Griesert, Herbert, 207
Grigg, Donald Wayne, 143
Grigg, Jody Owen 1978, 143
Grigg, Kelly Dawn 1975, 143
Grigg, Robert Henry 1970, 143
Grigsby, Christopher Hull 1949, 135
Grigsby, Don Ellsworth 1942, 135
Grigsby, Don Ellsworth, Jr. 1964, 135
Grigsby, Donald Edward 1918, 135
Grigsby, Heather Lea 1973, 135
Grigsby, Heidi 1972, 135
Grigsby, Shane 1973, 135
Grimes, Albert, 183
Grimes, Charles, 183
Grimes, Donald, 183
Grimes, Marvin, 183
Grimes, May, 183
Grimes, Pearl, 184
Grimes, Ray, 183
Grimm, J. Mahlon, 207
Groomes, Achsah 1852, 203
Grossman, John, 52
Grossnickle, Blain, 42
Grossnickle, Carol Ann 1944, 191
Grossnickle, Charles Basil, Rev., 191

Grossnickle, Dale Eugene 1971, 191

Grossnickle, George P., 32

Grossnickle, Harry, 33

Grossnickle, Julia Ann Catharine 1829, 29, 32, 34, 41, 43, 45, 46

Grossnickle, Julia Ann Catherine 1829, 29

Grossnickle, Louisa C. 1856, 32

Grossnickle, Sarah Ann, 32

Gue, No given name, 138

Gue, Sadie Elizabeth 1901, 174

Gunther, Bertha, 106

Guyton, Bradley Charles 1962, 192

Guyton, Darrell Thomas 1965, 192

Guyton, Gail Thomas 1940, 192

Guyton, Lydia, 208

Guyton, Sharon Lea 1964, 192

Gwartney, Sarah Ann, 94

—H—

Haggard, Adaline, 92

Hahn, Francis, 118

Haines, Bonnie, 123

Haines, Camrell, 123

Haines, Kenneth, 123

Haines, Lola M. 1896, 36

Haines, Maizie H. 1925, 126

Haines, Michael, 123

Haines, Nathaniel, 123

Haines, Sharon, 123

Haines, Walter Edward 1890, 126

Hall, Hazel Viola, 120

Hall, Martin, 96

Halliday, Glen 1897, 55

Hamblin, Omer, 13

Hamilton, James, 62

Hamilton, No given name, 42

Hamilton, Rhoda 1810, 90

Hanchett, Caroline 1874, 55

Hanklin, Judith Ann 1954, 172

Hanklin, William Maxwell Tees 1929, 171

Hanklin, William Maxwell Tees, II 1956, 172

Hannon, Elizabeth, 128

Harbaugh, Anna M. 1873, 47

Harbaugh, Hamilton, 47

Harbaugh, Susan Dorothy 1874, 47

Harding, David Michael 1950, 154

Harding, Paul Jeffrey 1946, 154

Harding, Warren George 1923, 154

Hargerhymer, Mary Magdalena 1759, 9, 10, 28

Harne, Brenda Lynn 1964, 191

Harne, Danny Lee 1962, 191

Harne, Jeffrey Glenn 1966, 191

Harne, Merhl Glenn, 191

Harne, Oliver Glenn 1895, 70

Harp, Amanda Catherine 1857, 68

Harp, Clara Virginia, 72

Harp, Edith 1882, 72

Harp, Jennie 1882, 72

Harp, Josiah, 68

Harrendon, William, 88

Harris, Edith, 183

Harrison, Cheryl Jeanne 1948, 157

Harryman, Shirley Laura, 128

Harshman, Ada Alice 1875, 189

Harshman, Amy Jo 1982, 39

Harshman, Anne Marie 1966, 191

Harshman, Charles, 33

Harshman, Charles Daniel 1955, 39
Harshman, Christie Dawn 1966, 39
Harshman, Cornelius, 189
Harshman, Elizabeth Ann 1968, 39
Harshman, Gareth Wayne 1950, 39
Harshman, Gaylen Patrick 1968, 39
Harshman, Harold David 1923, 38
Harshman, Harold David, Jr. 1946, 38
Harshman, Harry Herbert, 38
Harshman, Jeffrey Allen 1968, 38
Harshman, Katherine JoAnn 1970, 39
Harshman, Kimberly Diane 1967, 39
Harshman, Leslie Ann 1971, 38
Harshman, Melissa Ann 1959, 39
Harshman, Monica Jean 1975, 39
Harshman, Richard Lee 1941, 191
Harshman, Richard Lee, II 1965, 191
Harshman, Ronald Lee 1947, 38
Harshman, Sue Ellen 1962, 191
Hart, Anna, 106
Hartsock, Bertha E. 1892, 24
Hashhagen, Helen Florence, 76
Haupt, Simon David 1852, 17
Haupt, Simon Jacob 1888, 17
Hauver, Rae Irene 1901, 44
Hawse, Allen Roosevelt 1946, 129
Hawse, Beverly Michelle 1968, 129

Hawse, Michael Allen 1974, 129
Hawse, William, 129
Hayden, Rachel Shacklett, 96
Hayes, Thomas 1819, 97
Hays, Albert E., 31
Hays, Geraldine Reba 1901, 31
Healey, Rhoda, 70
Heffner, Joann Marie 1956, 39
Heffner, Paul Luther, 39
Hefner, Clifford 1922, 163
Heller, Kathleen Newton 1922, 39
Helm, Mary Elizabeth 1860, 58
Helm, Sarah Emily 1866, 59
Helsel, Deborah Gail 1964, 130
Helsel, James A., 130
Helwig, Amanda Lou 1951, 168
Hendershot, Ellen Jane, 54
Henson, Sarah 1780, 93
Herbat, No given name, 43
Herring, Edward L. 1817, 79
Hershberger, Lou Ellen 1899, 16
Hessong, Arthur Jacob 1920, 42
Hessong, Charles William 1926, 42
Hessong, George M. L. 1918, 42
Hessong, James Ellsworth 1870, 42
Hessong, James Ellsworth, Jr. 1908, 42
Hessong, John Thomas, 42
Hessong, John Thomas, III 1913, 42
Hessong, Joseph Ezra 1915, 42
Hessong, Naomi Elizabeth 1906, 42
Hessong, Parker Oliver 1924, 42
Hessong, Paul Andrew 1929, 42
Hessong, Robert Lee 1922, 42
Hessong, Ruby Matilda 1904, 42
Hessong, Ruth Sarah 1910, 42
Hewitt, George 1815, 136

Hewitt, Laura Richard 1855, 135
Hewitt, Melissa, 80
Hickman, Russell, 26
Hill, Lucille 1904, 158
Hilton, Mary Catharine 1928, 132
Hilton, Ray 1893, 132
Himes, Anna Margaret 1949, 39
Himes, Richard Maxwell, 39
Hines, Abraham 1812, 58
Hines, William, 58
Hipkins, Rufus Burkett 1911, 35
Hipkins, Walter 1890, 35
Hoff, Blanche Viola 1880, 13
Hoff, Isaac 1852, 13
Hoff, Lewis Calvin 1876, 13
Hoff, Lillie Montrose 1878, 13
Hoffman, Louise, 129
Hogan, George, 125
Holiday, Henry Clay, 98
Holz, Richard G., Dr., 121
Holz, Susan Marie 1959, 121
Hood, Larry, 168
Hooper, John William 1862, 32
Hoover, Claretta Virginia 1853, 189
Hopkins, Elizabeth, 76
Hopping, Albert 1862, 59
Hopping, Albert John 1837, 59
Hopping, Albert M. 1841, 60
Hopping, Alberta 1868, 60
Hopping, Anna 1862, 59
Hopping, Chalres Louis 1859, 59
Hopping, David S., Jr. 1831, 59
Hopping, David S., Sr., 58
Hopping, Eliza, 59
Hopping, Eliza 1840, 59
Hopping, Eliza 1861, 59
Hopping, Elizabeth 1837, 59
Hopping, Elizabeth 1859, 59
Hopping, Ellery Elwood 1857, 59
Hopping, Ezekiel 1826, 59

Hopping, Ezekiel R. 1822, 58
Hopping, Franklin 1835, 59
Hopping, Gladys 1867, 60
Hopping, James L. 1852, 58
Hopping, Jane 1824, 59
Hopping, John 1857, 58
Hopping, Letitia B. 1847, 60
Hopping, Mary Elizabeth 1865, 59
Hopping, Mary Ellen 1855, 58
Hopping, Mary M. 1823, 58
Hopping, Sarah, 59
Hopping, Sarah 1855, 59
Hopping, Sarah Ann 1830, 59
Hopping, William Horace 1853, 59
Hopping, William Morris 1866, 59
Horine, Mary Catherine 1843, 207
Hornbuckle, Mary Elizabeth 1925, 156
House, Mary, 92
Houser, No given name, 185
Hubble, Brenda Lee 1961, 165
Hubble, Keith Allen 1959, 165
Hubble, Kevin Richard 1957, 165
Hubble, Marvin W. 1932, 165
Hubble, Robert Lee 1952, 165
Huffman, Nancy J., 62
Hughbanks, James, 96
Hughes, Burgess, 185
Humbert, Anna Maria 1747, 65
Hummer, Roy Christopher, 76
Hummer, Ruth Lorraine 1927, 76
Hurley, Alfred Ellsworth 1937, 142
Hurley, Bruce Edward 1960, 142
Hurley, Connie Elaine 1966, 142
Hurley, Daniel c.1658, 141
Hurley, David Allen 1968, 142

Keller, Catherine, 66
Keller, Charlotte 1769, 65
Keller, Harry Nevin 1925, 174
Keller, John Jacob 1743, 65
Keller, Joyce Helen 1961, 174
Keller, Lola Virginia 1897, 36
Keller, Mary Jane 1845, 78
Keller, Paul Nevin 1959, 174
Keller, Sonja Mae, 45
Kemp, Janiele Anita 1962, 167
Kemp, Julia Emily, 209
Kemp, Julie Renee 1960, 167
Kemp, Mary, 29
Kemp, Mary 1794, 28
Kemp, Michael Allen 1959, 167
Kemp, Ralph Eugene 1938, 167
Kern, Will Browning, 158
Kiefer, Diana, 134
Kiefer, Patricia Dale 1943, 134
Kiefer, William James 1914, 134
Kiefer, William James, Jr. 1947,
134
Kindley, Charlotte 1804, 111,
114, 135, 136, 143, 145, 151
Kindley, George Frederick, 101
Kindley, John, 101
Kindley, William 1770, 111
King, Bertie May 1886, 129
King, Douglas M. 1963, 158
King, Harriet Ann 1807, 144,
151
King, Holly Ann 1965, 158
King, Jemima 1805, 114, 135
King, Leslie, 119
King, Richard M., 158
King, Sarah, 103
King, Sarah Elizabeth 1888, 138
Kingsley, Simeon, 97
Kinna, Mary E. 1860, 69
Kirchgassner, George, 132
Kirchgassner, Marjorie, 132
Kirchgassner, Patricia, 132

Kline, Arthur Franklin 1910, 189
Kline, Florence Geraldine, 194
Kline, Herman, 30
Kline, Joseph, 76
Kline, Louise, 190
Kline, Malinda, 41
Kline, Matilda, 42
Kline, Vera Naomi 1924, 25, 193
Kline, William Guy 1882, 76
Knapp, John, 97
Knox, Charles 1854, 74
Knox, David H., 208
Knox, David William 1820, 73
Knox, Effie J. C., 74
Knox, Emma 1859, 74
Knox, Mary 1848, 74
Knox, Sarah 1851, 74
Koogle, Barbara 1755, 66
Koon, George, 139
Korth, Ingrid, 156
Kosenski, Sharon, 124
Kramer, Philip, 208
Krantz, Beverly Kaye 1947, 157
Krantz, Henry Cornelius, Jr.
1917, 157
Krantz, Kenneth Edward 1941,
157
Kuhn, Elizabeth Ann, 44
Kuhn, Marian, 119
Kyber, No given name, 202

—L—

LaForce, David Rene, 98
Lajoie, Samuel, 208
Langwell, Charlotte, 208
Lantz, Christine, 83
Lape, Grace Ann 1884, 12
Latham, Althah Ernestine 1918,
155
Lawler, Mary Ann, 58
Lawson, Dianne Cecil 1941, 161

Miller, Elsie 1938, 125
Miller, Frederick 1933, 126
Miller, Glenn Michael 1958, 125
Miller, Glenn Scott 1974, 126
Miller, Helen G. 1941, 125
Miller, Herbert Allen 1945, 126
Miller, Herbert Gervis 1914, 125
Miller, James, 18
Miller, Joyce Ann 1937, 125
Miller, Mary 1943, 126
Miller, Michael Allen 1967, 126
Miller, Patricia Ann 1971, 126
Miller, Pearl B. 1885, 13
Miller, Susan Regina, 143
Miller, William David 1950, 126
Minnick, Charles E., 74
Minor, Victoria, 62
Miracle, Jesse, 107
Miracle, Rachel A., 107
Miss, Mary, 82
Miss, Sandra Lee, 82
Mitchell, Drucilla Iona, 134
Mitchell, James 1856, 59
Moats, Nancy Virginia 1946, 195
Mobley, Helen, 115
Molesworth, Albert, 138
Monahan, Pauline, 192
Montgomery, Theresa 1830, 95
Montlenone, Dawn Bliss 1979, 125
Montlenone, Michael, 125
Moore, Bryan Joseph 1941, 192
Moore, Bryan Joseph, III 1970, 193
Moore, George, 14
Moore, Marilyn R., 158
Morgan, Ann 1967, 193
Morgan, Cindy Lou 1956, 193
Morgan, Dwight Irving 1945, 193
Morgan, Evelyn Annabelle, 39
Morgan, Gloria Ann 1943, 192

Morgan, Irving Recher, 192
Morgan, Joyce Jean 1940, 192
Morgan, Judy Floretta 1949, 25, 193
Morgan, Kimberly Sue 1970, 193
Morgan, Paul Irving 1921, 25, 193
Morgan, Ralph Emerson 1889, 192
Morgan, Ralph William 1918, 192
Morgan, Ruth Rohann 1924, 193
Morton, Agnes 1776, 91
Morton, Samuel, 91
Moser, Rebecca, 70
Mosley, Frances, 91
Moss, Clara Belle 1943, 25
Moss, James 1906, 69
Mott, Richard Albert 1917, 134
Motter, Michael, 207
Motter, Michael 1790, 66
Mounce, James Robert 1964, 155
Mounce, Lloyd Michael 1942, 154
Mounce, Tammara Lynn 1967, 155
Mount, Ethel Hilda 1911, 121
Mount, Wilfred Edgar, 121
Mount, William T., Jr., 105
Moxley, Allison 1888, 116
Moxley, Ann Wilson 1847, 120
Moxley, Caleb, 104
Moxley, Donald, 141
Moxley, Donna Jeanne 1948, 170
Moxley, Elvira 1896, 116
Moxley, Ernest Walter 1882, 116
Moxley, Esther Lee 1898, 123
Moxley, Gloria Alvin 1930, 169
Moxley, Jemima 1825, 104
Moxley, Jesse Herman 1893, 116
Moxley, Jesse William 1855, 116
Moxley, Kelly Wayne 1969, 170

Moxley, Kevin Harold 1961, 169
Moxley, Kristen Leon 1964, 170
Moxley, Leonard Wayne 1941, 169
Moxley, Lester 1886, 116
Moxley, Lillie May 1890, 116
Moxley, Raymond Merson 1909, 169
Moxley, Risdon, 116
Moxley, Rosa Medora 1865, 117, 133
Moxley, Vivy 1900, 116
Mullican, Carl Oscar 1906, 168
Mullican, Carroll Lee 1943, 169
Mullican, Danny Lee 1959, 169
Mullican, David Scot 1960, 169
Mullican, Deborah Lynn 1952, 169
Mullican, Dennis Ray 1965, 169
Mullican, Marcia Ann 1952, 169
Mullican, Oscar Ray 1928, 168
Mullican, Oscar Thomas 1886, 168
Mullican, Robert Day 1932, 169
Mullineaux, Delma Viola 1893, 120
Mullineaux, Eldridge, 120
Mullineaux, Sarah E. 1837, 136
Mullinix, Asbury, 210
Mullinix, Aubrey, 119
Mullinix, Audree Virginia 1923, 128
Mullinix, Caroline Virginia 1854, 149
Mullinix, Clyta Beatrice, 119
Mullinix, Dorothy, 119
Mullinix, Edna Mae 1912, 83
Mullinix, Genevieve, 119
Mullinix, Granville Roland, 128
Mullinix, Kitty, 115
Mullinix, Larry Wayne 1948, 159

Mullinix, Leslie, 119
Mullinix, No given name, 115
Mullinix, Robert, 119
Mullinix, Sarah Elizabeth 1836, 210
Mullinix, Tammy Dawn 1974, 159
Mullinix, Thomas, 119
Murdoch, Richard Bruce, 105
Murphy, Bernard Joseph 1906, 71
Murphy, Eugene Francis, 130
Murphy, Ronald Wayne 1955, 130
Murray, No given name, 118
Musial, Sharon Ann 1952, 163
Myers, Ericka, 122
Myers, Frances 1907, 172
Myers, Mary Alice 1891, 26
Myers, Nicole, 122
Myers, No given name, 122
Myers, Tiffany, 122

—N—

Nachtman, Dorothy M., 207
Nash, George, 26
Nash, Milton, 116
Nash, William, 54
Nelson, Beverly Ann, 135
Nelson, William C., 135
Newman, Catherine, 46
Newton, William, 106
Nicholas, Ruth Marie, 77
Nicklas, Mary Vandevort 1910, 173
Nicodemus, Bradley T., 105
Nikirk, Elmer, Jr., 82
Nikirk, Goldye M., 82
Nikirk, Hallie Virginia, 82
Niswonger, Nettie 1878, 14
Noonan, Edward Joseph, 116

Norland, Derek Alan 1967, 195
Norland, Jerome Ferdinand 1942, 195
Norland, Leif Andrew 1970, 195
Norris, Franklin W., 194
Norwood, Allan Wayne 1937, 147
Norwood, Angie Beth 1967, 147
Norwood, Belt M. 1813, 145
Norwood, Beverly Lee 1938, 147
Norwood, Brent Everett 1971, 148
Norwood, Carolyn Yvonne 1943, 148
Norwood, Constance Sue Dawn 1948, 148
Norwood, Cynthia Kay 1962, 147
Norwood, Darryl Everett 1945, 148
Norwood, Deborah Lynn 1963, 147
Norwood, Doris Adabelle 1925, 147
Norwood, Ella, 148
Norwood, Evaleen, 148
Norwood, Fay, 146
Norwood, Garrison 1896, 148
Norwood, Joyce Anne 1938, 120, 147
Norwood, Julian Garrison 1930, 147
Norwood, Julian Garrison, Jr., 147
Norwood, Lisa Michelle 1971, 147
Norwood, Mabel, 146
Norwood, Mary E. 1844, 145
Norwood, Michael, 147
Norwood, Norval Lester 1891, 146
Norwood, Otis Calvin 1942, 40
Norwood, Rebecca, 147

Norwood, Sharon Lynn 1946, 148
Norwood, Stephen Douglas 1968, 40
Norwood, Tammy Sue 1968, 147
Norwood, William 1862, 146
Nus, Glen Fred 1895, 55

—O—

O'Conner, Eve Ann, 209
O'Connor, George Edward, 97
Osborn, James, 54
Oswalt, Frank, 11
Ott, Judith Lynn 1958, 125

—P—

Pace, David James, 92
Paine, Richard Daniel 1941, 154
Paine, Richard Daniel, Jr., 154
Palmer, George Oliver, 77
Palmer, John C., 42
Palmer, No given name, 194
Pappalardo, Mary Ann 1945, 72
Patterson, No given name 1804, 96
Paul, Rodger B., 17
Payne, Daniel Thomas 1958, 40
Payne, Janet Marie 1961, 40
Payne, Rex Allen 1956, 40
Payne, Sherri Lynn 1969, 40
Payne, Thomas Henry, Jr. 1932, 40
Pecawicz, Alan Eugene 1950, 155
Pecawicz, Brenda Inez 1949, 155
Pecawicz, John Walter 1915, 155
Pefley, Lydia A., 51
Penfield, Altana Adaline 1869, 55
Penny, Lillian, 155
Perkins, Minnie May 1878, 55

261

Perry, Cora Frances 1870, 16
Perry, William Alpheus, 12
Pflugradt, Bruce Alan 1954, 153
Pflugradt, Carl Paul 1900, 153
Pflugradt, Evelyn Damaris 1922, 153
Pflugradt, Gretchen Anne 1926, 154
Pflugradt, Susan Elaine 1965, 154
Pflugradt, William John Roger 1924, 153
Phebus, Dora E. 1877, 140
Pickett, Bridgett Lynn 1988, 122
Pickett, Bruce, 122
Pickett, No given name, 122
Pierce, George Michael 1856, 13
Pierce, No given name, 108
Pierce, Raleigh 1890, 13
Pierson, Mary 1795, 53
Pierson, Stephen, 53
Pigott, William O., 26
Pinney, W. M., 52
Place, George, 209
Plunkard, Carrie Manzella 1902, 37
Plunkard, Donna Jean 1948, 195
Poffenbarger, William, 11
Poffenberger, Ann Cordelia 1852, 76
Poffenberger, Elizabeth V., 42
Poffenberger, George J. 1824, 76
Poffenberger, Henry, 29
Poffenberger, Lawson, 207
Poffenberger, Mary Ann, 79
Polansky, Christina 1962, 125
Poole, Gail Lee 1948, 38
Porter, Janet Mae 1949, 148
Posner, Benjamin, 128
Posner, Donald Edward 1937, 128
Posner, Julie Lynn 1965, 128

Posner, Terri Dawne 1962, 128
Presley, Charles, 60
Pridemore, Fred Benny, 129
Pridemore, Fred Benny, Jr. 1956, 129
Prugh, David, 184
Prugh, Mary Catherine 1848, 184
Pryor, Cornelia Ann Elizabeth 1847, 47
Pryor, Donna Louise 1910, 30
Pryor, James D. 1898, 30
Pryor, Jasper V. 1899, 30
Pryor, Mary Jane, 157
Pryor, Milton A. 1897, 30
Pryor, Rohann, 190
Pryor, Rooklyn 1874, 30
Pryor, Samuel, 190
Purcell, Bradford Moore, 46
Purcell, Margaret Ann 1955, 46
Purdum, Anna O. 1858, 136
Purdum, Cornelia G. 1864, 136
Purdum, Edward E. 1860, 136
Purdum, Emma L. 1869, 136
Purdum, J. Marie 1900, 162
Purdum, Jemima 1855, 136
Purdum, John Fillmore 1851, 135
Purdum, John Lewis 1798, 114, 135
Purdum, Laura 1879, 136
Purdum, Lemuel W. 1853, 136
Purdum, Margaret, 136
Purdum, Rachel, 102
Purdum, Rachel Browning 1835, 171
Purdum, Roberta Grant 1865, 158
Purdum, Rufus King 1827, 135
Purdum, Samuel W. 1853, 136
Purdum, Sarah Rebecca 1829, 114, 127

Purdum, Virginia L. 1862, 136
Purdum, William Reich 1866, 136

—Q—

Quickel, John Allan 1962, 142
Quickel, Matthew Allan 1984, 142
Quitmyer, Bessie Beatrice 1901, 55

—R—

Rauth, Amanda Joan 1964, 46
Rauth, Ellen Louise 1930, 46
Rauth, Evylon Beatrice 1959, 46
Rauth, Leslye Louise 1963, 46
Rauth, Lucinda Catherine 1961, 46
Rauth, Philip Anthony 1906, 46
Rauth, Philip Anthony 1925, 46
Rawles, Carl 1966, 126
Rawles, Cody Allen 1986, 126
Rawles, Jennifer Hope 1981, 126
Rawles, Jessica 1989, 126
Rawles, Marci Ann 1984, 126
Rawles, Robert Cleon 1964, 126
Rawles, Robert Jessie 1935, 125
Rawles, William Douglas 1960, 125
Rebert, Albert Francis 1916, 161
Rebert, Debra Louise 1954, 161
Rebert, Dennis Alan 1958, 161
Rebert, Nelson Wayne 1952, 161
Recher, Sophia, 34
Reed, Charles Junior 1940, 122
Reiblich, Carrie C. 1882, 137
Rein. *See* Rine
Remsberg, Henry, 80
Remsberg, John, 13
Remsberg, Lewis Hamilton 1828, 13

Remsburg, Annie Malinda 1861, 14
Remsburg, Charles Edward 1863, 14
Remsburg, Charles Reuben 1869, 11
Remsburg, Helen R. 1895, 15
Remsburg, Jennie Rebecca 1859, 13
Remsburg, Lydia A. R. 1829, 80, 81
Remsburg, Mabel R. 1892, 15
Remsburg, Malissa Catherine 1857, 13
Remsburg, Mary, 82
Remsburg, Mary Elizabeth 1855, 13
Renn, Lillie 1871, 117
Renn, M. Luther, 117
Renn, Tillie M. 1871, 117
Rennie, Donald, 56
Repass, Anita 1970, 39
Repass, Larry 1950, 39
Reyborn, Katherine 1805, 51
Rhea, No given name, 187
Rhinehart, Edwin, 38
Rhinehart, Kelly Marie 1968, 38
Rhinehart, Lauri Ann 1967, 38
Rhoderick, Irma Lucille, 130
Rhodes, Charlotte, 50
Rhodes, No given name, 108
Rice, Betty Jane 1926, 37
Rice, Olive Elizabeth 1937, 169
Richardson, Julian Leigh, 154
Ridenour, Henry, 206
Riggs, Almeda 1931, 35, 133
Riggs, Andrew Hilton 1973, 132
Riggs, Carolyn Patricia 1975, 132
Riggs, Charles Larry 1948, 132
Riggs, James Brian 1950, 132

Riggs, James Brian, Jr. 1972, 132
Riggs, Jesse Lee 1925, 132
Riggs, Jessica Christine 1975, 132
Riggs, Julie Marie 1957, 132
Riggs, Lester Baker 1903, 35, 132
Rine, Elizabeth d/1833, 2, 102, 106, 111
Rippeon, Austin Delmar 1932, 168
Rippeon, Austin Delmar, Jr. 1958, 168
Rippeon, Hope Dayon 1974, 168
Rippeon, Peggy Lou 1933, 40
Rippeon, Wesley Pierre DeVoe 1960, 168
Ritasse, Jacque Nadine 1967, 132
Ritasse, Jeffrey Scott 1969, 132
Rittase, William Harvey 1934, 131
Ritter, Mary, 184
Roberts, Judy Mae 1947, 163
Roberts, Nila, 18
Robertson, James Stephen, 169
Robertson, Robert L., 169
Robinson, Brian, 123
Robinson, Ester, 53
Robinson, Jessica, 123
Robinson, No given name, 123
Robinson, Priscilla, 209
Rogers, Grace, 131
Rohrback, Daniel A. 1845, 207
Rohrback, Emma Mary 1870, 207
Rohrer, Grace Eleanor 1920, 72
Ropp, Evelyn Earlene 1926, 195
Rosapepe, Karen Ann 1945, 159
Rose Hill Farm, 81
Rose, Connie 1942, 36

Rosencrantz, Paul Burlin 1922, 165
Routsong, Lillie Mae, 77
Routzahn, Adam, 79
Routzahn, Alma B. 1891, 76
Routzahn, Ann 1946, 193
Routzahn, Ann Ludwig, 31
Routzahn, Ann Magdalena 1816, 81
Routzahn, Anna Elizabeth 1907, 31
Routzahn, Anna Elizabeth Catherine 1864, 78
Routzahn, Beulah Katharine 1896, 77
Routzahn, Calvin Wesley 1873, 24
Routzahn, Carlton 1848, 75
Routzahn, Carrie B. 1872, 75
Routzahn, Catharine 1814, 73, 75
Routzahn, Chad Paul 1972, 25, 193
Routzahn, Charles David 1851, 75
Routzahn, Clark Austin 1940, 24
Routzahn, Cyrus Raymond 1900, 31
Routzahn, Daniel 1783, 67
Routzahn, Edith M. 1882, 75
Routzahn, Edna Marie 1901, 77
Routzahn, Eliza Ann 1864, 77
Routzahn, Elmer E. 1886, 75
Routzahn, Emma Frances 1857, 77
Routzahn, Esta May 1866, 78
Routzahn, Evelyn Glendora 1916, 190
Routzahn, George Levi 1826, 75
Routzahn, George Markwood 1888, 77

Schroyer, Eva Catherine, 46
Schuettler, Charles Peter 1919, 124
Self, Elihu H., 89
Sellers, Cresent Carol 1973, 164
Sellers, Edward Leroy 1948, 164
Sellers, James Ira, 107
Sellman, Anna, 185
Sellman, Frank C. 1872, 185
Sellman, Joseph 1863, 185
Sellman, Joshua 1868, 185
Sellman, Lawman 1869, 185
Sellman, Marshall H. 1873, 185
Sellman, Matilda B. 1857, 184
Sellman, May 1875, 185
Sellman, Ninasau 1866, 185
Sellman, Rachel 1859, 184
Sellman, Walter, 184
Sellman, Walter 1860, 185
Sellman, William 1832, 184
Sellman, William Chapman 1856, 184
Sessa, Brian David 1963, 162
Sessa, David J. 1938, 161
Sessa, Jennifer Danielle 1972, 162
Sessa, Kenneth Gregory 1969, 162
Sessa, Valerie Irene 1964, 162
Sever, Earl Franklin, 77
Shafer, John A., 35
Shank, Franklin Peter 1887, 72
Shank, George Franklin 1910, 72
Shank, John Jacob, 72
Shank, Margaret Catherine 1917, 72
Shank, Myree Virginia 1907, 72
Sheetenhalm, Delilah, 103
Shellhorse, John, 141
Shiers, Wanda Kaye 1956, 166
Shifflet, Shelby Jean 1941, 147
Shipley, Elizabeth, 184

Shipley, Norman, 122
Shipley, Robin, 122
Shoemaker, George W., 104
Shoemaker, Helen Gertrude 1909, 195
Shoemaker, Jonas, 208
Shoemaker, Magdalena, 74
Shoemaker, Margaret Gertrude, 116
Shoemaker, No given name, 115
Shuester, Susan 1735, 49
Shuff, Benjamin, Jr. 1837, 32
Shuff, Doris Jane, 195
Shuff, Lucretia 1862, 32
Shuff, Margaret V. 1863, 191
Shuff, Margaret Virginia 1863, 46
Shull, Clarence John, III 1947, 164
Shurts, Anneta 1866, 62
Shurts, Catherine V. 1861, 61
Shurts, Cora Ada 1879, 62
Shurts, Henry Clay 1859, 61
Shurts, Huldah Delise 1856, 61
Shurts, Joseph B. 1862, 61
Shurts, Laura 1853, 61
Shurts, Lewly Ardena 1871, 62
Shurts, Sarah E. 1854, 61
Shurts, William Worley 1826, 61
Shurts, William Worley 1869, 62
Sibert, Elizabeth, 207
Sidler, Georgia, 142
Sidler, Jennifer Cheryl 1971, 148
Sidler, John Carl 1946, 148
Sigler, Percy Allen, 69
Sikken, Christa 1946, 173
Simmons, Larry 1946, 126
Simpson, Connie 1946, 37
Sisney, Lydia Jane 1822, 60
Slaughter, Dell Pemberton 1892, 158

Spurrier, Stella, 144
Stacy, Elizabeth Dasher, 142
Stanley, Mildred Elizabeth 1909, 129
Stanley, Roy 1953, 166
Stauffer, Margaret Virginia 1920, 134
Steele, Thomas, 36
Steepleton, Susan, 51
Stephenson, G. W., 14
Stephenson, Lucinda, 92
Stephenson, Peyton S., 92
Stephenson, Washington, 92
Stevenson, Lydia, 62
Stevenson, Robert G. 1918, 17
Stewart, Alice, 11
Stine, Eleanor F. 1894, 69
Stine, Hannah Catherine, 77
Stitley, Gary Wayne 1944, 163
Stitzel, August Joseph, 128
Stockslager, John W. 1872, 75
Stogden, Edith 1887, 57
Stokes, Alice May 1859, 59
Stone, Alfred Finney 1887, 15
Stone, George H. 1906, 15
Stottlemyer, Jennie, 31
Stottlemyer, Sarah Ann 1842, 32
Strite, Beverly Marie 1956, 190
Strite, Jay Benjamin, 190
Strite, Jay Benjamin, Jr. 1958, 190
Strite, Thomas Alan 1962, 190
Stubbs, Alice, 60
Stubbs, Edward, 60
Stubbs, Horace, 60
Stubbs, Laura, 60
Stubbs, Oscar, 60
Stubbs, Samuel, 60
Stubbs, William, 60
Stubbs, Zimrial, 60
Stull, Bonnie, 123
Stull, Brian Keith, 123

Stull, Charles 1929, 122
Stull, Charles, Jr., 122
Stull, Deborah, 122
Stull, Dorothy 1931, 123
Stull, Eloise 1923, 122
Stull, Gary U. 1899, 122
Stull, Gary U., Jr. 1927, 122
Stull, George 1940, 123
Stull, Lois 1938, 123
Stull, Mary 1930, 123
Stull, Michael, 123
Stull, Miriam 1928, 122
Stull, Pamela, 123
Stull, Stanley 1934, 123
Stup, Alison Elizabeth 1949, 163
Stup, Corey Stephen 1973, 163
Stup, Darryl Leslie 1943, 163
Stup, Elizabeth 1917, 37
Stup, George Josiah 1917, 163
Stup, George Larry 1939, 163
Stup, Joel Lynn 1975, 163
Stup, Lauren Davis 1973, 163
Stup, Linda Jeanne 1940, 163
Stup, Stephen Jay 1951, 163
Summers, Charles, 23
Summers, Chester, 23
Summers, Isaac J. 1838, 23
Summers, John, 94
Summers, Joshua, 71
Summers, Katie, 23
Summers, Leo, 36
Summers, Melissa Alverta 1873, 71
Summers, William H. 1866, 23
Sutherland, No given name, 118
Swan, Elizabeth 1780, 94
Swan, John, 94
Swank, Lydia A. Pefley, 51
Swanson, Julia Elminda, 56
Swartout, Tiffany 1966, 126
Swartzbaugh, Betty 1938, 124

—W—

Wachtel, Clyde C., 31
Wachtel, Louise 1916, 31
Waddell, Phyllis M., 14
Wakenight, Abraham, 208
Waldron, Dora, 106
Walker, Alice Catherine 1864, 105
Walker, Bessie Pauline 1897, 172
Walker, Blanche Willard 1892, 171
Walker, Charlotte 1814, 103
Walker, Dwight Talmadge 1903, 161, 172
Walker, Dwight Talmadge, Jr. 1929, 172
Walker, Edward, 102, 104
Walker, Edward 1830, 104
Walker, Eleanor Jeanette 1861, 105
Walker, Elizabeth Ann 1944, 173
Walker, Ernest Artman 1904, 173
Walker, Esther May 1893, 171
Walker, George Washington Wesley 1837, 171
Walker, Hester, 105
Walker, James 1810, 103
Walker, Jane Rebecca 1866, 105
Walker, Jemima Florence 1869, 105
Walker, Jesse 1820, 104
Walker, Jesse Clinton 1853, 105
Walker, John Calvin 1858, 105
Walker, June Wanita 1932, 172
Walker, Louise, 105
Walker, Lydia A. N. 1856, 105
Walker, Mary 1827, 104

Walker, Mary Ann 1936, 165, 173
Walker, Mary E. 1845, 104
Walker, Reuben 1812, 103
Walker, Rhoda 1825, 104
Walker, Rufus Wesley 1902, 172
Walker, Samuel Wesley 1892, 162
Walker, Sarah 1823, 104
Walker, Wava Jane 1934, 173
Walker, Wesley Day 1900, 172
Walker, Wilbur Bryan 1908, 173
Walker, Wilfred Taft 1908, 173
Walker, William 1817, 104
Walker, William Alfred Baker 1867, 171
Walker, William F. 1942, 172
Walker, William Norris 1847, 105
Walker, William Paul 1898, 172
Walker, William Richard 1940, 173
Walker, Willing Wendell 1910, 173
Walsh, Thomas Eugene, 69
Walter, John, 130
Waltman, M. H., 112
Waltman, Mary Austen 1827, 111
Ward, Clay E. 1901, 131
Warfield, Henry Clark 1942, 129
Warfield, Jason Edward 1979, 121, 169
Warfield, John O., 129
Warfield, Julie Marie 1981, 129
Warfield, Kristin Leeann 1984, 121, 169
Warfield, Merhle Basil 1927, 169
Warfield, Merhle Wayne 1950, 120, 169
Warfield, Raymond Curtis 1952, 169

Warner, Edward A. 1872, 113
Warner, Ralph A. 1913, 113
Warnick, Gail, 122
Warnick, No given name, 122
Warnick, Susan, 122
Warren, James, 91
Warrenfels, Mary Ann Rebecca 1836, 16
Warrenfels, Minerva 1842, 15
Warrenfels, Samuel, 13
Warthen, Bessie Vierna 1886, 141
Wathen, Gabriel 1789, 95
Wathen, Sarah Wintersmith 1823, 95
Watkins, Addie 1902, 122
Watkins, Albert Dewey 1899, 115
Watkins, Alexander Paul 1938, 170
Watkins, Alvin Rudell 1921, 126
Watkins, Alvin Rudell, Jr. 1946, 126
Watkins, Anna Louise 1903, 115
Watkins, Anna Reba 1908, 123
Watkins, Asa Hull 1887, 133
Watkins, Barbara Ann 1938, 121
Watkins, Bernard Lee 1960, 127
Watkins, Betty Lee 1924, 120
Watkins, Bradley Ellsworth 1947, 134
Watkins, Bradley Mitchell 1974, 134
Watkins, Bruce Edward 1957, 121
Watkins, Caleb H. 1806, 115, 116
Watkins, Carrie G. 1871, 139
Watkins, Catherine Marie 1963, 170
Watkins, Clarence E., 106
Watkins, Cora Elaine 1901, 115

Watkins, Debra Lee 1958, 121
Watkins, Dennis Wayne 1955, 131
Watkins, Denton 1795, 102, 106
Watkins, Dorothy, 108
Watkins, Dorothy 1917, 106
Watkins, Earl Lee, 140
Watkins, Edward, 207
Watkins, Edward Evan 1906, 108
Watkins, Edward Taylor, 106
Watkins, Eloise Nadine 1925, 131
Watkins, Ernest, 107
Watkins, Evan R., 108
Watkins, Fillmore C. 1852, 140
Watkins, Frances, 107
Watkins, George Victor 1904, 107
Watkins, George Washington 1869, 106
Watkins, Glenda Eileen 1950, 127
Watkins, Grover Sim 1892, 116
Watkins, Hamilton 1847, 107
Watkins, Harold, 108
Watkins, Harriet 1874, 108
Watkins, Harry 1874, 108
Watkins, Hattie 1873, 107
Watkins, Helen Elizabeth 1917, 125
Watkins, Herbert Taylor 1910, 107
Watkins, Inza Isidore, 108
Watkins, Iva M. 1897, 132
Watkins, J. Latimer, 152
Watkins, Jack, 108
Watkins, James Russell 1908, 129
Watkins, Janice Pearl 1917, 118
Watkins, Jepe 1821, 106

Watkins, Jeremiah Columbus
1841, 120
Watkins, Jesse 1872, 107
Watkins, Jessie Nadine 1921,
135
Watkins, John 1881, 152
Watkins, Joseph Grant 1866, 130
Watkins, Joyce, 107
Watkins, Kenneth, 106, 108
Watkins, Laura Blanche 1884,
108
Watkins, Laura Dorcas 1858,
152
Watkins, Lawrence 1893, 107
Watkins, Lester Basil 1910, 123
Watkins, Lester Edsel 1927, 131
Watkins, Lester Steele, 130
Watkins, Lois Allene 1915, 106
Watkins, Lois Evelyn 1931, 123
Watkins, Lois Virginia 1914, 118
Watkins, Lucy Marian 1914, 124
Watkins, Margaret Rae 1919,
118
Watkins, Marjorie Nell 1922,
106
Watkins, Marlene Yvonne 1936,
129
Watkins, Mary, 152
Watkins, Mary 1830, 107
Watkins, Mary Jean 1931, 121
Watkins, Mary Winifred 1876,
107
Watkins, Matilda 1820, 106
Watkins, McKendree 1833, 107
Watkins, Merhle 1896, 107
Watkins, Mildred Colleen 1933,
124
Watkins, Milton 1873, 140
Watkins, Milton B. 1845, 107
Watkins, Minnie E. 1876, 140
Watkins, Miranda 1828, 107

Watkins, Myra Lavinia 1896,
115
Watkins, Nellie Mae 1897, 115
Watkins, Norma, 108
Watkins, Norman Sylvester
1900, 121
Watkins, Oakley Massarene
1895, 117
Watkins, Opal 1907, 107
Watkins, Patricia Lynn 1967,
170
Watkins, Paul, 107
Watkins, Pearl, 108
Watkins, Priscilla 1824, 106
Watkins, Ralph, 107
Watkins, Raymond 1885, 117
Watkins, Robert, 125
Watkins, Roland, 152
Watkins, Rose Eveline 1915, 134
Watkins, Rudell Edward 1932,
121
Watkins, Rudy Edward 1898,
120
Watkins, Ruth, 152
Watkins, Sally Fay 1939, 134
Watkins, Shirley Lee 1933, 121
Watkins, Stella Florence 1872,
107
Watkins, Steven Edsel 1952, 131
Watkins, Sylvester 1869, 120
Watkins, Thomas Ellsworth
1862, 117, 133
Watkins, Thomas Ellsworth
1922, 118
Watkins, Tobias Calvin 1865,
116
Watkins, Velma Winifred 1906,
140
Watkins, Virgie I. 1899, 117
Watkins, Wannie Blanche 1879,
107

Watkins, Wayne Sellman 1938, 170

Watkins, William Edward 1916, 107

Watkins, William Eldridge 1867, 115

Watkins, William Henry 1867, 106

Watkins, William T. 1863, 108

Watkins, Winifred Lenore 1906, 107

Weast, Hiram, 105

Weast, No given name, 35

Weast, Susan Elizabeth, 35

Weast, Tracy Ann, 35

Weaver, Mary V., 207

Webster, Agnes, 12

Weddle, Deloris, 192

Wells, Jeannette, 26

Welsh, Gary 1947, 37

Welsh, Martha 1837, 182

Welsh, Philip, 182

Wenner, Margaret E. 1835, 111

Werking, Donna Jean 1952, 38

Werking, Margaret 1908, 36

Werner, David, 202

Wessa, Delilah 1771, 89

Wessa, Samuel, 89

West, Kimberly Ellen 1960, 143

Whetstone, Allen, 107

White, Carolyn Maye 1942, 165

White, Dorothy, 39

White, Lewis, 145

White, Lillian, 145

White, Murr, 145

White, Paul, 145

Whitter, Nellie M., 82

Whorley, Mabel Christine 1901, 17

Wilcom, Daniel Christopher, 36

Wilcom, Donald Lee, 36

Wilcom, Mary, 36

Wilcom, No given name, 35

Wilcom, Ruth Elizabeth, 35

Wile, Catherine 1785, 66

Wiles, George, 10

Wiles, Peter 1795, 10

Wilhide, Elsie, 31

Wilhite, Daisy Laurine 1896, 16

Wilkinson, Marilyn Paige 1948, 154

Willard, Ann Kelly, 121

Willard, Dewalt J. 1739, 207

Williams, Alezan 1798, 88

Williams, Downey, 127, 128

Williams, Fannie Lois 1876, 201

Williams, Katherine Elizabeth 1895, 127

Williams, Leah Marie 1893, 128

Williams, Mary Margaret 1941, 40

Willier, Helen, 157

Wilson, Roxana, 182

Winebrenner, Carole Ann, 130

Wise, Frances M. 1883, 23

Wiseman, Susannah, 97

Wisner, Mildred, 127

Wisner, Paul, 127

Wisner, Ruby L. 1953, 126

Wolf, Jane, 120

Wolf, Oneita Grace 1919, 191

Wolfe, Elizabeth, 104

Wolgamot, Catherine, 87

Wolgamot, Hester, 87

Wolgamot, Hester 1744, 88

Wolgamot, Joseph, 87

Wood, George Palmer, III, 131

Wood, Melvin P., 105

Woodfield, Beatrice, 119

Woodfield, Dorothy, 119

Woodfield, Eldridge, 115

Woodfield, Emory Cross 1889, 115

Woodfield, George, 115

Woodfield, Joseph Leslie 1891, 119
Woodfield, Peggy 1928, 131
Woodfield, Rose, 115
Woodfield, Ruth Virginia 1942, 175
Woodfield, Shirley Ann 1931, 167
Woodfield, Thomas Griffith 1856, 115, 119
Woodfield, Vincent, 119
Woodfield, Willard, 119
Woodfield, William Robert, 131
Worley, Mary 1786, 57
Worman, Harry, 105
Wortman, No given name, 111
Wright, David Patrick 1967, 155
Wright, Elward, 129
Wright, Patrick L. 1940, 155
Wright, Robert Ashby 1961, 155
Wright, Terence L. 1967, 129
Wright, Thomas 1968, 155

—Y—

Yaste, Elizabeth Ann 1830, 28

Yaste, Samuel 1800, 28
Yingling, Charles Ralph 1915, 191
Yingling, Karen Lea 1961, 191
Yingling, Kathy Lynn 1956, 191
Youkins, No given name, 187
Young, Margaret M. 1864, 17
Young, Mary Virginia, 144
Young, Sarah F., 144
Youtsey, Mary 1800, 28

—Z—

Zimmerman, Anita Kay 1960, 192
Zimmerman, Carroll, 192
Zimmerman, Carroll Gordon, 209
Zimmerman, Dean Ashley 1961, 192
Zimmerman, Edgar Allen 1909, 209
Zimmerman, Hester A. M. 1851, 36
Zimmerman, Miriam A., 209
Zollers, No given name, 126